The Sayyid Qutb Reader

Anyone who wants to understand what militant Muslims think has to understand what they read—and they read Sayyid Qutb, the intellectual father of Islamic fundamentalism. Qutb, an Egyptian literary critic and philosopher who was appalled by American decadence, gained prominence in the Muslim Brotherhood, was imprisoned by Nasser, and hanged in 1966. Through his death and prolific writings he became a martyr for the cause of political Islam. His work is virtually unknown outside the Muslim world, but Qutb is at the heart of the intellectual rationale for jihad and violence in the name of Islam.

The Sayyid Qutb Reader is the first collection of his selected works available to the general public. As such, this valuable introduction to Qutb's core intellectual ideas should be read by anyone who wants to understand one of the most important conflicts of our age.

Albert Bergesen is Professor of Sociology at the University of Arizona.

The Sayyid Qutb Reader

Selected Writings on Politics, Religion, and Society

Edited by
Albert J. Bergesen

 Routledge
Taylor & Francis Group

NEW YORK AND LONDON

First published 2008
by Routledge
270 Madison Ave, New York, NY 10016

Simultaneously published in the UK
by Routledge
2 Park Square, Milton Park, Abingdon, Oxon OX14 4RN

Routledge is an imprint of the Taylor & Francis Group, an informa business

© 2008 Taylor & Francis

Typeset in Garamond 3 by
RefineCatch Limited, Bungay, Suffolk
Printed and bound in the United States of America on acid-free paper by
Edward Brothers, Inc.

Library of Congress Cataloging-in-Publication Data
Qutb, Sayyid, 1903-1966.
    [Essays. English. Selections]
    The Sayyid Qutb reader : selected writings on politics, religion, and society /
edited by Albert J. Bergesen. – 1st ed.
        p. cm.
    ISBN 978–0–415–95424–2 (hardback : alk. paper) –
ISBN 978–0–415–95425–9 (pbk. : alk. paper)   1. Islam.   I. Bergesen,
Albert.   II. Title.
    BP88.Q74A2 2007
    320.5'57–dc22
    2007034647

ISBN 10: 0–415–95424–X (hbk)
ISBN 10: 0–415–95425–8 (pbk)

ISBN 13: 978–0–415–95424–2 (hbk)
ISBN 13: 978–0–415–95425–9 (pbk)

Contents

Preface

It has been said that perhaps no writer has occupied so central a place within the universe of political Islam in the second half of the twentieth century as Egypt's Sayyid Qutb[1], and if one wants to understand the mind of radical Muslims, one needs to know what they read, or have read, and they read Sayyid Qutb.[2] In general, his work has been divided into three general periods.[3] The earliest (1920–1947) centers on more literary works where he wrote poems, criticism, and novels. The second (1948–1954) constitutes his first militant Islamic period, when he wrote *Social Justice in Islam*, the first parts of his Qur'anic commentary, *In the Shade of the Qur'an*, and numerous militant articles for journals. His final phase (1957–1966) took place while he was in prison and involved his most radical Islamist writing, including revisions of both *Social Justice in Islam*[4] and multiple volumes of *In the Shade of the Qur'an*, along with his call to action, *Milestones*. At present, though, there is no collection of his selected works available for students, scholars, and the interested public. This volume attempts to fill that void.

Part One comprises two introductory essays that provide a summary of his life and ideas. Chapter One identifies the political and cultural contexts that might have influenced his thinking including the years in prison, Egyptian national politics, the twentieth-century Islamic Revival and possible similarities with the Protestant Reformation, and assumptions of Islamic civilization itself. Chapter Two is an introduction to three of his core ideas about the interface of Islam, existing society, and *jihad*.

Part Two contains a selection of his writings which come from the later period of his career when his attention turned to questions of religion, politics, and society.[5] These include selections from *Milestones* (nd. [1964]), *In the Shade of the Qur'an*, (1999–2004), *Social Justice in Islam* (2000), and his memoirs as a young boy growing up in Egypt, *A Child from the Village* (2004). All of the selections reprinted here are whole chapters from larger works. Nothing has been added or subtracted. With the *Milestones* selection, though, I was only able to gain permission to reprint short sections, and hence there is selection in what was reprinted.

Acknowledgements

A couple of years ago I offered a course at Stanford on the global *jihad* and looked for a collection of readings of Sayyid Qutb. I couldn't find one, let alone any of his books in bookstores. At that point I decided a collection of Qutb's basic writings was needed, and suggested such a book to Routledge's Rob Tempio, who was very enthusiastic and worked hard to get the project approved. For that I'm very grateful. Michael Kerns took over the project and has been a great help. I also want thank my wife Susie who had to put up with endless talk around the kitchen table over the intricate points of religion and politics as I tried to grasp Qutb's basic ideas. Whether my understanding is close to what he meant will be up to the readers to decide. All I can say is that I tried, without bias, to represent his basic ideas as accurately as possible.

Permissions acknowledgements

The publishers would like to thank the following for their permission to reprint their material:

Kazi Publications, Inc. for permission to reprint sections from Sayyid Qutb, *Milestones*, on pages, 7, 8, 9, 12, 45, 47, 55–65, 70–75, 82, 83, 124, 125, 130, 159, and 160.

The Islamic Foundation, for permission to reprint pages 1–64 from Sayyid Qutb, *In the Shade of the Qur'an*, Volume VII, Surah 8 and pages 37–98 and pages 262–316 from Volume VIII, Surah 9.

Islamic Publications International for permission to reprint Chapter 1 (pages 19–35) from Sayyid Qutb, *Social Justice in Islam*.

Syracuse University Press, for permission to reprint Chapter 11 (pages 125–134) from Sayyid Qutb, *A Child from the Village*.

Part 1
Life, context, and core ideas

1 Sayyid Qutb in historical context

Albert J. Bergesen

Sayyid Qutb was born in 1906 in the town of Musha in Middle Egypt.[1] He was the eldest of five children. His family was well known. It included his brother Muhammad, known for his writing on Islamic topics and activism, a sister, Hamidah, who was involved with the Muslim Brothers and imprisoned for seven years, and another sister, Aminad, also involved in the propagation of Islam and writing for numerous periodicals. Little seems known about his third sister. Qutb went to local schools and at the age of ten is said to have memorized the Qur'an because his mother wanted him to attend the al-Azhar University, a center of Sunni learning. His father al-Hajj Qutb Ibrahim was a delegate to Mustafa Kamil's National Party and subscribed to the party journal *al-Liwa* (the Standard). There were many political meetings at his father's house where he was exposed to anti-British Egyptian nationalism and seems to have become politically aware at an early age. At the age of 13 the family moved to Cairo; in 1929 he went to Dara al-Ulum's Teacher College and in 1933 he got his BA in education. He excelled at school and in studying literature and poetry.

After college he went to work for the Ministry of Public Instruction, and from 1940–1948 served as an inspector for the Ministry. He drafted many reform projects and had a parallel career as a man of letters, a social critic, and a journalist. He loved poetry, and wrote short stories and novels. At least three of this works were autobiographical (*A Child From the Village, The Four Apparitions*, and *Thorns*). The last was a veiled account of a deep disappointment in love, from which he seems to have become a dedicated bachelor.

After 1945 his writing shifted from literature to nationalism, political events, and social problems. He irritated King Farouk who wanted him imprisoned. In 1948 the Ministry of Education sent him to study American systems of education, and he received an MA in education from Teachers College at the University of Northern Colorado. There, shocked by what he perceived as sexual promiscuity and the worship of the dollar, he seems to have rediscovered his religion. At this point he turned his attention to the question of Islam and politics.

In 1951 he returned to Egypt and began to frequent meetings of the Society of Muslim Brothers, which he joined. He was very positive about the Revolution of 1952 that brought Nasser to power and met with him often. But soon the Muslim Brothers and Nasser's regime parted ways. In 1954 a Muslim Brother tried to assassinate Nasser. By then Qutb had become editor-in-chief of a Muslim Brethren weekly (*Al-Ikhwan al-Muslimin*), which was banned in 1954 and many of the Brethern, including Qutb, were then imprisoned in response to the assassination attempt. Tried in 1955, he was sent to Tura prison for a 25-year term, where he was tortured and spent much of his time in the infirmary.

While in prison he wrote extensively on Islamic topics. Between 1953–1964 he wrote a 30-volume commentary on the Qur'an, *In the Shade of the Qur'an*. In 1962 he started drafts of *Milestones*, which has been compared to Lenin's *What is to Be Done*. Qutb was kept in prison until 1964, when after the intervention of the President of Iraq, he was released. *Milestones* was also published that year. Upon his release he was offered a place to live in Iraq, but declined. Eight months later along with his brother Muhammad and sisters Haminah and Aminah (and many other Muslim Brethren), he was again jailed; the charge was armed revolt and terrorism. On 29 August 1966, along with two other Brethren leaders, Sayyid Qutb was hung. His writings have lived on and he has become a martyr for Islam in the eyes of many.

His distinctly Islamist thinking seems to have been concentrated from the mid-1940s up to his death in 1966, and is a reflection of, and contribution to, the social turmoil and cultural milieu in which he wrote. His ideas can be better understood if we place them in a number of contexts, ranging from the most immediate, that is, his prison years, to the broader Egyptian nationalist struggles, to the even broader twentieth-century Islamic Revival, and finally to the cultural assumptions of Islamic civilization itself. We can begin with the effect of his prison experience.

The prison experience

Joining the Muslim Brothers in 1951, Qutb was given positions of responsibility: head of the Propaganda Section, a position in the Orientation Office, and membership on the Executive Committee. He was also "the only civilian to attend the first meetings of the Revolutionary Command Council"[2] and was an important intermediary between the Brothers and Nasser himself. But almost immediately after Nasser came to power the Free Officers and Muslim Brothers parted company, and it would only "take Nasser two years to deprive the Brothers of what they considered their revolution."[3] In 1954 the Brothers were banned, and Qutb withdrew his support from the regime as Nasser dramatically consolidated his power. In 1954 Qutb was reported to have been seen with Communists distributing political tracts. He was arrested for three months and then released. But following a Brother's assassination attempt on Nasser, Qutb was re-arrested, and in 1955 charged with subversive activity, anti-government agitation, and pamphleteering.[4] He was sent to prison where he remained until 1964, being considered, "one of Nasser's personal targets."[5]

Scholars have linked the prison years to a further radicalization of his thinking.[6] He seems to have been particularly affected by the murder of a number of Muslim Brothers in 1957, leading some to argue that "Qutb's most radical work appear to date from after this event."[7] "At the end of May 1957 various developments convinced them [the Muslim Brothers in Nasser's prisons] that they were about to be exterminated. Fearing that they would be killed if they reported for the normal daily work detail (rock-breaking), they refused to do the forced labour, locking themselves in their cells on 1 June. Armed soldiers broke into the cells and massacred twenty-one of them. The authorities said that they had put down a rebellion."[8]

This government violence against the Islamist cause has been linked to Qutb's changing views concerning the religious character of the Nasser regime. "These twenty-one new martyrs—added to the victims of the 1954 hangings, and to Hasan al-Banna himself, the martyr *par excellence*, who was assassinated by King Farouk's police in 1949—made a deep impression on the man who sat writing relentlessly in his sickbed. Sayyid Qutb was horrified by the barbarism of the camp guards, and the inhumanity with which they had let the wounded die. Various witnesses report that it was then that he lost his last remaining illusions as to the Muslim character of the Nasser regime."[9] It has also been suggested that, "this period constituted the beginning of his radical contemplation that resulted in the belief of *al-hakimiyyah* [sovereignty] of God and *al-jahiliyyah* [state of ignorance from the guidance of God] of societies that were to be taken up by quite important radical organizations such as *al-Takfir was al-Hijrah* and *al-Jihad.*"[10]

It has also been suggested that some of the effect of prison on his ideas was simply due to isolation. "Qutb's prison experience hardly provided any training in moderation and the isolation from outside political society must have encouraged the tendency toward the theoretical and radical consistency that marks his later thought."[11] Whether he would have developed his vision without prison is unknown, but we do know that during this period his writing became more radical, as in his revision of *Social Justice in Islam* to make it a more theocratic work, the first parts of *In the Shade of the Qur'an*, and the composition of his call to action, *Milestones*.

Prison censors may have also affected the form of his exposition, on analogy with the vague and indirect manner of Gramsci's *Prison Notebooks*.[12] With this in mind one is struck when reading, say, *Milestones*, by it's sometimes abstract, vague, and somewhat elusive call to arms. For example, he speaks of Islam as, "a social setup that takes the necessary action to liberate mankind"[13] leaving open what is exactly meant by "necessary action." Is he referring to elections, pamphleteering, persuasion, or to more violent activities such as terrorism, assassination, bomb throwing, or seizing state power? Given prison censorship it might not have been possible to put such techniques of political change in explicit terms, hence the encoded reference to taking "the necessary action". Sometimes what is clearly understood as revolutionary action is put in terms where the actor is, somewhat generically, "Islam", and the opposition isn't so much Nasser, but the "*jahili* system," which could be both a general condition of ignorance of the guidance of God or the specifics of the Egyptian government. Similarly, the relationship between a revolutionary ideology for a vanguard party which might have to use violence is also put quite abstractly by Qutb, who argues, "Islam's theoretical foundation—belief—materializes in the form of an organized and active group" and that, "through 'preaching' and 'the movement' material objects are tackled" such that this combination of "preaching" and the "movement" will "confront 'the human situation' with all the necessary methods."[14]

It may though simply be the case that his level of abstract theoretical discourse reflects his philosophical and theological bent of mind. If this is the case, such coded material was no doubt possible because of it's embeddedness within broader webs of cultural framing that link terms and phrases to more clearly understood nationalist anti-colonial concerns. That is, his discourse gains a particular meaningful resonance because it is embedded within the larger re-adjustment of the Muslim world to the international system since the nineteenth century, and the discourse about that, in turn, is more understandable because such issues are themselves framed by the Weltanschauung of textural critique and commentary that comprises the history and essence of Islamic civilization.

As prison no doubt affected his ideas, it is also no doubt true that prison and execution elevated him to martyrdom for the Islamist cause, which in turn increased the saliency of his theories about jihadic politics against existing Arab regimes. His ideas have gone on and influenced generations of Islamist militants throughout the Muslim world. "[An] influential interpretation of Qutb's ideas was that of Shuki Mustafa, who drew the implication of the doctrine of *jahiliyyah* to its logical extreme. If Egyptian society was *jahiliyyah* and rotten to the core, then it must be excommunicated (*takfir*, a lapsed Muslim . . .). . . . By far, the most influential disciple of Qutb was Muhammad Abd al-Salam Faraj (1954–1982), who was head of the Cairo branch of the Tanzim al-Jihad

(*jihad* organization) that killed President Anwar al-Sadat. Faraj articulated his ideas in a pamphlet, *The Neglected Duty*. He quickly built upon Qutb's argument."[15] To this list could be added the Egyptian Ayman al-Zawahiri, the Saudi Osama bin Laden, and others.[16]

Egyptian politics

The prison experience stands on its own as a context that seems to have crystallized and radicalized Qutb's ideas. But it is also true that the social fact of imprisoned Muslim Brothers is clearly part of the broader Arab/Egyptian political struggles of the mid-twentieth century. From the immediacy of a decade in prison to a century of political/ideological struggles over the future shape of Egypt, Qutb is part of a wider twentieth-century context of contentious political factions, parties, and interest groups. These included the Wafd party in the early twentieth century, organized around Sa'd Zaghlul who was inspired by the reformism of Muhammad 'Abduh, the regime of Nasser who made overtures to the Soviet Union and expounded an ideology of pan-Arab socialism, and, of course, the Muslim Brothers, created by Hasan al-Bana in 1928, who argued for the restoration of Islam in all aspects of Egyptian life. Politically the competitive relations between the Muslim Brothers and Nasser's Free Officers provide the immediate context for Qutb's imprisonment, while their struggle over ideologies of political governance provide a broader context for his developing ideas.

While known for its desire to Islamize all aspects of Egyptian life, it is important to remember that the Muslim Brothers had also been active in many of the important political events of twentieth-century Egyptian and Arab history. They volunteered to participate in the 1936–1939 Palestinian revolt and again in the 1948 Palestinian War, where they had a "violent opposition to the 1949 Armistice Agreement (as a result of which they were driven underground for the first time)."[17] Interestingly, and perhaps tellingly for later developments, the Muslim Brothers were initially close to the Free Officers. Anwar Sadat, who had known Nasser since their military college days in the 1930s, had met with al-Bana in 1940, and al-Bana, through Sadat, went on to have contact with Nasser in 1944. It has been suggested that along with other Free Officers, Nasser was a member of the Brothers (using a pseudonym) such that, "the chief popular base for Nasser's success was provided by the Muslim Brothers and their sympathizers . . . [and it was] in tight cooperation with the Brothers that the Free Officers successfully launched their 'revolution' on July 23, 1952."[18] While initially allies, there was a natural political antagonism between Nasser and the Muslim Brothers for they were both contenders for power in Egypt.

Given their competition, the religious Brothers and the socialist Nasserites shared a surprising number of similarities. Both had an anti-Western outlook, as did almost all political parties and ideological persuasions in the Arab world in the 1950s. Because of a variety of neo-colonial practices, such as trying to maintain control of the Suez Canal, the Western powers were still considered unwanted influences in Arab politics. Qutb's particular anti-Western outlook took the form of arguing for the superiority of Islam over other Western religions (Christianity and Judaism), philosophies (Greek rationalism, empiricism, and science) and political creeds from liberal democracy to Marxism, communism, and socialism. Pan-Arabism was also important within the overall Nasserite ideology, and made a temporary political appearance with the union of Syria and Egypt as the United Arab Republic (1958–1961). While Qutb's thinking could be considered pan-Arabist, he actually argues for a community of believers which would transcend national boundaries. Social welfare was a central ideological plank in Nasser's socialist program and central to Qutb as well, as seen in his earliest Islamist book, *Social Justice in Islam*, and both the Muslim Brothers and secular parties had branches in numerous Arab countries: the Ba'ath Party in Iraq, Jordan, Lebanon and Syria, and the Muslim Brothers in Syria, Jordan, Saudi Arabia, Palestine, and of course, Egypt. Finally, there is Arab public opinion. Nasserite positions were very popular throughout the Arab world, such that, "in the court of Arab public opinion, the Nasserites decisively won the argument [against the United States]."[19] Similarly, Qutb's writings also enjoyed a great popularity not only in Egypt but throughout the Muslim world.

Perhaps it was all these similarities that made Nasserites and Muslim Brothers such heated enemies, and the fact that such ideologically different contenders for power shared such similar characteristics may very well be a product of the zeal for self-governance that griped the Arab world after the Second World War. The creation of the UN, the rise of African and Asian nations, the recession of European colonialism, the rising importance of Middle Eastern oil, and a growing young urban population all contributed to sentiments of national self-determination.[20] It was already a heady climate for political change when Qutb returned to Egypt with a recommitment to Islam and a renewed involvement in Egyptian nationalist politics. "By the mid–1950s, then, politically conscious Arabs were inclined to be restless and impatient. They had gained nominal independence and now wanted the real thing."[21] This would certainly seem to characterize Qutb, the Muslim Brothers, and Nasser and his Free Officers, and it was in this context that Qutb moved toward a growing political radicalism.

His ideas were both affected by, and contributed to, Egyptian political struggles. For instance, the older question of responding to, or reaching an accommodation with the West, was now replaced by the question of exactly what self-rule would look like. Should the emerging autonomous Egyptian state have a pan-Arabist orientation and work toward something like the United Arab Republic, or should it be more strictly nationalist with secular democratic, military, dynastic, or one-party rule, or should it be an Islamic-based polity? On this ideological plane, contending positions were as much among Egyptian Muslims, as between them and the West, and this, in turn, raised the question of the moral status of domestic conflict and anarchy, that is, the classic Sunni fear of revolt and disorder (e.g. *fitna*).

The right to revolt against a Muslim ruler who was despotic, was "not readily acceptable to traditional Sunni political theory, haunted as it was by the trauma of civil war of the type that tore the Islamic community apart in the mid-seventh century. Hence the predilection of the *ulama* [religious authorities]—later reinforced by material dependence upon the authorities—for a sort of pessimistic realism: even an evil ruler is better than anarchy."[22] Similarly, religiously justified struggle/striving/fighting had traditionally been conducted against non-Muslims, and was often led by a caliph or some established leader within the Muslim community.[23] Ataturk, though, had abolished the Caliphate in 1924 and in Egypt the government financially supported the Islamic clerics at al-Azhar University, who in turn supported the Nasser regime. From the point of view of traditional Islam, then, it would have been difficult to both religiously justify and motivate, jihadic resistance to a practicing Muslim ruler or call for jihadic political opposition without a caliph or clerics from al-Azhar. There were, of course, secular grounds for resistance as found in Marxist and socialist theories of revolution,[24] but a distinctly Islamic position calling for a regime change was much more tenuous. This seems particularly to have been the case for religiously justified resistance to a government of practicing Muslims originating within the Egyptian army and serving the national interest by doing battle with the ex-colonial powers of Britain and France during the Suez Crisis of 1956.

One way to legitimate and motivate a struggle against a regime of devout Muslims from a distinctly Islamic perspective, would be to create a new formulation of the classic notion of a struggle in the cause of God, or *jihad*. Such an Islamic justification of jihadic politics against fellow Muslim leaders would be difficult because, for one, it would no longer be defensive, unless one wanted to argue that Egypt's government was somehow attacking its own citizens. While by twists and turns such a case could be made about a ruler like Nasser, a more reasonable position would be to abandon the defensive war prerequisites and adopt a new, more offensive or proactive, theory of jihadic politics, which is also a return to the initial religious foundation of the Islamic conquest of the seventh century. Qutb's fundamentalism isn't limited to application of *shari'a* law, but includes a reformulation of the earliest mix of religion and fighting that was the moral cornerstone of the seventh century Muslim expanse beyond the Arabian Peninsula.

Qutb built upon Ibn Taymiyya's (1268–1328) justification for fighting the Mongol rulers who had conquered Baghdad but who were practicing Muslims. Taymiyya reasoned that while they professed the Islamic creed (There is no god but God, and Muhammad is his messenger), performed the five prayers and observed the fast of Ramadan, this wasn't enough to make them true Muslims. "Here Ibn Taymiyya introduced a new criterion. A professed Sunni Muslim ceases to be one when he fails to keep (or in the case of a Muslim ruler, apply) the shari'a. . . ."[25] Now, in Qutb's application, Nasser's government, while composed of faithful Muslims in terms of their private religious practices, was not actually a true Muslim regime because the government did not apply the *shari'a*. Hence they were fair game for the application of the doctrine of *jihad*; and hence fair game to be overthrown. A modern Islamic theory of domestic resistance and revolutionary politics by Muslims, within a Muslim state, against political rule by fellow practicing Muslims, was formulated.

On the plane of theorizing political resistance, Qutb generated an Islamic theory "to legitimize revolt in terms of main stream Sunni thought."[26] As a disciple of Qutb's would latter comment: "One cannot account for the first Muslim Empire unless one takes into consideration the prophecy of Muhammad; the groundwork for the French Revolution was laid by Rousseau, Voltaire, and Montesquieu; the Communist Revolution realized the plans set by Marx, Engels, and Lenin; Nazism grew out of a soil labored by Hegel, Fichte, and Nietzsche. The same holds true for us as well,"[27] and the same point would now hold for Qutb, as grounds for resistance, revolt, and revolution were being set in Islamic, not Marxian or socialist, terms.

The Islamic revival

Like the prison experience of 1955–1964 and mid-twentieth century Egyptian politics, the late nineteenth/twentieth century Islamic Revival also seems to have had a clear effect upon Qutb's thought. The change in Islamic thinking and practices associated with the term the "Islamic Revival" has many aspects, including the analogy some make with the Protestant Reformation.[28] "Just as the leaders of the Reformation in Europe set in motion revolutionary religious and political changes while contrasting a presumably purer past with present corruption, so may today's Islamists be revolutionary in impact as they preach a return to the past."[29] And as Qutb's prison experience was part of Egyptian politics, so is that politics part of the broader intellectual movement of reaction against Western influence. "Between 1800 and 1920, the British, the French, the Russians, the Dutch, the Italians, and the Germans annexed or asserted influence over almost the entire Muslim community."[30] Qutb's ideas can also be considered part and parcel of not only the trauma of prison and the politics of Egyptian nationalism, but also of the historical shift within Islam variously referred to as the rise of modernist Islam, the idea of Islam in a liberal age,[31] the Islamic revival,[32] or the notion of an Islamic Reformation.[33]

The Revival/Reformation thesis is often seen in the shift from more other-worldly religious orientations, as embodied in Sufism, toward more this-worldly orientations, as represented by Wahhabism, Salafism, and Qutbian fundamentalism, and the analogy between radical Islamic Fundamentalism and radical Puritan Protestantism.[34] From a Weberian perspective,[35] this can be seen as a shift from more mystical, ritualistic, and other-worldly practices (as more predominant in Catholicism and Sufism) to more reform and protest practices and more this-worldly orientations (as more predominant in radical Protestantism and Islamic Fundamentalism). "It is there in the grand narrative of the Egypto-Arab tradition. It is there in Jamal al-Din al-Afghani's (1838/39–1897) admiration for the achievements of the European Protestants in Christianity for their willingness to ignore the advice of their priests, in going back to first principles, and making up their minds, as he urged Muslims to do, using their own efforts. 'Verily', he was to say many times quoting the Qur'an, 'God does not change the state of a people until they change themselves inwardly'. He identified himself, of course, with Martin Luther. This activism for individuals was present in his friend and pupil, Muhammad 'Abduh (1849–1905), who was probably the first major thinker in the modern Arab world to emphasize the caliphate of man. . . . This activism was present, too, in the emphasis of 'Abduh's leading disciple, Rashid Rida (1869–1935) on *jihad*, or positive effort, being the essence of Islam. This was, he argued, a principle contained both in Islam and in modern civilization. This activism was there, of course, when the movement for reform, shocked by the corruption and complacency of Egypt's elites, both '*ulama* and lay folk, began to be manifest as a radical popular movement, an Islamist movement, the Muslim Brotherhood. It was there, too, in the second phase of the Brotherhood's existence in the call of Sayyid Qutb (1906–1966) for Muslims to commit themselves to *jihad* against the *jahili*, Islamically ignorant, elements which pervaded it."[36]

In both Islamic Revival and Protestant Reformation there appears to have been similar declines in traditional religious authority. Experts have noted the decline in the Sufi tradition of mysticism, cults, and the worship of tombs, shrines, and saints, and with Protestantism a similar disregard for saints, indulgences, church hierarchy, and ritual in general. Williams argued that the more radical Protestant sects were interested in *restitutio* (restitution of what was perceived to have been the original order of the faith community) rather than *reformatio* which involved reforming the existing religious order, and something along these lines could be said of the reforms proposed by earlier modernists such as al-Afghani, 'Abduh, or Rida, and the later more radical Islamist fundamentalists such as Mawdudi, al-Bana, and Qutb.[37] They seem more interested in *restitutio*, the renewal of the polity in the form of the initial community of the Prophet and his Companions, rather than merely reforming (*reformatio*) traditional Sufi mystical traditions.

Within the Sunni tradition religious authority had been largely established through the *madhhabs* (schools of jurisprudence), but by the nineteenth century, "the most striking element was the widespread abandonment of *taqlid* (following) of the *mudhhabs* in favor of various form of *ijtihad* (independent judgment). This then, is one parallel with the European Reformation."[38] Clearly Qutb fits this pattern of independent judgment. His interpretation of the Qur'an is not based upon previous interpretations of medieval jurists, imams, or clerics, but of his own independent opinion. Where there are noticeable influences, they are more likely to be from his contemporaries. Accompanying, and in some sense facilitating this independence of judgment, is the fact that Qutb was not a trained cleric, but a literary critic, as Mawdudi was a Pakistani journalist by training, and al-Bana an Egyptian school teacher. None of these twentieth century figures in the emergence of Islamic Fundamentalist thinking were trained in traditional Islamic institutions of higher learning. "[I]n premodern Muslim societies we do not find the Protestant model of scriptural interpretation—the believer along with the sacred text, without the mediation of tradition. Instead, it was necessary for the average believer to turn to qualified authorities. Experts did not attempt to read the text in an individualistic fashion but relied on the many-layered discoveries of their predecessor."[39] But since the nineteenth century writers increasingly used "the techniques of Protestant Christianity, [and] appealed to scriptural authority, and [as such] rejected centuries of historical tradition."[40] Qutb would clearly seem to be part of such a movement.

The Revival/Reformation comparison also suggests more than just reformist attacks upon established religious practices, as "the eclipse of Sufi beliefs and practices in the Islamic world . . . parallels the eclipse of central elements of Catholic belief and practice in early Protestantism."[41] This can be seen in Rashid Rida's (1865–1935) comment that what is needed is to combine "religious renewal and earthly renewal, the same way Europe has done with religious reformation and modernization."[42] Qutb's twentieth-century thinking, then, could be seen as having origins in the nineteenth century, as shifts in Muslim attitudes can be seen in both South Asian and Egyptian lines of thought. "The feeling of personal responsibility before God, and the need to act on earth to achieve salvation, ran through the many manifestations of reform in [nineteenth century] India."[43]

Intellectual movements accompanied by political violence were also not new with Qutb and the Muslim Brothers. There had been uprisings on the Muslim sub-continent, including the Indian "mutiny" of 1857, and the *fatwa's* of Shah Waliullah, an Indian Muslim cleric, against the Hindus. There was also the Sudanese Mahdi's revolt in the late nineteenth century and the eighteenth century Wahhabist revolt in Saudi Arabia. Prior to Qutb, then, there had clearly been a century or more of reaction, revolt, and religious revitalization movements in Muslim lands. "In all these cases, anger and a sense of injustice compounded by continued social and economic crisis resulted in movements coalescing around charismatic religious figures who used the language of Islam to articulate a variety of diverse grievances and to suggest a solution. The solution almost always relied on a rejection of current Islamic practice and political structures and actors in favor of a reversion to a pure and unpolluted 'truth'."[44]

While there are many possible reasons for this broad shift in thinking, the change in schooling seems particularly applicable to Qutb. "A world-view that had sustained Sufism through many centuries was replaced—largely as a result of 'modern education'—with a rationalistic world-view among elites that was incompatible with many of the understandings on which Sufism is based."[45] As a result Muslims increasingly characterized Sufism's other-worldly orientation as "un-Islamic", "a deviation from Islam", "an anachronism", "an archaism", "an obscurantism", "obscurantist in comparison with modern rationality", or "an anachronism in the modern age."[46] As a result, "established and aspiring elite families were obliged to put their children through these modern systems of education to equip them for the new career paths created by modernizing and colonial states. The education given at venerable institutions such as the Azhar in Cairo . . . had for centuries been the path to position and respect, but with modernity led only to increasingly ill-paid and low-status occupations."[47] This description of social change seems to fit Qutb's life, for although he was very devout he became a literary critic, secular writer, and an employee of the Egyptian education ministry. And if it is true that "many of these 'modern schools' produced graduates who were . . . familiar with the thinkers of the European Enlightenment,"[48] that seems an apt description of Qutb's early love of distinctly modernist literature, novels, poetry, and literary criticism.

Islamic civilization

Nesting Qutb's thought in ever larger political and ideological contexts comes to an end at the level of Islamic civilization as a whole. "Throughout the ages Muslim religious spokesmen have confronted Muslim rulers – ever so circumspectly at times, but occasionally in thundering condemnation,"[49] and the tension between Qutb and Nasser can be seen as part of a much longer tradition of religiously based political struggle. These would also include, "Ahmad Sirhindi in India against the syncretism of the Mogul ruler Akbar; Muhammad ibn Abd al-Wahhab against the champions of popular religious customs in the eighteenth-century Najd; Uthman dan Fodio against the venal ulama and semi-pagan rules of West Africa; or Muhammad Ahmad, the Sudanese Mahdi, against a corruption government and also popular religious customs."[50] Here, "anyone who can . . . achieve a standing as a valid religious spokesman is in a position to pose a serious organized threat to government,"[51] and religious vocabularies of resurgence involving ideas of "renewal" (*tajdid*) and "reform" (*islah*) have appeared throughout Muslim history. "The renewer-reformer . . . has claimed the right to make his own judgment based directly on an independent analysis of the Quran and Sunna,"[52] which is precisely Qutb, with his interpretations of classic Islamic concepts such as *jahiliyyah* (state of ignorance of God), *jihad* (struggle in the cause of God), and *hakimiyyah* (sovereignty), all formulated under the Islamic tradition of *ijtihad* (independent analysis and reasoning). At this most macro of contexts three civilizational traditions can be seen which once identified are relevant to a fuller understanding of the concept of *jihad* that is so central to Qutb's writings.

First, one can find precursors to *jihad* in the pre-Islamic traditions of Northern Arabia, a stateless area where aggrieved parties would look to large, powerful, pastoral nomadic groups for revenge and protection.[53] In such an environment of rivalrous tribes, a semi-Hobbesian world of ritualized raiding and conflict was a normal state of affairs, and raids of this sort were separated from more serious wars which were over things such as grazing territories or access to wells. "There appear to have been definite 'rules of the game' in raiding that both sides were expected to observe in the interests of fairness; attacking noncombatants with lethal intent, for example, was considered bad form and was generally avoided."[54] Such "rules of the game" could have served as a cultural template out of which the distinctly Islamic notion of *jihad* was later constructed. As Donner and others have noted, traditions of fighting and struggle in the cause of God seem to have precursors within the tribal traditions of pre-Islamic Arabia. On the other hand contemporary attacks by terrorists in the name of global *jihad* do not seem to be directly derivable from pre-Islamic traditions of tribal conflict, with their prohibitions on violence against innocents, non-combatants, women, children, and so forth. "The contemporary jihadists—the violent wing among the fundamentalists—seem different. It is hard to avoid the impression that for them the point is simply violence and killing, while care for the unfortunate, generosity, and socially and politically constructive activities, in general, are all matters of indifference."[55]

Second, the mix of religion and politics so characteristic of Qutb is, as almost all commentators point out, at the heart of Islam and appears to originate in the very founding of the faith itself. The key fact here is that Muhammad received his revelations within a stateless polity. "Muhammad was active among warring tribes and had to take political and military action if he was to accomplish his mission. The religion could not survive without communal embodiment, and the community could not survive without defense. Hence it had to have political organization."[56] Therefore, mixing religion and politics, as in the modern notion of "Political Islam," is not new. This could be considered a classic instance of what the sociology of organizations calls an organizational founding effect, where environmental constraints become incorporated within an emerging organization's structure and culture, and continue to persist even after their initial founding conditions no longer apply. "Thanks to the environment in which it originated, Islam was thus embodied in a political organization almost from the start: the *umma* [community of the faithful] was a congregation and a state rolled together. Christians originated with dual membership. As believers they belonged to the church and were administered by the clergy; as citizens they belonged to the Roman Empire and were ruled by Caesar. Islam originated without this bifurcation. As believers *and* as citizens they were members of the *umma* and ruled by the Prophet, thereafter by his successors."[57] From a civilizational perspective, then, Qutb doesn't seem to have hijacked Islam for political purposes as much as called for a return to Islam's original religio-political compact.

Qutb could be considered something of a "strict constructionist" in the sense of those who favor a literal, or fundamentalist interpretation of the American Constitution. Interestingly, the moral fury of American conservatives over purported departures from the initial eighteenth-century constitutional blueprint concerning the separation of powers is analogous to Qutb's strong desire to enforce a strict constructionist interpretation of the seventh-century Muslim amalgam of powers. He wanted a polity where the religious and the political are fused; American strict constructionists want a modern polity modeled on the principles lived by the founding fathers of the Republic. Qutb wanted to reorganize the world according to how the founding fathers of Islam lived: the political-religious constitution, so to speak, of the first generation of Muslims. The implications of such strict constructionist interpretation obviously depends on the character of the initial social compact. In the American case it was a separation of powers; in the Muslim case it was a merger of the political and the religious.

Third, given a stateless polity accompanied by inter-tribal raiding, and resistance to Muhammad's monotheistic revelations, it makes sociological sense that the Qur'an would contain permissions and even exhortations concerning the use of violence and fighting (e.g. "Prescribed for you is fighting, though it be hateful to you". Q. 2:216). There has been much discussion as to the true meaning of *jihad*, and the famed "sword verses" (such as Q. 9:5) continue to be debated.[58] While the origin and precise Qur'anic meaning of *jihad* is open to question, the Muslim conquests of the seventh century, and the juridical writing of the eighth century, began to apply the term to military action. Qutb's theory of proactive *jihad* to create a universal Islamic community is not new with him, nor with struggles with Nasser, nor as an instance of a possible Islamic Reformation. Civilizationally, *jihad* is a contested concept that has taken on implications of violence from the very beginning of the Muslim era, and as we have seen, perhaps even earlier.

There is a final civilizational perspective, the view of Islam from the point of view of the West. The classic critique of the Western view was Edward Said's book *Orientalism*. "My contention is that without examining Orientalism as a discourse one cannot possibly understand the enormously systematic discipline by which European culture was able to manage—and even produce—the Orient politically, sociologically, militarily, ideologically, scientifically, and imaginatively during the post-enlightenment period."[59] He further argued that, "because of Orientalism the Orient was not (and is not) a free subject of thought or action."[60] This assumption has become important in studies of Islamic thought and has served as an inspiration for the establishment of post-colonial studies.[61]

Qutb's intellectual presence now raises the issue of what could be called Reverse Orientalism. If we can call the original Western bias, Orientalism1, the essentialist reading of Muslims as lethargic, child-like, feminine, and devoid of energy and initiative, then today's critics point to what could be called Orientalism2—the depiction of Muslims as overly aggressive and violent. "Islam is not violence, nor are Muslims intrinsically prone to violence. The stereotype amounts to a slur, and it must be addressed . . . Islamists, or Muslim "fundamentalists," are thought to be single-mindedly pitted against the secular state; suicide bombings and hostage-taking are viewed as critical, if not the decisive, component of the modern Muslim-Western encounter."[62] The stereotype many argue needs to be overcome today is no longer the Muslim with a child-like passivity, but just the opposite: the violent and aggressive Muslim. "I suggest that the principal reason for the negative view of Islam is the predominance in popular thinking of the . . . [view] that Islam emanates from a hostile, 'Arab' Middle East."[63]

It is as if the Orientalist bias has been turned on its head. Where earlier the root of Western stereotypes of the Muslim Orient was centered on "its backwardness, its silent indifference, its feminine penetrability, its supine malleability,"[64] today's bias is that "the dominant stereotype is . . . Muslims [are] intrinsically prone to violence."[65] To believe the critics, the West has gone from depicting the Middle East as silent and lacking initiative (when supposedly it wasn't) to depicting it as violent and aggressive (when, supposedly it isn't). In Orientalism1 the charge was passivity; in Orientalism2 the charge is aggressiveness, raising the question of where the truth lies. Part of the problem is events. Given a couple centuries of colonial domination, ideas of passivity arise; given a few decades of terrorist attacks by radical Islamist groups, ideas of aggressiveness are proposed. Where the truth lies remains contested terrain.

2   Qutb's core ideas

Albert J. Bergesen

Qutb theorizes an organic connection between religion and politics based upon his understanding of the early days of the Prophet and his Companions in seventh-century Arabia. He argues that the manner in which religion and politics were connected in the first generation of Muslims constitutes a viable model for today. For him what emerged then was a society and political system based upon the divine revelations of the Qur'an, and while over time there has been a drift from this intimate relationship, it still constitutes the best model for political organization and social life. As he notes, "what an amazing phenomenon in the history of mankind: a nation emerging from the text of a Book, living by it, and depending on its guidance as the prime source!", by which he is referring to, "the first group of Muslims [who] molded their lives according to this concept which comes directly from the Qur'an. They led mankind in a manner unparalleled in history, either before or after [but then] . . . later generations drifted away from the Qur'an, . . . [such that] today we see mankind in a miserable condition."[1]

His proposal to alleviate today's human misery is a "new attempt at the revival of Islamic life," which most importantly is a practical sociological matter, not just one of psychological religious belief. "The real problem in grasping the significance and the spirit of the Qur'anic teachings does not lie in understanding its words and sentences [. . .] The problem lies in the capacity of our minds to reconstruct feelings, ideas, and experiences like the feelings, ideas and experiences of the first generation of Muslims . . . in the thick of the struggle. Theirs was a struggle of *jihad*, of striving within oneself and striving with other people. It was a fight against temptations and a battle against enemies."[2] For Qutb the battle for the establishment of God's path for mankind is eternal and will persist as long as there is willful opposition backed by the political power and the material force of the state and it's society.

His program to bring mankind back to Islam and realize the fundamental relationship between God and man, is based upon three interconnected concepts or ideas. First, there are the divine revelations of the Qur'an, and the *Islamic concept* of life that they specify and imply. Second, there are socio-political obstacles in the form of existing socio-political systems, from race and economic relations to the power of the modern state. All of this he characterizes as *jahiliyyah* (ignorance of God). This existing state of the world actively opposes God's will. Third, given that such *jahili* societies actively resist the implementation of the word of God, there must be an equivalent power, in the form of an Islamic social movement, to remove these socio-political obstacles, thereby liberating mankind to realize the way of life God has designed. In short, there is (1) a goal to be realized, (2) obstacles to be overcome, and (3) a means to overcome these obstacles and realize that goal. These notions can be explicated in a little more detail.

The goal: realizing *the Islamic concept*

We begin with Qutb's concept of religion, and with what he refers to as the Islamic concept and the Oneness of God. "The Islamic concept rests on the principle that the Divine Being is distinct from His creation. Divinity belongs exclusively to Allah Most High, while creatureliness is common to everyone and everything else. Since Allah Most High is the only Divine Being, it follows that the Divine attributes belong to Him alone. And since everyone and everything else is His creation, it also follows that they are all devoid of Divine attributes. Thus there are two distinct orders of existence, namely, the independent existence of Allah Most High and the dependent existence of all others as His creatures. The relationship between Allah and everything else is that of the Creator to His creatures and of the Lord to His servants. This is the first principle of the Islamic concept and all other principles follow from it. Because the Islamic concept rests on this basic principle, the Oneness of God is its most important characteristic."[3]

This radical transcendence acts to absolutely naturalize the world, which God created as a natural non-divine reality. Divinity is entirely separate and takes the form of a totally transcendent God. This assumption of a radical bifurcation of existence has two important implications. First, knowledge of God's will is only obtainable through God's revelations to humanity as given to prophets from Abraham and Moses to Jesus and Muhammad. This, and only this, is the manner in which the will of God is known. All the prophets are important, but Muhammad, as the last, brings together, sums up, and finalizes all the prophetic messages that preceded him. As recorded in the Qur'an this is the message of God for mankind, and to believe in God is to work toward realizing God's plan.

To more fully understand the Islamic concept, we can begin with his conception of the uniqueness of Islam, which centers on the belief in the radical Oneness of God which makes, by implication, other religions, ideologies, and philosophies open to errors, and hence not reliable guides for human life. From the point of view of the Oneness of the divine, the simplest error other religions can make is believe in multiple divines, whether formal polytheisms such as the ancient Egyptian trinity Horus, Isis, and Osiris, contemporary Hinduism, or all sorts of paganisms, idol and animistic nature worship. The critique from Oneness also includes pre-Islamic Arabia, where, "they also worshipped planets and stars as the Persians also did. Sa'ed says, 'The tribe of Hamir worshipped the sun, Kanah the moon, and Tamin Alderbran, Lakhm, and Judham worshiped Jupiter, Tayy the Dog-star, Qays, Sirius, and Asad, Mercury.' "[4] He also devalues Islamic philosophy, because of its non-divine origin. "It is not possible to find a basis for Islamic thought in the modes and products of European thought, nor to reconstruct Islamic thought by borrowing from Western modes of thought or its products."[5] Therefore, "the so-called 'Islamic Philosophy' was nothing more than a discordant note in the harmonious melody of the Islamic belief. Such intellectual gymnastics merely produced confusion in people's minds and polluted the purity of the Islamic concept, narrowing its scope and rendering it superficial, dry, complicated, and incomprehensible. . . . [in short] 'Islamic philosophy'. . . . [is] completely foreign to Islam."[6]

A second error religions can make is limiting the Oneness of God to a specific human group. "Belief in the Oneness of Allah was the religion of Abraham. . . . When Moses, peace be upon him, came as a Messenger to the children of Israel, he came with the message of the Oneness of Allah, but the children of Israel, before and after Moses, corrupted this concept and changed the meanings of the words from their intended meanings. They made Allah into a national deity of the Israelites, the Lord God of Israel. . . ."[7] For Qutb, the message of God is for all humanity. The radical bifurcation of the universe into the divine and only divine—making God the one and only one—has a mirror opposite Oneness principle on the side of the natural—a radical Oneness to all of humanity. The God that is all and everything, is for all and everyone, and to claim God is a God of a particular people is to violate the Oneness on both the divine and the natural plane. Because of one God there should only be one global community of believers—no social, class, tribal, ethnic, national, regional, racial, ethnic, or gender differences within humanity. As God's creation, humanity shares a common status in relation to God the creator, making distinctions amongst humanity a violation of their singular relationship to their singular God.

A god for a particular people, subdivides the potential Oneness of the global *umma* (community of believers) into peoples, nations, states, groups, races and so forth, and the Oneness of God into de facto, separate gods, for if there is a god for this group, then that isn't the god for other groups, which, if they are to have religion, would mean they would have to have their own gods. This group has god X, that group god Y, and another god Z, and with that the Oneness on both sides of the ontological divide is lost. Multiple worshiping communities (the division of the Oneness of the human *umma*) and multiple gods (the division of the Oneness of God), was the precondition of the world before the call to Islam in the seventh century, and it is the condition of the world today that has regressed back to the state of pre-Islamic existence.

Third, Oneness can be lost when some attributes of God are shared with humans. The mixing of the divine and the natural can be bottom up or top down. Bottom up is worshipers claiming to be able to fuse, or somehow merge with God, and in a variety of mystical practices this would characterize many religions, including Sufi Islam. Top down is the Christian error, assuming that Jesus is a compound Godhead. "Jesus, peace be upon him, came with the message of the Oneness of Allah, but Christians ended up with a belief in the Trinity. They still claim that the Godhead is One entity divided among three persons: the Father, the Son, and the Holy Ghost . . . [therefore] we can safely state that the Islamic concept is the only concept resting on the foundation of a complete and pure belief in the Oneness of Allah."[8]

For Qutb, this occurred because Christianity was Romanized more than Rome was Christianized, which resulted in a modification of the original Oneness of Jesus' prophetic message. Qutb endorses the line of thinking that at the Council of Nicea the newly converted Christian Emperor Constantine wanted a cohesive religio-political formulation that fit the Empire and would meld the theological factionalism of Christian sects into a common unified platform: a godhead composed of the separate entities of father, son, and holy ghost, as expressed in the Nicean Creed. "Religious passions were exploited to keep the Empire together, exposition of faiths were intended to halt disputes between the contending factions, and doctrines were propounded to unite heretics to the Orthodox Church and to the central government . . . [and] as a result of these compromises, the Church adopted many distorted concepts."[9] With Christian Trinitarianism the Oneness of God was lost and Qutb would cynically compare the purported monotheism of Christianity with the polytheism of ancient Egypt. "The conception of the trinity in the new faith must have seemed to the Egyptians a mere duplication of their own triads, the most famous of which was, of course, the triad of Osiris, Isis, and Horus."[10]

The subsequent European world view was of a reality where it is possible to be wholly human and wholly divine, which meant a world where hints of the divine are understood to be able to penetrate, or somehow be embodied within the fiber of nature. Now religious rulings could also be rulings about the natural world. The immanental doctrine of the Catholic Church paved the way for Church objections, on religious grounds, to scientific propositions about the nature of the physical world, as in the famous case of Galileo. With the Islamic Oneness assumption this problem couldn't have arisen for physical nature is seen as God's creation, outside of and independent of the divine essence. Nature was created as a here and now reality whose laws and principles can, and should, be discovered by mankind. God, on the other hand, is clearly above and beyond his physical creation, and therefore human scientific claims about nature have no implication for God, or the divine, as "the Islamic concept rests on the principle that the Divine Being is distinct from His creation."

For Qutb, such Roman induced divine immanentalism, along with centuries of Church, hence human, created doctrine, edicts, and dogma, ended up leading European thought down an erroneous path. "Christianity was born in the shadow of the pagan Roman Empire. Later, when the Roman Empire adopted Christianity as the state religion, it did great violence to the teachings of Jesus, distorting them beyond recognition."[11] Therefore, "when the astronomers and physicists started to correct the errors contained in these "facts," the origins of which was human rather than divine, the church took a very harsh stand against them . . . [and so] in order to get rid of the authority of the Church, they [European thinkers] eliminated the God of the Church."[12] In short, Europe turned toward only secular thinking.

Half a century after Qutb's death, Pope Benedict XVI seems to have come to a similar conclusion, when he noted that Islam, "is capable of offering a valid spiritual basis for the life of the peoples, a basis that seems to have slipped out of the hands of old Europe, which thus, notwithstanding its continued political and economic power, is increasingly viewed as a declining culture condemned to fade away."[13] Qutb observed that, "the enmity of European thought to religion and to the methodology of religion consists not simply in the philosophical system, schools of thought, and subjects of study that were established in opposition to religion, but rather lies at the very heart of European thought . . . [where] since the Renaissance, the general trend of the Western mode of thought was criticism of the Catholic Church and its doctrines, and with the passage of time, to object to all religion and religious doctrines per se."[14] His thinking is strikingly echoed in a summary of Pope Benedict's view by the primate of the Benedictine order. "Western society has become detached from the roots of its creator. This is the basic view of the Pope, and it is my view also. What the Muslims say about the decadence of Europe is partly right, and that's because we think we have to set up everything as if God doesn't exist."[15] "Secularism may be one of the great developments in history, but the secularism that holds sway in much of the West—that is, in Western Europe—is flawed; it has a bug in its programming. The mistaken conviction that reason and faith are two distinct realms has weakened Europe and has brought it to the verge of catastrophic collapse."[16] These observations by a Western commentator were foreshadowed by Qutb who earlier argued that European thought, "has taken an inimical stand not merely against the doctrines of the Church . . . but against all religious ideas and concepts in general. Indeed, its enmity extended beyond religious ideas and concepts to the very essence of religious thought."[17] This was echoed half a century later by the Pope who argued, "Europe is losing its soul. Not only are we no longer Christian; we're anti-Christian. So we don't know who we are."[18]

For Qutb, such a European identity crisis arose because their sources of knowledge began with a basis in scripture, then in reason (rationalism), then in sensations (empiricism), and finally in materialism (Marxism). All of these attempted to realilze ultimate values (divine knowledge) through secular knowledge (trial and error, constantly revised scientific knowledge). For Qutb, the two cannot be mixed. What is required for human values, a fixed absolutism, yields error in science; what is required for science, trial and error and changing beliefs, yields errors in human values (no absolute guide, no real values of any permanent sort). The result of this unhappy marriage has been the various conundrums, contradictions, and unnecessary oppositions that characterize Western thought. Plato had ideas above matter; Christians a soul over the body; and Marx matter over ideas. But for Qutb, Islam honors both and sees no contradiction because Islam has only one basis: God, within which all other sources of knowledge have their place. None is downgraded nor raised to be a deity. European secularity came at the expanse of a transcendent religious foundation resulting in material well-being at the expense of a sense of divine origin. This is a modern pathology which Qutb argues can only be cured by the worldwide re-establishment of Islam.

Finally, there is the fourth departure from Oneness, the nature of which constitutes his most significant contribution to political theory. "One consequence of belief in the Oneness of Allah is that Allah Most High is the Lord and Sovereign of men not merely in their beliefs, concepts, consciences, and rituals of worship, but in their practical affairs . . . the Muslim believes that there is no true ruler above him except Allah, no legislator for him except Allah, no one except Allah to inform him concerning his relationships and connections with the universe, with other living creatures, and with one's fellow human beings. This is why the Muslim turns to Allah for guidance and legislation in every aspect of life, whether it be political governance, economic justice, personal behavior, or the norms and standards of social intercourse."[19]

This link between daily politics and religion, which is the heart of what is meant by Qutbian political Islam, can be seen when he argues, "obedience to laws and judgements is a sort of worship, and anyone who does this lords over others."[20] He assumes, "sovereignty over people is a major attribute of divinity,"[21] which means humanity's self-sovereignty, man's rule over man, (from kingship to democracy), is usurping that which is an attribute of God. This constitutes a partnering with God, and thereby a violation of the Oneness assumption. If only God is to exercise sovereignty over people, then when humans claim sovereignty over each other this implicitly takes people away from God. This, of course is the mirror opposite of the Western separation of the religious and the political; leave to Caesar what is Caesar's and to God what is God's. But in Qutbian Islam, what is Caesar's is God's, and to leave it to Caesar is to take it from God. The logic is as follows.

First, God's plan, law, or rules, that is what God wants for humanity, as revealed to Muhammad and recorded in the Qur'an, should obviously be followed. Second, to exercise some level of political authority is to exercise sovereignty, and if sovereignty is a core attribute of God, then following the Oneness assumption, it is not to be divided, split, partioned, or shared with others. Therefore, only God is to exercise sovereignty (only God's laws are to be followed), not those of the state, or school board, or county planning commission, such that exercising state, school board, or planning commission sovereignty, is, by definition, a usurpation of a prerogative of God. "Anyone who serves someone other than God in this sense is outside God's religion, although he may claim to profess this religion."[22] This is the fourteenth-century Ibn Taymiyya principle, re-articulated for today's political conditions. The Mongols, after converting, were psychologically Muslims—they said prayers, and so forth—as was Nasser and Sadat. But the Mongols didn't rule on the basis of *shari'a*, and neither did Nasser or Sadat. Therefore, the Mongols were apostate Muslims, or psychologically but not sociologically Muslims, and so too were Nasser and Sadat. In the West professing religion is sufficient; having faith is having belief. But for Qutb having faith is having a political community where authority relations are governed by Qur'anic principles. One is about personal and private belief; one is about collective public political structure.

The link between the political and the religious hinges on the act of submitting to another, that is, political sovereignty and religious worship. When Qutb argues, "some people worship others in some form or another" he is using a religious designation (worship) for a political relation (sovereign authority). It is the key to the fusion of the institutional spheres that makes for what is described in the West as "political Islam." To Qutb, though, it is just religion, or politics; for they are both the same, once one assumes an equivalence between deferral to God in worship and deferral to a political office in sovereignty. Worship is acknowledging a sovereign and sovereignty demands worship from others. Following the Oneness principle, if, "sovereignty . . . is a major attribute of divinity," then for God to be God, and the faithful to be faithful, there can only be submission to God. Qutb does not leave some sovereignty to Caesar and some to God. Sovereignty is an attribute of God; to split it amongst other objects of deferral, thereby worshiping other deities, is to exist in a state of sociological polytheism, which he captures with the term *jahiliyyah*.

This is because exercising political sovereignty involves a partnering with God (the office holder is demanding of others something that should only be demanded by God, namely, submission to His sovereignty). If the office holder is guilty of usurping one of God's attributes, we have a condition of multiple divine attributes in operation, hence we have a situation of polytheism, hence we have a direct challenge to monotheism, and hence a challenge to Islam. People who submit are also guilty, for they, in acknowledging the authority of a political office holder implicitly recognize the partitioning of a major attribute of divinity (sovereignty) between God and the State. "Islam is not merely 'belief'. . . . Islam is a declaration of the freedom of man from servitude to other men. Thus it strives from the beginning to abolish all those systems and governments which are based on the rule of man over men and the servitude of one human being to another."[23]

This reasoning runs counter to the Western political mind, hence it is often derided as a political hijacking of religious belief. But that conclusion is predicted upon the assumption that the political and the religious are ontologically separate spheres. Fusing that which should be separate is making religion into political religion; separating that what should be fused makes monotheistic religion into heretical polytheism. For Qutb, the deviation isn't the fusing of the naturally separate, but the unnatural separation of the inherent unity of sovereignty under God. The deviant position is the Western position, of leaving to Caesar what is, in fact, God's.

The Western idea of a separation of institutional spheres, leaving Caesar's sovereignty to Caesar and God's sovereignty to God, is, for Qutb, a direct challenge to God. Such an assumption has tremendous consequences, for now ordinary, stable, non-aggressive political institutions, say an ideal perfect democracy, is not only not ideal or perfect, but is an aggressive act of taking worshipers away from God by establishing another deity (the State) that demands worship (obeying its laws). Obeying the law (being a good citizen) is now denying God (being a heretic).

The implication is clear. To have a truly monotheistic religion is to have Islam. To be a Qutbian Muslim is to challenge existing political forms of sovereignty. Qutbian Islam, therefore, is an active set of practices; it is not just performing traditional religious rituals. This means that to bear behavioral witness that "there is no deity but God" means to take political action, for if there is no deity but God, there is no sovereignty but God, and to bear witness to that is to avoid submission to other sovereignties, which means to defy existing secular political authorities.

Religion as mere belief is not enough; nor is holding religious ideas in the mind. "The nature of the Islamic concept is not to remain hidden in the human mind. It must be translated immediately into action and become a concrete reality in the world of events. The believer cannot be content to have his faith remain concealed in his heart, because he feels compelled to make his faith an effective force in changing his own life and the lives of the people around him."[24] In effect, religion is as religion does, and Qutb's acts upon the world. "Indeed, the Islamic concept is not like a theory, or an ideal dream, or spiritual mysticism, which may remain passively in the depths of the human heart. It is a practical 'plan' designed to be implemented. As long as it is not implemented, its value remains purely academic, and that is not its intent. It keeps stirring in the heart of the Muslim, spurring him to work in order to realize its goals in the world of events."[25] To realize goals in events is to act, and given the emphasis upon sovereignty, it is to act politically as a social movement. "Islam . . . is intended to penetrate into the veins and arteries of a vital society and to be a concrete organized movement."[26] As he asserts, "philosophical systems have rarely, if ever, played a significant role in the daily lives of human beings. Religious beliefs have always motivated people to action, propelling them toward definite goals, through the wilderness of time and the darkness of the way, whereas philosophical systems have not."[27]

Qutb's Islam is more than just a cognitive plan. It is more like a moral calling, or a compelling and demanding personal ethic. "Thus the Islamic concept keeps the mind of the Muslim restless, always calling him to action from the depths of his consciousness, telling him to get up and go out and actualize this concept in the real world. It refines his sensibilities in order to bring the entire power of his belief and will to bear upon the reconstruction of a society so that the Islamic faith may be realized in the lives of people."[28] To have Qutbian faith is to act. "So, faith is not merely feelings in the heart or ideas in the mind, with no application in life, nor is faith merely rituals of worship, without action in society. . . . The Muslim, under the inspiration of the Islamic concept, feels personally responsible to be a witness to the universal and eternal *din* [the way or path] of Islam. He cannot rest, nor can his conscience be satisfied, nor does he feel that he has fully expressed his thanks to Allah Most High for His great favor in making him a Muslim, nor can he even hope to be saved from Allah's punishment here and in the Hereafter, unless he has given complete testimony to the truth of Islam through his life, effort, and wealth."[29]

For Qutb such testimony progresses through stages, starting with the psychologically more inner and private, and ending with the sociologically more political. "The first manifestation of this testimony is within one's own self. One must bring one's personal life, in every detail, in line with one's concept and belief. . . . Secondly, one expresses one's testimony by inviting others to this way of life through clear exposition of the Islamic concept. . . . Thirdly, our . . . responsibility, similar to the responsibility of the Messengers of Allah to dispel others' ignorance and error, motivates us to convey this message to one and all . . . [and] lastly, one gives testimony through one's efforts to establish the way of life prescribed by Allah, to build the system that proceeds from the Islamic concept, and to organize the affairs of man, and of all peoples, on the basis of this system."[30] In turn, these forms of testimony build upon each other. "Once the negative attitudes are removed from a person's mind, he is impelled toward work and dynamic action. Islam is not satisfied merely with removing the negative attitudes, but rather reinforces positive attitudes by teaching that Allah's will, among human beings, works through themselves and through their actions."[31] Faith and political action are one. "Islam also teaches that Allah is not pleased with mere thoughts in the minds of men and words on their tongues. He does not let a people alone until they translate their faith into action, and He continues to show them His signs until their reward from Him comes in the form of clear guidance."[32]

The essence of the Islamic concept, then, centers upon two core ideas. God has a plan for mankind as revealed through the Prophet Muhammad which has not, importantly, been distorted as have earlier prophetic revelations (Judaism and Christianity). Second, testimony to faith should be manifest in behavioral action to change society and bring it in accord with God's plan, rules, or laws. Therefore, to return mankind to God is a world revolutionary project, "moreover, believers in the Oneness of God, by returning to the system of life that this belief entails and calling others to it are in a position to offer the whole world something possessed by no other religion, ideology, system, constitution, or philosophy. This is the grand opportunity for them to play a great and significant role in transforming the entire world."[33]

The obstacle—*jahili* societies

What stands in the way of realizing God's plan for mankind? And, therefore, what should be the target when faith is translated into action? For Qutb the answer is human devised social relations and political systems, whose authority relations center on human submission to other humans, or the sovereignty of some humans over others. This, as noted earlier, is a usurpation of God's sovereignty on earth. To submit to anyone other than God is to violate the Oneness of God's sovereignty; in Qutb's words, it creates a "servitude of servants." To exercise authority over another is, therefore, to "lord over others" even if this is the consensual authority of a perfect democracy. To characterize this condition he employs the term *jahiliyyah* (ignorance of God) which has been traditionally been used as a characterization of pre-Islamic Arabia.

How pre-Islamic Arabia is also the twenty-first century involves two of Qutb's key points. First, the issue isn't traditionalism, meaning turning the clock back to the seventh century, but fundamentalism, meaning employment of an abstract set of fundamental social and political relations. Second, the notion of ignorance of God is less the psychology of polytheism—belief in multiple gods, and more a sociology of polytheism—submission to multiple sources of authority. Where the emergence of Islam can be seen as a monotheism of belief, Qutb emphasizes the sociological dimension of Oneness. One God is, yes, one belief; but one God is also one source of political sovereignty. For Qutb the Oneness at the heart of monotheism is, of course, about number of gods, idols, or worship sites, but also, and more importantly, Oneness defines, "the Muslim's way of life and the kind of system established by this way of life."[34] Religion is belief (psychology) but more importantly a community (sociology), for Islam was revealed "in order to initiate a special kind of *umma* (community)," and further not just for the Arabs alone but one that is, "unique and distinctive, namely an *umma* that came to lead mankind, to establish the way of Allah on earth, and to save people from the misery brought about by the misguided leadership, erroneous ways, an false concepts."[35] That is, both the pre-Islamic *jahiliyyah* of the seventh century and, given the falling away from Islam, the *jahiliyyah* of today, for, "*Jahiliyyah* is based on rebellion against God's sovereignty on earth. It transfers to man one of the greatest attributes of God, namely sovereignty, and makes some men lords over others. It is now not in that simple and primitive form of the ancient *jahiliyyah*, but takes the form of claiming that the right to create values, to legislate rules of collective behavior, and to choose any way of life rests with men, without regard to what God has prescribed. The result of this rebellion against the authority of God is the oppression of His creatures."[36]

From the assumption of the Oneness of God comes an assumption about our world that is not only belief vs. unbelief, but political systems that submit and those that don't submit to God. "There are only two possibilities for the life of a people, no matter in what time and place they live. These are the state of guidance or the state of error, whatever form the error may take; the state of truth or the state of falsehood, whatever may be the varieties of falsehood; the state of light or the state of darkness, regardless of the shades of darkness; the state of obedience to the Divine guidance or the state of following whims, no matter what varieties of whims there may be; the state of Islam or the state of *jahiliyyah*, without regard to the forms of *jahiliyyah*; and the state of belief or the state of unbelief, of whatever kind. People live either according to Islam, following it as a way of life and a socio-political system, or else in the state of unbelief, *jahiliyyah*, whim, darkness, falsehood, and error."[37]

In the Christian West such a separation of religion and politics was established early on: "And Jesus answering said unto them, Render to Caesar the things that are Caesar's, and to God the things that are God's."[38] But for Qutb, sovereignty is not to be left to Caesar but resisted, overcome, and replaced by God's rightful sovereignty. "This *jahiliyyah* is based on rebellion against God's sovereignty on earth. It transfers to man one of the greatest attributes of God, namely sovereignty, and makes some men lords over others. . . . [the principle that] 'There is no deity except God' . . . is abhorrent to those who are in power in any age and place."[39] Put another way, there is no sovereignty except God's sovereignty, which is abhorrent to those of any age who are in sovereign positions. "In systems other than Islam, some people worship others in some form or another. Only in the Islamic way of life do all men become free from the servitude of some men to others and devote themselves to the worship of God alone."[40] Again, the meaning of freedom and servitude differ depending on the foundational assumption about the fusing of institutional spheres. If the religious and the political are supposed to be fused, then the exercise of secular political sovereignty is to exercise tyranny. It is submitting people to an inappropriate power and hence putting them in a condition of servitude. If the spheres are to be separated then political submission within a system of secular authority relations is not only unproblematic, but a freedom from being folded into a totalitarian submission to only God. Here what is Caesar's is always what is Caesar's; but if Caesar is exercising what is God's, then that yields servitude to Caesar. For existing political systems the implication is clear as, "only Islam refers back all legislative power and sovereignty to Allah and thereby brings people from servitude to the servants into the service of their lord,"[41] and since there is no evidence of political systems where Allah has all legislative power, "mankind today is drowned in the servitude of servants."[42]

Qutb's theory equates a Oneness of God with a Oneness of political sovereignty, the violation of which yields the rule of multiple gods (religious *jahiliyyah*) and a rule of multiple political authorities/sovereignties (political *jahiliyyah*). "Sovereignty is one of the most important attributes of Allah. The person who refuses to attribute sovereignty, either in theory or practice, to anyone besides Allah is a Believer, while the one who does so is an Unbeliever."[43] If the concept of no deity but God means no submission to any political office or authority but God, then, "to believe in the Uniqueness and Oneness of Allah . . . means that human beings must take the rules and laws for their lives from no one other than Allah."[44] There is then a monotheism of the mind, psychological belief in no deity but God, and a monotheism of worship/sovereignty, sociological submission to no power/deity but God.

If, *jahiliyyah* social formations, "take the form of claiming that the right to create values, to legislate rules of collective behavior, and to choose any way of life rests with men,"[45] then traditional Muslim countries engage in poly-sovereign practices, and as such, do not behaviorally acknowledge that there is no deity but God, and therefore are, in fact, unbelieving countries. In the West a sociological instantiation of faith is left out of the formal doctrine, by and large. In Qutbian Islam, it is included. In the West faith is belief, realized in the personal, and the private, as in the psychological transformation of conversion. In Qutbian Islam, faith is a social system, realized in public law, political procedure, and political sovereignty. Therefore, it is a matter of sociological, not psychological transformation; social movements, vanguard parties, revolution, political force, and system change—not so much individual conversion.

Qutb, as mentioned before, is following in the footsteps of Ibn Taymiyya's critique of Mongol rule in the fourteenth century. Here heresy wasn't so much a loss of faith in a psychological sense (the Mongols converted to Islam), but in the sociological sense of the loss of God's sovereignty in the functioning operation of their existing political systems (the Mongols ruled on the basis of some of their pre-Islamic legal traditions). Qutb and Taymiyya would agree that, "only Islam refers back all legislative power and sovereignty to Allah and thereby brings people from servitude to the servants into the service of their Lord. . . . In systems where legislative power and sovereignty belong to human beings, there is a kind of slavery of people to other people, but in Islam, and only in Islam, all people without exception, are liberated from such slavery and serve their creator alone."[46]

What this means is that, not just the Pharaohs, or Mongols, or Nasser and Sadat, but all historical forms of human political sovereignty, whether ancient Greek democracy, republicanism, kingship, dictatorship, or one-party rule, constitute attacks upon divine sovereignty, for in all of these we see a "servitude of servants," not humans serving their God. What is to be done is to "eliminate all human kingship."[47] meaning all forms of God-devoid social and political systems through the material instantiation of the Oneness of God. But not as a theocracy, where the few rule in God's name, nor as the rule of priests, Church, Imams, or holy men. God's law is to be followed by all. This is what the world must strive to attain and has not seen for centuries, as, "the Muslim community . . . vanished at the moment the laws of God became suspended on earth."[48]

The solution: *jihad*

Given the goal, realizing the Oneness of God, and the obstacle of existing *jahili* societies, what is the person of religion to do? The Qutbian answer lies at the heart of the idea of Islamic fundamentalism; return to the fundamentals, regenerate, as a political template, the religio-political system of the first Muslim who read the Qur'an to, "find out what the Almighty Creator had prescribed for him and for the group in which he lived, and for his life and the life of the group."[49] This can be done because the Qur'an isn't a book of "stories" or "literature" or "history" or a "book of intellectual content" but instead, "it comes to become a way of life, a way dedicated to God . . . a faith not hidden in intellects or books, but expressing itself in a dynamic movement which changed conditions and events and the course of life."[50]

That, of course, was then, which brings us to the contemporary Qutbian predicament. What keeps mankind from realizing this ideal social system? "We are also surrounded by *jahiliyyah* today, which is of the same nature as it was during the first period of Islam, perhaps a little deeper."[51] The response to this condition should be to, "return to that pure source from which those people derived their guidance, the source which is free from any mixing or pollution . . . from it we must derive also our concepts of life, our principles of government, politics, economics and all other aspects of life."[52] Again, nothing is left to Caesar. God is about economics, government, law, and politics. "We must return to it with a sense of instruction for obedience and action and not for academic discussion and enjoyment . . . [for] our primary purpose is to know what way of life is demanded of us by the Qur'an . . . the kinds of morals and manners . . . the kind of legal and constitutional system it asks us to establish in the world."[53]

To do this, Qutb argues, "we must also free ourselves from the clutches of *jahili* society, *jahili* concepts, *jahili* traditions and *jahili* leadership. Our mission is not to compromise with the practices of *jahili* society, nor can we be loyal to it. *Jahili* society, because of its *jahili* characteristics, is not worthy to be compromised with. Our aim is first to change ourselves so that we may later change the society. Our foremost objective is to change the practices of this society."[54]

There is to be no Roman Compromise; no leaving political sovereignty to Caesar, for, "they should worship Him [God] alone," that is, no more, "servitude of servants . . . [for] ascribing sovereignty only to God meant that the authority would be taken away from the priests, the leaders of tribes, the wealthy and the rulers, and would revert to God."[55] To take authority away from "the priests, the leaders of tribes, the wealthy and the rulers" is to engage in radical social change, to create an ideal world where only "God's authority would prevail in the heart and conscience . . . and in the affairs of life such as business, the distribution of wealth and the dispensation of justice."[56]

Qutbian religion, then, is a direct challenge to the established political order, for "the proclamation there is no deity except 'Allah' was a challenge to that worldly authority which had usurped the greatest attribute of God, namely, sovereignty."[57] Islam, "was a rebellion against all modes of behavior which have been devised under this usurpation and was a declaration of war against that authority which legislates in ways not permitted by God."[58] Who then qualifies as an object of this "declaration of war."? Anyone, everyone; for all human history except the short period of the first generation of Muslims, has engaged in the usurpation of God's sovereignty. Human history has been composed of nothing but man-made sovereignties—kingdoms, empires, tribes, clans, and now nation-states.

God's message to all these historical forms has been resisted, including the call to the tribal order of pre-Islamic Arabia. "The Arabs . . . greeted this call—this revolutionary message—with anger, and fought against it with that vigour which is known to everyone."[59] The call, "no deity except God" is not about building an Islamic/Arab world power. "The way is not to free the earth from Roman and Persian tyranny in order to replace it with Arab tyranny. All tyranny is wicked! The earth belongs to God, and it cannot be purified for Him unless the banner "No deity except God," is unfurled across the earth. Man is servant to God alone, and he can remain so only if he unfurls the banner, No deity except God . . . no sovereignty except God's, no law except God, and no authority of one man over another, as the authority in all respects belongs to God."[60]

Such a faith is not only a social creed, "the 'grouping' of men which Islam proclaims is based on this faith alone, the faith in which all peoples of any race or color . . . are equal under the banner of God,"[61] but a declaration of war on social and economic inequality for God, "knew that true social justice can come to a society only after all affairs have been submitted to the laws of God and the society as a whole is willing to accept the just division of wealth prescribed by Him."[62]

The result is a kingdom on earth, not in heaven, for faith in God was complete, "when people recognized their sustainer and worshiped Him alone, when they became independent not only of other human beings, but also their own desires . . . then God, through this faith and through the Believers, provided everything which was needed. God's earth became free of 'Romans and Persians', not so that the authority of 'Arabs' might prevail, but only so that God's authority might be established and that the earth might be cleared of all the rebels against Him, whether they were Roman, Persian or Arab."[63]

This means that even during the early Arab conquest it was God, not politics, that was in command. It was about a growing submission to God. With God's help, "mankind was uplifted in its social order, in its morals, in all of its life, to a zenith of perfection which had never been attained before and which cannot be attained afterwards except through Islam. All this was possible because those who established this religion in the form of a state, a system of laws and regulations, had first established it in their hearts and lives in the form of faith, character, worship, and human relationships."[64] He continues, "when their hearts became free of pride of lineage, of nationality, of county, of tribe, of household—in short, when God Most High saw them to be morally pure. . . . since they were pure in faith, the requirement for which is that God's sovereignty alone extend over hearts and consciences in human relationships and morals, in life and possessions, in morals and manners."[65] It was only because of the call to Islam that the Muslim community arose. "Had this call come in its initial stages as a national call or a social movement or a reformist attempt, or had it attached other labels to the call of *"La ilaha illa Allah,"* then this blessed system would never have been for the sake of God alone."[66]

How is this community to be realized? The obstacles aren't just matters of false belief, for *jahiliyyah* (ignorance of God) isn't pure belief, a psychology, but is, instead, a sociology, for, "it always takes the form of a living movement in society. . . . It is an organized society and there is a close cooperation and loyalty between its individuals, and it is always ready and alive to defend its existence consciously or unconsciously. It crushes all elements which seem to be dangerous to its personality."[67] *Jahiliyya* is a living social formation, a sociological structure with power and intention.

If the obstacle to Qutbian faith is "a living social formation with power and intention" that "crushes all elements which seem to be dangerous to its personality," then a forceful opposition is required. If the obstacles were merely stubborn psychological patterns of belief as indifference, atheism, or polytheism, then the path of verbal persuasion would be appropriate. But pure persuasion, or pure theory, can't confront political power. "When *jahiliyyah* takes the form, not of a 'theory' but of an active movement in this fashion, then any attempt to abolish this *jahiliyyah* and to bring people back to God which presents Islam merely as a theory will be undesirable, rather useless. . . . *Jahiliyyah* controls the practical world, and for its support there is a living and active organization. In this situation, mere theoretical efforts to fight it cannot even be equal, much less superior, to it."[68]

Because, Qutb argues, Islam provides appropriate means for appropriate situations, then some form of struggle through fighting becomes the next logical step. "When the purpose is to abolish the existing system and to replace it with a new system which in its character, principles and all its general and particular aspects, is different from the controlling *jahili* system, then it stands to reason that this new system should also come into the battlefield as an organized movement and a viable group. It should come into the battlefield with a determination that its strategy, its social organization, and the relationship between its individuals should be firmer and more powerful than the existing *jahili* system."[69] The call to religion is, at one and the same time, the call for political change. From the perspective of the Western separation of politics and religion this involves a radical distortion of religion; from Qutb's point of view it means a fundamental understanding of what religion is really about. "The theoretical foundation of Islam, in every period of history, has been to witness '*La ilaha illa Allah*' – 'there is no deity except God' – which means to bear witness that the only true deity is God, that He is the Sustainer, that He is the Ruler of the universe, and that He is the Real Sovereign; to believe in Him is one's heart, to worship Him Alone, and to put into practice His laws."[70]

The call for political opposition and social change through a vanguard or revolutionary party now becomes clear. "A person who bears witness that there is no deity except God and that Muhammad is God's Messenger should cut off his relationship of loyalty from the *jahili* society, which he has forsaken, and from *jahili* leadership, whether it be in the guise of priests, magicians or astrologers, or in the form of political, social or economic leadership."[71] The call for an alternative society and political order, on analogy with that of the first generation of Muslims, is also clear: "there is no other way for the revival of Islam in the shade of *jahiliyyah*, in whatever age or country if appears, except to follow its natural character and to develop it into a movement and an organic system."[72]

This isn't traditionalism, a turning the clock back to the seventh century, as much as it is a realization of a particular form of political life, in whatever century that needs to be constructed. "Throughout every period of human history the call toward God has had one nature. Its purpose is 'Islam', which means to bring human beings into submission to God, to free them from servitude to other human beings so that they may devote themselves to the One True God, to deliver them from the clutches of human lordship and man-made laws, value systems and traditions so that they will acknowledge the sovereignty and authority of the One True God and follow His law in all spheres of life. The Islam of Muhammad – peace be on him – came for this purpose, as well as the messages of the earlier Prophets."[73] If the revelations given to Muhammad were to show mankind how to live, and that manner of life cannot be found today on this earth, then it becomes obvious that, "today we see mankind in a miserable condition . . . [and what needs to be done is] to establish the way of Allah on earth."[74] The means to accomplish this is *jihad*.

If religion is a form of social system, and if its obstacle is an alternative social system, then the means for its removal is political activity including "striving through fighting." Again, for Qutb, "the word 'religion' includes more than belief; 'religion' actually means a way of life, and in Islam this is based on belief. . . . Anyone who understands this particular character of this religion will also understand the place of *jihad bis saif* (striving through fighting), which is to clear the way for striving through preaching. . . . He will understand that Islam is not a 'defensive movement' in the narrow sense which today is technically called a 'defensive war.' "[75] *Jihad* and faith are so fundamentally linked that, "persons who attempt to defend the concept of Islamic *jihad* by interpreting it in the narrow sense of the current concept of defensive war . . . lack understanding of the nature of Islam and its primary aim . . . to spread the message of Islam throughout the world."[76]

Even when it seems like *jihad* is being used for political purposes, for defense, even for the defense of Medina, this is not the case, for "the reason for *jihad* was not merely to defend Medina. Indeed, its defense was necessary, but this was not the ultimate aim. The aim was to protect the resources and the center of the movement – the movement for freeing mankind and demolishing the obstacles which prevented mankind from attaining this freedom."[77] Defensive *jihad*, actually, diminishes the Islamic way of life. "Those who say that Islamic *jihad* was merely for the defense of the 'homeland of Islam' diminish the greatness of the Islamic way of life and consider it less important than their 'homeland'."[78]

This brings us back to the idea of existing political orders as resistance and obstacle. "How could the message of Islam have spread when it faced such material obstacles as the political system of the state, the socio-economic system based on races and classes, and behind all these, the military power of the government?"[79] Given social and political power resisting the call for submission to God, "it would be naive to assume that a call is raised to free the whole of humankind throughout the earth, and it is confined to preaching and exposition."[80] Preaching might be used when there are no obstacles, "but when . . . obstacles and practical difficulties are put in its way, it has no recourse but to remove them by force so that when it is addressed to peoples' hearts and minds they are free to accept or reject it with an open mind."[81]

In Qutb's world view, this isn't a cynical use of religion to attain a geopolitical end; it is politics to realize a religious state of affairs. *Jihad* is only about religion. It is not a triggered defensive maneuver given to attacks upon Muslim lands or Arab countries. "It is immaterial whether the homeland of Islam—in the true Islam sense, *Dar al-Islam*—is in a condition of peace or whether it is threatened by its neighbors. When Islam strives for peace, its objective is not that superficial peace which requires that only that part of the earth where the followers of Islam are residing remain secure. The peace which Islam desires is that the religion (i.e. the law of the society) be purified for God, that the obedience of all people be for God alone, and that some people should not be lords over others."[82]

For Qutb, *jihad* is neither a defensive response to an outside trigger nor a product of geopolitics, national liberation struggles, regime change, party politics, or palace coups. "What kind of man is it who after listening to the commandment of God and the Traditions of the Prophet . . . still thinks that it [*jihad*] is a temporary injunction related to transient conditions and that it is concerned only with the defense of the borders?"[83] If *jihad* isn't defensive or political, then what is it? It is a witnessing of the faith; it is inherent in the faith; to have the faith is to struggle for its sociological implementation in an existing *jahili* world.

"In the verse giving permission to fight, God has informed the Believers that the life of this world is such that checking one group of people by another is the law of God, so that the earth may be cleansed of corruption. 'Permission to fight is given to those against whom war is made, because they are oppressed, and God is able to help them. These are the people who were expelled from their homes without cause except that they said that our Lord is God. *Had God not checked one people by another, then surely synagogues and churches and mosques would have been pulled down, where the name of God is remembered often.* Thus, this struggle is not a temporary phase but an eternal state – an eternal state, as truth and falsehood cannot coexist on this earth. Whenever Islam stood up with the universal declaration that God's lordship should be established over the entire earth and that men should become free from servitude to other men, the usurpers of God's authority on earth have struck out against it fiercely and have never tolerated it. It became incumbent upon Islam to strike back and release man throughout the earth from the grip of these usurpers."[84]

Striving through fighting isn't religion in the service of politics, but politics in the service of religion. That is, "the reasons for *jihad* . . . are these: to establish God's authority in the earth; to arrange human affairs according to the true guidance provided by God; to abolish all the Satanic forces and Satanic systems of life; to end the lordship of one man over others since all men are creatures of God and no one has the authority to make them his servants or to make arbitrary laws for them. These reasons are sufficient for proclaiming *jihad*."[85] Further, it has always been this way going back to the earliest days, as he quotes Ibn Qayyim on the stages of *jihad*. The Prophet, "was commanded to migrate, and later permission was given to fight. Then he was commanded to fight those who fought him, and to restrain himself from those who did not make war with him. Later he was commanded to fight the polytheists until God's religion was fully established."[86]

Therefore, "the *jihad* of Islam is to secure complete freedom for every man throughout the world by releasing him from servitude to other human beings so that he may serve his God. Who is One and Who has no associates. This is in itself a sufficient reason for *jihad*. These were the only reasons in the hearts of Muslim warriors. If they had been asked the question 'Why are you fighting?' none would have answered, 'My country is in danger; I am fighting for its defense' or 'The Persians and the Romans have come upon us', or 'We want to extend our dominion and want more spoils.'[87] Instead, they would have answered, 'God has sent us to bring anyone who wishes from servitude to men into the service of God alone, from the narrowness of this world into the vastness of this world and the Hereafter, and from the tyranny of religions in to the justice of Islam.' "[88]

Jihad, then, is really about testifying, witnessing, and manifesting faith. It isn't a political tool. *Jihad* is inherent in Islam, argues Qutb. "These are the reasons inherent in the very nature of this religion. Similarly, its proclamation of universal freedom, its practical way of combating actual human conditions with appropriate methods, its developing new resources at various stages, is also inherent in its message from the very beginning – and not because of any threat of aggression against Islamic lands or against the Muslims residing in them. The reason for *jihad* exists in the nature of its message and in the actual conditions it finds in human societies, and not merely in the necessity for defense, which may be temporary and of limited extent."[89] As such Qutb argues, Islam has a right to initiate *jihad*, for it is, "in the very nature of Islam to take initiative for freeing the human beings throughout the earth from servitude to anyone other than God . . . [and] Islam has a right to remove all those obstacles which are in its path so that it may address human reason and intuition with no interference and opposition from political systems . . . [meaning that] Islam has the right to take the initiative . . . hence it is the duty of Islam to annihilate all such systems, as they are obstacles in the way of universal freedom"[90]

From this point of view, "wherever an Islamic community exists which is a concrete example of the Divinely-ordained system of life, it has a God-given right to step forward and take control of the political authority so that it may establish the Divine system on earth, while it leaves the matter of belief to individual conscience. When God restrained Muslims from *jihad* for a certain period, it was a question of strategy rather than of principle."[91] *Jihad*, then, isn't about attacks on the Muslim community, for such an entity, in Qutb's sense of the term, doesn't exist. *Jihad*, instead, is about fighting to remove obstacles to the establishment of an Islamic community in the first place.

Given *jahili* society is world wide, and is, in effect, the state of the world, and further possesses not only the material power but a will to resist, a religious movement for change, "comes into conflict with the *jahiliyyah* which prevails over ideas and beliefs, and which has a practical system of life and a political and material authority behind it, the Islamic movement had to produce parallel resources to confront this *jahiliyyah*. This movement uses the methods of preaching and persuasion for reforming ideas and beliefs; and it uses physical power and *jihad* for abolishing the organizations and authorities of the *jahili* system which prevents people from reforming their ideas and beliefs but forces them to obey their erroneous ways and make them serve human lords instead of the Almighty lord. This movement does not confine itself to mere preaching to confront physical power."[92]

Therefore, "the effort expended in establishing the Islamic system for the benefit of all people, both Muslims and non-Muslims alike, is termed *jihad*. *Jihad* is thus struggle for the initiation and establishment of this system, which aims at securing freedom of conscience and belief for every person on earth. And this freedom can only be attained by establishing a just government and a just legal and social system, which calls to account anyone who tries to abolish freedom of speech and freedom of belief from the land."[93]

The call for *jihad* is clear. "Islam is . . . a way of life represented in a social set-up that takes the necessary action to liberate mankind. Other communities try to prevent it from addressing their individuals to convince them of adopting its way of life. Therefore, it becomes imperative that Islam should try to remove those regimes that impede the freedom of mankind."[94] That is, "to fight for Islam is to fight for the implementation of this way of life and its systems. Faith, on the other hand, is a matter for free personal conviction, after the removal of all pressures and obstacles."[95] This is a universal fight. "It is not possible that Islam will confine itself to geographical boundaries, or racial limits, abandoning the rest of mankind and leaving them to suffer from evil, corruption and servitude to lords other than God Almighty."[96] Therefore, "when we understand the nature of Islam, as it has already been explained, we realize the inevitability of *jihad*, or striving for God's cause, taking a military form in addition to its advocacy form."[97]

Significance of these ideas

The circle is now complete. Qutb's Islamic concept specified a goal and identified obstacles the nature of which dictated a path for their removal by force. How significant are these ideas? That remains to be seen, for what lasts is largely decided by history. What can be said, though, is that his ideas remain very prominent in the world of militant Islam and particularly in jihadic theory, as seen in the frequency in which Qutb is quoted on *jihadi* websites.[98] Will his ideas, though, resonate within the wider Salafi, Islamist, and Muslim worlds?[99] Again, we will have to wait and see. But some analogy with radical ideas in the West can be tentatively drawn.

In the nineteenth century militant political theory generated by the West spoke of the permanent revolution, unending class struggle, and issued a call for the liberation of mankind from servitude to others. Qutb's call is similar in some regards, but different in others, specifically its focus is upon religion rather than economics. Here the contradictions which drive his theory of history are belief vs. unbelief, that is, Islam vs. *jahiliyyah*, and not capital vs. labor. And today what is read in many militant circles is Qutb, not Marx; what is discussed is Islamic fundamentalism, not revolutionary socialism. The new framework seems less about who does and doesn't own the means of production, and more about who does and doesn't believe in the path of God. Political power, governance, and rule seems less and less about which economic class will predominate than whether God's law will rule, and political struggle seems less and less about tensions between positions defined with the economic division of labor (class struggle) and more and more about tensions between believers and unbelievers.

Even what is considered to be ideology covering the true laws of history seem up for grabs. For example, from the perspective of the reigning paradigm of revolutionary change in the West, Marxism, the true and the real are economic forces, with religious belief occupying the status of superstructure, a fig leaf masking what is really going on. When considering the Crusades or latter-day Western imperialism, Qutb claims that to see these as economic issues underneath is to mask their real nature. He wishes to turn economic determinism on its head; the real struggle is between believers, not matters of economics, as "the struggle between the Believers and their enemies is in essence a struggle of belief."[100] That is, the real base is religion and the real superstructure is the economy. Marx is turned on his head. "The enemies of the Believers may wish to change this struggle into an economic or political or racial struggle, so that the Believers become confused concerning the true nature of the struggle and the flame of belief in their hearts becomes extinguished."[101] For him the purported economic struggles are but a mystification as to what is really going on; an ideology; a fig leaf. "The Believers must not be deceived, and must understand that this is a trick. The enemy, by changing the nature of the struggle, intends to deprive them of their weapon of true victory . . . the victory of the freedom of spirit."[102]

A case in point is provided. Certainly a radical Western perspective on the Crusades and Western imperialism would be that they were really a matter of economic, not religious, motives. In received radical eschatology the economic is the base, the real, and the religious is the superstructure, the illusion, the mask, the ideology covering the true motives. But not for Qutb. "We see an example of this today in the attempts of Christendom to try to deceive us by distorting history and saying that the Crusades were a form of imperialism." To the radical imagination in the West, to see a movement that was religious as really economic is to unveil and get to the real truths. But to the radical imagination of Qutb, it is just the opposite. "The truth of the matter is that the latter-day imperialism is but a mask for the crusading spirit, since it is not possible for it to appear in its true form, as it was possible in the Middle Ages."[103]

Think of Western colonialism. Think of the United States in Iraq. What is a deep radical analysis from the West: oil, economics, geopolitics; these are the real reasons for Western imperialism. But for Qutb, this is "but a mask for the crusading spirit," that is, the economic is the ideological overlay; the religious is the real, the base, the new foundation. To the Western mind the old paradigm still holds. Religion here is but a front; Islam has been hijacked by political actors; it is political Islam; not just Islam. The economic remains the real; the religious the mask. Maybe; but for many the religious is the real and all other motives are but "masks" to be "unveiled" as nothing but the "crusading spirit". In the West the true spirit is that of the economic stuggle: it is still capital vs. labor on a global scale. But for Qutb the struggle is between *jahiliyyah* and Islam; between the tyranny of man over man vs. the freedom of submission to God. Proletarian rule whether as socialism, or with a withered-away state, as some ideal world of pure communism, is still the servitude of servants, still the tyranny of man over man, still the absence of the divine guidance in the organization of human affairs, still, then, a system in need of opposition and transformation.

Is this a delusion, or the start of a new post-Western form of radical theory? Again, history will tell. There are, though, some signs that ideas of populist and fundamentalist Islam are gaining currency amongst the downtrodden in the world's global south. A cogent observer from the Western Left, Mike Davis, notes that, "for the moment at least, Marx has yielded the historical stage to Mohammed and the Holy Ghost. If God died in the cities of the industrial revolution, he has risen again in the postindustrial cities of the developing world".[104] Said a socialist leader from the developing world, "We [the Left] have become embourgeoisified. We have cut ourselves off from the people. We need to reconquer the popular quarters. The Islamicists have seduced our natural electorate. They promise them heaven on earth."[105] Perhaps the Islamist promise is the age old opiate of the masses; but perhaps it is a new theoretical foundation for the expression social discontent and political transformation in the developing world.

If so, then we may be witnessing the birth of new, non-Western contenders in the field of militant ideology. And perhaps their most surprising non-Western qualities are (1) the prominence of religion as the foundational base and accordingly the derivation that (2) the great contradictions that drive historical development are within the religious sphere (*jahiliyyah* vs. Islam) and finally, (3) that resistance and revolution take a religious form as *jihad*. This new world of post-Western radical theory remains beyond the grasp of Western intellectuals, running so contrary to their core epistemological belief of the separation of the religious and the political, and the primacy of the economic as the base and religion as the superstructure. For the Western mind raised on the

Enlightenment belief that religion is a hindrance, not a stimulant, to revolutionary social change, the new role of religion remains a puzzle. It is easier to look backward than forward; easier to designate radical Islamic theory as traditionalism, turning clocks backwardism, or as a defensive reaction to modernity as an Islamo-fascism. And, maybe this is so.

But maybe it might be a new turn in world political thinking? Again, the sage observations of Mike Davis. In the nineteenth century, "in the slums of St. Petersburg, Buenos Aires and even Tokyo, militant workers avidly embraced the new faiths of Darwin, Kropotkin and Marx. Today, on the other hand, populist Islam and Pentecostal Christianity (and in Bombay, the cult of Shivaji) occupy a social space analogous to that of early twentieth-century socialism and anarchism."[106] Whether this new role of religion is part of an emerging theoretical paradigm for revolutionary change, or not, there is a body of Islamist theory that needs to be seriously engaged if one wants to understand the militant turmoil of the Muslim world and the growth of populist Islam in the mega cities of the global South. In this regard there is no better place to begin than with a selection of the writings of Sayyid Qutb.

Part 2
Selected writings

3 Milestones

Mankind today is on the brink of a precipice, not because of the danger of complete annihilation which is hanging over its head—this being just a symptom and not the real disease—but because humanity is devoid of those vital values which are necessary not only for its healthy development but also for its real progress. Even the Western world realises that Western civilization is unable to present any healthy values for the guidance of mankind. It knows that it does not possess anything which will satisfy its own conscience and justify its existence.

It is essential for mankind to have new leadership!

The leadership of mankind by Western man is now on the decline, not because Western culture has become poor materially or because its economic and military power has become weak. The period of the Western system has come to an end primarily because it is deprived of those life-giving values which enabled it to be the leader of mankind.

Islam cannot fulfill its role except by taking concrete form in a society, rather, in a nation; for man does not listen, especially in this age, to an abstract theory which is not seen materialized in a living society. From this point of view, we can say that the Muslim community has been extinct for a few centuries, for this Muslim community does not denote the name of a land in which Islam resides, nor is it a people whose forefathers lived under the Islamic system at some earlier time. It is the name of a group of people whose manners, ideas and concepts, rules and regulations, values and criteria, are all derived from the Islamic source. The Muslim community with these characteristics vanished at the moment the laws of God became suspended on earth.

If Islam is again to play the role of the leader of mankind, then it is necessary that the Muslim community be restored to its original form. [. . .]

I am aware that between the attempt at 'revival' and the attainment of 'leadership' there is a great distance, as the Muslim community has long ago vanished from existence and from observation, and the leadership of mankind has long since passed to other ideologies and other nations, other concepts and other systems. This was the era during which Europe's genius created its marvellous works in science, culture, law and material production, due to which mankind has progressed to great heights of creativity and material comfort. It is not easy to find fault with the inventors of such marvellous things, especially since what we call the 'world of Islam' is completely devoid of all this beauty. [. . .]

How is it possible to start the task of reviving Islam?

It is necessary that there should be a vanguard which sets out with this determination and then keeps walking on the path, marching through the vast ocean of *jahiliyyah* which has encompassed the entire world. [. . .]

It is necessary that this vanguard should know the landmarks and the milestones of the road toward this goal so that they may recognize the starting place, the nature, the responsibilities and the ultimate purpose of this long journey. [. . .]

I have written *"Milestones"* for this vanguard, which I consider to be a waiting reality about to be materialized. [. . .]

The message of Islam brought by the Messenger of God, Muhammad—peace be on him—was the last link in the long chain of invitations toward God by the noble Prophets. Throughout history, this message has remained the same: that human beings should recognise that their true Sustainer and Lord is One God, that they should submit to Him Alone, and that the lordship of man be eliminated. Except for a few people here and there in history, mankind as a whole has never denied the existence of God and His sovereignty over the universe; it has rather erred in comprehending the real attributes of God, or in taking other gods besides God as His associates. This association with God has been either in belief and worship, or in accepting the sovereignty of others besides God. Both of these aspects are *shirk* [1] in the sense that they take human beings away from the religion of God, which was brought by the Prophets. After each Prophet, there was a period during which people understood this religion, but then gradually later generations forgot it and returned to *jahiliyyah*. They started again on the way of *shirk*, sometimes in their belief and worship and sometimes in their submission to the authority of others, and sometimes in both. [. . .]

It is therefore necessary that Islam's theoretical foundation—belief—materialize in the form of an organized and active group from the very beginning. It is necessary that this group separate itself from the *jahili* society, becoming independent and distinct from the active and organized *jahili* society whose aim is to block Islam. [. . .]

Since this movement comes into conflict with the *jahiliyyah* which prevails over ideas and beliefs, and which has a practical system of life and a political and material authority behind it, the Islamic movement had to produce parallel resources to confront this *jahiliyyah*. This movement uses the methods of preaching and persuasion for reforming ideas and beliefs; and it uses physical power and *jihad* for abolishing the organizations and authorities of the *jahili* system which prevents people from reforming their ideas and beliefs but forces them to obey their erroneous ways and make them serve human lords instead of the Almighty Lord. This movement does not confine itself to mere preaching to confront physical power, as it also does not use compulsion for changing the ideas of people. These two principles are equally important in the method of this religion. Its purpose is to free those peoples who wish to be freed from enslavement to men so that they may serve God alone. [. . .]

Thus, when they speak about *jihad*, they speak clumsily and mix up the various stages, distorting the whole concept of *jihad* and deriving from the Qur'anic verses final principles and generalities for which there is no justification. This is because they regard every verse of the Qur'an as if it were the final principle of this religion. This group of thinkers, who are a product of the sorry state of the present Muslim generation, have nothing but the label of Islam and have laid down their spiritual and rational arms in defeat. They say, "Islam has prescribed only defensive war"! and think that they have done some good for their religion by depriving it of its method, which is to abolish all injustice from the earth, to bring people to the worship of God alone, and to bring them out of servitude to others into the servants of the Lord. Islam does not force people to accept its belief, but it wants to provide a free environment in which they will have the choice of beliefs. What it wants is to abolish those oppressive political systems under which people are prevented from expressing their freedom to choose whatever beliefs they want, and after that it gives them complete freedom to decide whether they will accept Islam or not. [. . .]

The Islamic *jihad* has no relationship to modern warfare, either in its causes or in the way in which it is conducted. The causes of Islamic *jihad* should be sought in the very nature of Islam and its role in the world, in its high principles, which have been given to it by God and for the implementation of which God appointed the Prophet—peace be on him—as His Messenger and declared him to be the last of all prophets and messengers.

This religion is really a universal declaration of the freedom of man from servitude to other men and from servitude to his own desires, which is also a form of human servitude; it is a declaration that sovereignty belongs to God alone and that He is the Lord of all the worlds. It means a challenge to all kinds and forms of systems which are based on the concept of the sovereignty of man; in other words, where man has usurped the Divine attribute. Any system in which the final decisions are referred to human beings, and in which the sources of all authority are human, deifies human beings by designating others than God as lords over men. [. . .]

The way to establish God's rule on earth is not that some consecrated people—the priests—be given the authority to rule, as was the case with the rule of the Church, nor that some spokesmen of God become rulers, as is the case in a 'theocracy'. To establish God's rule means that His laws be enforced and that the final decision in all affairs be according to these laws.

The establishing of the dominion of God on earth, the abolishing of the dominion of man, the taking away of sovereignty from the usurper to revert it to God, and the bringing about of the enforcement of the Divine Law (*shari'a*) and the abolition of man-made laws cannot be achieved only through preaching. Those who have usurped the authority of God and are oppressing God's creatures are not going to give up their power merely through preaching; if it had been so, the task of establishing God's religion in the world would have been very easy for the Prophets of God! [. . .]

This religion is not merely a declaration of the freedom of the Arabs, nor is its message confined to the Arabs. It addresses itself to the whole of mankind, and its sphere of work is the whole earth. God is the Sustainer not merely of the Arabs, nor is His providence limited to those who believe in the faith of Islam. God is the Sustainer of the whole world. This religion wants to bring back the whole world to its Sustainer and free it from servitude to anyone other than God. In the sight of Islam, the real servitude is following laws devised by someone, and this is that servitude which in Islam is reserved for God alone. Anyone who serves someone other than God in this sense is outside God's religion, although he may claim to profess this religion. [. . .]

It is not the intention of Islam to force its beliefs on people, but Islam is not merely 'belief'. As we have pointed out, Islam is a declaration of the freedom of man from servitude to other men. Thus it strives from the beginning to abolish all those systems and governments which are based on the rule of man over men and the servitude of one human being to another. When Islam releases people from this political pressure and presents to them its spiritual message, appealing to their reason, it gives them complete freedom to accept or not to accept its beliefs. [. . .]

Anyone who understands this particular character of this religion will also understand the place of *jihad bis saif* (striving through fighting), which is to clear the way for striving through preaching in the application of the Islamic movement. He will understand that Islam is not a 'defensive movement' in the narrow sense which today is technically called a 'defensive war.' This narrow meaning is ascribed to it by those who are under the pressure of circumstances and are defeated by the wily attacks of the orientalists, who distort the concept of Islamic *jihad*. [. . .]

If we insist on calling Islamic *jihad* a defensive movement, then we must change the meaning of the word 'defense' and mean by it 'the defense of man' against all those elements which limit his freedom. These elements take the form of beliefs and concepts, as well as of political systems, based on economic, racial or class distinctions. When Islam first came into existence, the world was full of such systems, and the present-day *jahiliyyah* also has various kinds of such systems.

When we take this broad meaning of the word 'defense,' we understand the true character of Islam, and that it is a universal proclamation of the freedom of man from servitude to other men, the establishment of the sovereignty of God and His Lordship throughout the world, the end of man's arrogance and selfishness, and the implementation of the rule of the Divine *shari'a* in human affairs.

As to persons who attempt to defend the concept of Islamic *jihad* by interpreting it in the narrow sense of the current concept of defensive war, and who do research to prove that the battles fought in Islamic *jihad* were all for the defense of the homeland of Islam—some of them considering the homeland of Islam to be just the Arabian Peninsula —against the aggression of neighboring powers, they lack understanding of the nature of Islam and its primary aim. Such an attempt is nothing but a product of a mind defeated by the present difficult conditions and by the attacks of the treacherous orientalists on the Islamic *jihad*. [. . .]

How could the message of Islam have spread when it faced such material obstacles as the political system of the state, the socio-economic system based on races and classes, and behind all these, the military power of the government?

It would be naive to assume that a call is raised to free the whole of humankind throughout the earth, and it is confined to preaching and exposition. Indeed, it strives through preaching and exposition when there is freedom of communication and when people are free from all these influences, as "There is no compulsion in religion; but when the above-mentioned obstacles and practical difficulties are put in its way, it has no recourse but to remove them by force so that when it is addressed to peoples' hearts and minds they are free to accept or reject it with an open mind.

Since the objective of the message of Islam is a decisive declaration of man's freedom, not merely on the philosophical plane but also in the actual conditions of life, it must employ *jihad*. It is immaterial whether the homeland of Islam—in the true Islamic sense, *Dar al-Islam*—is in a condition of peace or whether it is threatened by its neighbors. When Islam strives for peace, its objective is not that superficial peace which requires that only that part of the earth where the followers of Islam are residing remain secure. The peace which Islam desires is that the religion (i.e. the Law of the society) be purified for God, that the obedience of all people be for God alone, and that some people should not be lords over others. [. . .]

These are the logical positions consonant with the character and purposes of this religion, and not what is understood by the people who are defeated by present conditions and by the attacks of the treacherous orientalists.

God held back Muslims from fighting in Mecca and in the early period of their migration to Medina, and told them, "Restrain your hands, and establish regular prayers, and pay *zakat*". Next, they were permitted to fight: "Permission to fight is given to those against whom war is made, because they are oppressed, and God is able to help them. These are the people who were expelled from their homes without cause. The next stage came when the Muslims were commanded to fight those who fight them: "Fight in the cause of God against those who fight you." And finally, war was declared against all the polytheists: "And fight against all the polytheists, as they all fight against you;" "Fight against those among the People of the Book who do not believe in God and the Last Day, who do not forbid what God and His Messenger have forbidden, and who do not consider the true religion as their religion, until they are subdued and pay *jizyah*." Thus, according to the explanation by Imam Ibn Qayyim, the Muslims were first restrained from fighting; then they were permitted to fight; then they were commanded to fight against the aggressors; and finally they were commanded to fight against all the polytheists. [. . .]

What kind of a man is it who, after listening to the commandment of God and the Traditions of the Prophet—peace be on him—and after reading about the events which occurred during the Islamic *jihad*, still thinks that it is a temporary injunction related to transient conditions and that it is concerned only with the defense of the borders?

In the verse giving permission to fight, God has informed the Believers that the life of this world is such that checking one group of people by another is the law of God, so that the earth may be cleansed of corruption. "Permission to fight is given to those against whom war is made, because they are oppressed, and God is able to help them. These are the people who were expelled from their homes without cause, except that they said that our Lord is God. *Had God not checked one people by another, then surely synagogues and churches and mosques would have been pulled down, where the name of God is remembered often*." Thus, this struggle is not a temporary phase but an eternal state—an eternal state, as truth and falsehood cannot co-exist on this earth. Whenever Islam stood up with the universal declaration that God's Lordship should be established over the entire earth and that men should become free from servitude to other men, the usurpers of God's authority on earth have struck out against it fiercely and have never tolerated it. It became incumbent upon Islam to strike back and release man throughout the earth from the grip of these usurpers. The eternal struggle for the freedom of man will continue until the religion is purified for God. [. . .]

The reasons for *jihad* which have been described in the above verses are these: to establish God's authority in the earth; to arrange human affairs according to the true guidance provided by God; to abolish all the Satanic forces and Satanic systems of life; to end the lordship of one man over others, since all men are creatures of God and no one has the authority to make them his servants or to make arbitrary laws for them. These reasons are sufficient for proclaiming *jihad*. However, one should always keep in mind that there is no compulsion in religion; that is, once the people are free from the lordship of men, the law governing civil affairs will be purely that of God, while no one will be forced to change his beliefs and accept Islam.

The *jihad* of Islam is to secure complete freedom for every man throughout the world by releasing him from servitude to other human beings so that he may serve his God, Who is One and Who has no associates. This is in itself a sufficient reason for *jihad*. These were the only reasons in the hearts of Muslim warriors. If they had been asked the question, "Why are you fighting?" none would have answered, "My country is in danger; I am fighting for its defense" or "The Persians and the Romans have come upon us", or, "We want to extend our dominion and want more spoils". [. . .]

Those who say that Islamic *jihad* was merely for the defense of the 'homeland of Islam' diminish the greatness of the Islamic way of life and consider it less important than their 'homeland'. This is not the Islamic point of view, and their view is a creation of the modern age and is completely alien to Islamic consciousness. What is acceptable to Islamic consciousness is its belief, the way of life which this belief prescribes, and the society which lives according to this way of life. The soil of the homeland has in itself no value or weight. From the Islamic point of view, the only value which the soil can achieve is because on that soil God's authority is established and God's guidance is followed; and thus it becomes a fortress for the belief, a place for its way of life to be entitled the 'homeland of Islam', a center for the movement for the total freedom of man. [. . .]

The need for *jihad* remains, and will continue to remain, whether these conditions exist or not!

In pondering over historical events, we should not neglect the aspects inherent in the nature of this religion, its declaration of universal freedom, and its practical method. We ought not to confuse these with temporary needs of defense. [. . .]

It is in the very nature of Islam to take initiative for freeing the human beings throughout the earth from servitude to anyone other than God; and so it cannot be restricted within any geographic or racial limits, leaving all mankind on the whole earth in evil, in chaos and in servitude to lords other than God. [. . .]

There is also a great difference in the idea that Islam is a Divinely-ordained way of life and in the idea that it is a geographically-bounded system. [. . .]

This Islam has a right to remove all those obstacles which are in its path so that it may address human reason and intuition with no interference and opposition from political systems. According to the second idea, Islam is merely a national system which has a right to take up arms only when its homeland is attacked.

In the case of either concept, Islam has to strive and to struggle; but its purposes and its results are entirely different, both conceptually and practically.

Indeed, Islam has the right to take the initiative. Islam is not a heritage of any particular race or country; this is God's religion and it is for the whole world. It has the right to destroy all obstacles in the form of institutions and traditions which limit man's freedom of choice. It does not attack individuals nor does it force them to accept its beliefs; it attacks institutions and traditions to release human beings from their poisonous influences, which distort human nature and which curtail human freedom. [. . .]

Islam is not merely a belief, so that it is enough merely to preach it. Islam, which is a way of life, takes practical steps to organize a movement for freeing man. Other societies do not give it any opportunity to organize its followers according to its own method, and hence it is the duty of Islam to annihilate all such systems, as they are obstacles in the way of universal freedom. Only in this manner can the way of life be wholly dedicated to God, so that neither any human authority nor the question of servitude remains, as is the case in all other systems which are based on man's servitude to man. [. . .]

Lastly, all the existing so-called 'Muslim' societies are also *jahili* societies.

We classify them among *jahili* societies not because they believe in other deities besides God or because they worship anyone other than God, but because their way of life is not based on submission to God alone. Although they believe in the Unity of God, still they have relegated the legislative attribute of God to others and submit to this authority, and from this authority they derive their systems, their traditions and customs, their laws, their values and standards, and almost every practice of life. [. . .]

This, and only this, is Islam. Islam is not a few words pronounced by the tongue, or birth in a country called Islamic, or an inheritance from a Muslim father.

> "No, by your Sustainer, they have not believed until they make you the arbiter of their disputes, and then do not find any grievance against your decision but submit with full submission." (4:65)

Only this is Islam, and only this is *Dar al-Islam*—not the soil, not the race, not the lineage, not the tribe, and not the family.

Islam freed all humanity from the ties of the earth so that they might soar toward the skies, and freed them from the chains of blood relationships—the biological chains—so that they might rise above the angels.

The homeland of the Muslim, in which he lives and which he defends, is not a piece of land; the nationality of the Muslim, by which he is identified, is not the nationality determined by a government; the family of the Muslim, in which he finds solace and which he defends, is not blood relationships; the flag of the Muslim, which he honors and under which he is martyred, is not the flag of a country; and the victory of the Muslim, which he celebrates and for which he is thankful to God, is not a military victory. It is what God has described:

> "When God's help and victory comes, and thou seest people entering into God's religion in multitudes, then celebrate the praises of thy Lord and ask His forgiveness. Indeed, He is the Acceptor of Repentance." (110:1–3)

The victory is achieved under the banner of faith, and under no other banners; the striving is purely for the sake of God, for the success of His religion and His law, for the protection of *Dar al-Islam*, the particulars of which we have described above, and for no other purpose. It is not for the spoils or for fame, nor for the honor of a country or nation, nor for the mere protection of one's family except when supporting them against religious persecution.

The honor of martyrdom is achieved only when one is fighting in the cause of God, and if one is killed for any other purpose this will not be attained. [. . .]

The fatherland is that place where the Islamic faith, the Islamic way of life, and the *shari'a* of God is dominant; only this meaning of 'fatherland' is worthy of the human being. Similarly, 'nationality' means belief and a way of life, and only this relationship is worthy of man's dignity.

Grouping according to family and tribe and nation, and race and color and country, are residues of the primitive state of man; these *jahili* groupings are from a period when man's spiritual values were at a low stage. The Prophet—peace be on him—has called them "dead things" against which man's spirit should revolt. [. . .]

Jahiliyyah is the worship of some people by others; that is to say, some people become dominant and make laws for others, regardless of whether these laws are against God's injunctions and without caring for the use or misuse of their authority.

Islam, on the other hand, is people's worshipping God alone, and deriving concepts and beliefs, laws and regulations and values from the authority of God, and freeing themselves from servitude to God's servants. [. . .]

The struggle between the Believers and their enemies is in essence a struggle of belief, and not in any way of anything else. The enemies are angered only because of their faith, enraged only because of their belief.

This was not a political or an economic or a racial struggle; had it been any of these, its settlement would have been easy, the solution of its difficulties would have been simple. But essentially it was a struggle between beliefs—either unbelief or faith, either *jahiliyyah* or Islam. [. . .]

The enemies of the Believers may wish to change this struggle into an economic or political or racial struggle, so that the Believers become confused concerning the true nature of the struggle and the flame of belief in their hearts becomes extinguished. The Believers must not be deceived, and must understand that this is a trick. The enemy, by changing the nature of the struggle, intends to deprive them of their weapon of true victory, the victory which can take any form, be it the victory of the freedom of spirit as was case of the Believers in the story of the Maker of the Pit, or dominance in the world—as a consequence of the freedom of spirit—as happened in the case of the first generation of Muslims.

We see an example of this today in the attempts of Christendom to try to deceive us by distorting history and saying that the Crusades were a form of imperialism. The truth of the matter is that the latter-day imperialism is but a mask for the crusading spirit, since it is not possible for it to appear in its true form, as it was possible in the Middle Ages. The unveiled crusading spirit was smashed against the rock of the faith of Muslim leadership which came from various elements, including Salahuddin the Kurd and Turan Shah the Mamluk, who forgot the differences of nationalities and remembered their belief, and were victorious under the banner of Islam.

"They were angered with the Believers only because they believed in God, the All-Powerful, the All-Praiseworthy."

Almighty God spoke the truth, and these treacherous deceivers are liars!

4 Prologue *Surah* 8, Al-Anfal (The spoils of war)

Like *Surahs* 2–5, discussed in Volumes I–IV, this *surah* was revealed in the Medina period of the Prophet's mission, while *Surahs* 6 and 7, discussed in Volumes V and VI, were revealed earlier when the Prophet was still in Mecca. As is already clear, our approach in this commentary is to follow the order adopted in the Qur'an, in preference to the chronological order of revelation. For one thing, it is not possible to be absolutely certain about the time of revelation of each *surah*, except in general terms indicating that one *surah* is a Meccan revelation and another belongs to the Medina period, but even then there are some differences of views. To try to determine the exact order of when each verse, passage or *surah* was revealed is practically impossible, despite the fact that in the case of a small number of verses we have confirmed reports concerning the exact time of revelation.

Valuable as the endeavour to trace the chronological order of revelation may be in trying to establish the pattern of progress of the Islamic movement at the time of the Prophet, the lack of clear and firm evidence makes this endeavour both hard and problematic. The conclusions that we may arrive at will always remain uncertain, and could lead to serious or erroneous results. Therefore, I have chosen to present the Qur'an in the traditional order given in the original copy finalized at the time of 'Uthman, the third Caliph. However, I try to look at the historical events associated with the revelation of each *surah*, knowing that this can only be done in general and tentative terms. In so doing, I am only trying to give a general and tentative idea of the circumstances leading to the revelation of each *surah*.

This *surah*, al-Anfal, or The Spoils of War, was revealed after *Surah* 2, The Cow, shortly after the Battle of Badr which took place in Ramadan, in the second year of the Islamic calendar, approximately 19 months after the Prophet's migration to Medina. However, when we say that it was revealed after *Surah* 2, our statement does not give a complete picture, because *Surah* 2 was not revealed in full on one occasion. Some of its passages were revealed early in the Medinan period, and some towards its end, stretching over a period of nearly nine years. The present *surah*, al-Anfal, was revealed sometime between these two dates, while *Surah* 2 was still in the process leading to its completion. This meant that a passage would be revealed and placed in its appropriate position, according to divine instruction given through the Prophet. Normally, however, when we say that a particular *surah* was revealed on such and such date, we are simply referring to the beginning of its revelation.

Some reports suggest that verses 30–36 were revealed in Mecca, since they refer to events that took place there before the Prophet's migration to Medina. This, however, is not a sufficient reason to draw such a conclusion. Many are the verses revealed in Medina that refer to past events from the Meccan period. In this *surah*, Verse 26 provides such a case. Moreover, Verse 36, the last one in the passage claimed to have been revealed in

Mecca, speaks of how the idolaters allocated funds to prepare for the Battle of Uhud, which took place after their defeat at Badr.

The reports that claim that these verses were a Meccan revelation also mention a conversation that is highly improbable. They mention that "Abu Talib, the Prophet's uncle who provided him with protection, asked the Prophet: 'What are your people plotting against you?' He answered: 'They want to cast a magic spell on me, or to banish or kill me.' He said: 'Who told you this?' The Prophet replied: 'My Lord.' Abu Talib then said: 'Your Lord is a good one. Take care of him.' The Prophet said: 'I take care of Him! No, it is He who takes good care of me.' By way of comment on this, Verse 26 was revealed, saying: *'Remember when you were few and helpless in the land, fearful lest people do away with you: how He sheltered you, strengthened you with His support and provided you with many good things so that you might be grateful.'* " (Verse 26)

Ibn Kathir mentions this report and discounts it, saying: "This is highly improbable, because this verse was revealed in Medina. Besides, the entire event, when the Quraysh convened a meeting of its notables to discuss how they could get rid of the Prophet and the suggestions they made of imprisoning, banishing or killing him, took place on the eve of the Prophet's migration, about three years after Abu Talib's death. When Abu Talib died, the Prophet lost his uncle who had given him full support and protection. The Quraysh were thus able to abuse him and concoct a plot to kill him."

Muhammad ibn Ishaq, a very early biographer of the Prophet, transmits a couple of long reports on the authority of Ibn ʿAbbas, the Prophet's cousin who was an eminent scholar, concerning these plots by the Quraysh. He concludes by saying: "God then gave him permission to depart. After he settled in Medina, He revealed to him the *surah* entitled *al-Anfal*, reminding him of His grace: *'Remember how the unbelievers were scheming against you, seeking to keep you in chains or have you slain or banished. Thus they plot and plan, but God also plans. God is above all schemers.'* " (Verse 30)

This report by Ibn ʿAbbas fits well with the general text of the complete *surah*, and its reminders to the Prophet and his companions of His grace. When they remember these aspects of God's grace, they are motivated to fulfil their duty, fight the enemies of their faith and stand firm. Hence, to say that the whole *surah* was revealed after the Muslims' migration to Medina is more accurate.

Characteristics of the Islamic approach

This *surah* takes up the Battle of Badr as its subject matter. This battle, its circumstances, results and effects on human history constitute a major landmark in the progress of the Islamic movement. God describes this battle as *'the day when the true was distinguished from the false, the day when the two hosts met in battle.'* (Verse 41) He also makes it the parting point not merely in this life or in human history, but also in the life to come. He says in the Qur'an: *"These two adversaries have become engrossed in contention about their Lord. For the unbelievers garments of fire shall be cut out; and scalding water will be poured over their heads, melting all that is in their bellies and their skin. In addition, there will be grips of iron for them. Whenever, in their anguish, they try to get out, they are returned there, and will be told: 'Taste the torment of fire.' God will certainly admit those who believe and do righteous deeds into gardens through which running waters flow, wherein they will be adorned with bracelets of gold and pearls, and where silk will be their raiment. For they were guided to the best of words; and so they were guided to the way that leads to the One to whom all praise is due."* (22: 19–24) Some reports suggest that these verses speak of the two hosts that met in battle at Badr. This confirms that this battle provides the criterion by which people shall be distinguished in the life to come. This statement by God Almighty is sufficient to give us a clear idea of the importance of that day of battle. We will try to give an idea of its great value as we discuss the battle, the events leading to it and its outcome.

Exceptionally important as that battle is, its true value cannot be clearly seen unless we understand its nature and realize that it was merely one episode of *jihad*. To appreciate it fully we also need to understand the motives and objectives of *jihad*; and we certainly cannot understand those unless we fully understand the nature of Islam itself.

In his priceless book *Zad al-Ma'ad*, Imam Ibn al-Qayyim includes a chapter with the title, The Progress of the Prophet's Guidance on Dealing with the Unbelievers and the Hypocrites from the Start of His Mission to the End of His Life. This is given below in a highly summarized form:

> The first revelation given to the Prophet by his Lord—limitless is He in His glory— was his order to him, *"Read in the name of your Lord who created man out of a germ-cell"* (96: 1–2) This was the start of his prophethood. The instruction to him was to read within himself. At that point, He did not order him to convey anything to anyone. He subsequently revealed to him: *"You who are enfolded, arise and warn!"* (74: 1–2) This means that God made him a prophet by telling him to read, and He gave him his mission by saying, *"You who are enfolded, arise and warn!"* (74: 1–2) God then ordered him to warn his immediate clan. Subsequently, he gave the same warning to his own people, then to the surrounding Arabian tribes, then all Arabs, then mankind generally.
>
> For more than a decade after the start of his prophethood, Muhammad [peace be upon him] continued to advocate the faith without resorting to fighting or the imposition of any loyalty tax, i.e. *jizyah*. Throughout this period he was ordered to stay his hand, forbear patiently and overlook all opposition. Later, God gave him permission to migrate [from Mecca to Medina] and permitted him to fight. He then instructed him to fight those who wage war against him and to maintain peace with those who refrain from fighting him. At a later stage, God ordered him to fight the idolaters until all submission is made to God alone.
>
> After the order was given to the Prophet to strive and fight for God's cause [i.e. *jihad*], unbelievers were in three categories with regard to their relations with him: those with whom he was in peace and truce, combatants fighting him, and those under his protection [i.e. *Ahl al-Dhimma*]. God ordered him to honour his treaties with those whom he had a peace treaty, as long as they honoured their commitments. If he feared treachery on their part, he was to revoke the treaty but would not fight them until he had informed them of the termination of their peace treaty. On the other hand, he was to fight those who violated their treaties with him.
>
> When *Surah 9, al-Tawbah*, was revealed, it outlined the policy towards all these three categories. The Prophet is ordered there to fight his enemies from among the people of earlier faiths until they submit to his authority, paying the loyalty tax, *jizyah*, or embrace Islam. He is also ordered in the same *surah* to strive hard against the unbelievers and the idolaters. He strove against the unbelievers with arms, and against the hypocrites with argument and proof.
>
> A further order to the Prophet in *Surah 9* was to terminate all treaties with unbelievers, classifying such people into three groups. The first group he was ordered to fight, because these were the ones who violated their treaties with him and who were untrue to their commitments. He fought them and was victorious. The second group consisted of those with whom he had a peace treaty which they had honoured fully, and the treaty was to run for a specific term. They had given no support to any person or group who opposed the Prophet. With these he was to honour the peace

treaty until it had run its course. The third group included those with whom the Prophet had no treaty and no previous fighting engagements, as well as those who had an open-ended agreement. The Prophet was instructed to give these groups four months' notice, after which he was to fight them. The Prophet acted on these instructions, fought those who violated their treaties, and gave four months, notice to those who had no treaty or had one without a specific term. Those who honoured their treaty were to have it honoured by the Prophet until the end of its term. All these embraced Islam before the end of their term. As for those who pledged loyalty to him, they were to pay the loyalty tax, *jizyah*.

Thus, after the revelation of *Surah* 9, the unbelievers were in three different categories with regard to the Prophet's relations with them: combatants, or bound by a specified-term treaty, or loyal. The second category embraced Islam shortly thereafter, leaving the other two groups: combatants who feared him, and those who were loyal. Thus, all mankind were divided into three classes: Muslims who believed in the Prophet's message; those at peace with him who enjoyed security; and those who were hostile and feared him.

As for the hypocrites, he was instructed to accept from them what they professed, leaving the final verdict on them to God. He was to strive against them with informed argument. He was further instructed to turn away from them and to be hard so that he would deliver his message to them in a way that they could not refute. He was forbidden to pray for them when they died, or to visit their graves. He was informed that if he were to pray for them to be forgiven, God would not forgive them.

Such was the Prophet's policy towards his opponents, both unbelievers and hypocrites.[1]

This excellent summary of the different stages of the development of *jihad*, or striving for God's cause, reveals a number of profound features of the Islamic approach which merit discussion; but we can only present them here very briefly.

The first of these features is the serious realism of the Islamic approach. Islam is a movement confronting a human situation with appropriate means. What it confronts is a state of ignorance, or *jahiliyyah*, which prevails over ideas and beliefs, giving rise to practical systems that are supported by political and material authority. Thus, the Islamic approach is to confront all this with vigorous means and suitable resources. It presents its arguments and proofs to correct concepts and beliefs; and it strives with power to remove the systems and authorities that prevent people from adopting the right beliefs, forcing them to follow their errant ways and worship deities other than God Almighty. The Islamic approach does not resort to the use of verbal argument when confronting material power. Nor does it ever resort to compulsion and coercion in order to force its beliefs on people. Both are equally alien to the Islamic approach as it seeks to liberate people from subjugation so that they may serve God alone.

Secondly, Islam is a practical movement that progresses from one stage to the next, utilizing for each stage practically effective and competent means, while at the same time preparing the ground for the next stage. It does not confront practical realities with abstract theories, nor does it use the same old means to face changing realities. Some people ignore this essential feature of the Islamic approach and overlook the nature of the different stages of development of this approach. They cite Qur'anic statements stating that they represent the Islamic approach, without relating these statements to the stages they addressed. When they do so, they betray their utter confusion and give the Islamic approach a deceptive appearance. They assign to Qur'anic verses insupportable rules and principles, treating each verse or statement as outlining final Islamic rules. Themselves a product of the sorry and desperate state of contemporary generations who have nothing of Islam other than its label, and defeated both rationally and spiritually, they claim that Islamic *jihad* is always defensive. They imagine that they are doing Islam a service when they cast away its objective of removing all tyrannical powers from the face of the earth, so that people are freed from serving anyone other than God. Islam does not force people to accept its beliefs; rather, it aims to provide an environment where people enjoy full freedom of belief. It abolishes oppressive political systems depriving people of this freedom, or forces them into submission so that they allow their peoples complete freedom to choose to believe in Islam if they so wish.

Thirdly, such continuous movement and progressive ways and means do not divert Islam from its definitive principles and well-defined objectives. Right from the very first day, when it made its initial address to the Prophet's immediate clan, then to the Quraysh, and then to the Arabs and finally putting its message to all mankind, its basic theme remained the same, making the same requirement. It wants people to achieve the same objective of worshipping God alone, submitting themselves to none other than Him. There can be no compromise over this essential rule. It then moves towards this single goal according to a well-thought-out plan, with progressive stages, and fitting means.

Finally, we have a clear legal framework governing relations between the Muslim community and other societies, as is evident in the excellent summary quoted from *Zad al-Ma'ad*. This legal framework is based on the main principle that submission to God alone is a universal message which all mankind must either accept or be at peace with. It must not place any impediment to this message, in the form of a political system or material power. Every individual must remain free to make his or her absolutely free choice to accept or reject it, feeling no pressure or opposition. Anyone who puts such impediments in the face of the message of complete submission to God, must be resisted and fought by Islam.

The liberation of mankind

Writers with a defeatist and apologetic mentality who try to defend Islamic *jihad* often confuse two clearly different principles. The first is that Islam comes out clearly against forcing people to accept any particular belief, while the second is its approach that seeks to remove political and material forces that try to prevent it from addressing people, so that they may not submit themselves to God. These are clearly distinct principles that should never be confused. Yet it is because of their defeatism that such writers try to limit *jihad* to what is called today 'a defensive war'. But Islamic *jihad* is a totally different matter that has nothing to do with the wars people fight today, or their motives and presentation. The motives of Islamic *jihad* can be found within the nature of Islam, its role in human life, the objectives God has set for it and for the achievement of which He has sent His final Messenger with His perfect message.

We may describe the Islamic faith as a declaration of the liberation of mankind from servitude to creatures, including man's own desires. It also declares that all Godhead and Lordship throughout the universe belong to God alone. This represents a challenge to all systems that assign sovereignty to human beings in any shape or form. It is, in effect, a revolt against any human situation where sovereignty, or indeed Godhead, is given to human beings. A situation that gives ultimate authority to human beings actually elevates those humans to the status of deities, usurping God's own authority. As a declaration of human liberation, Islam means returning God's authority to Him, rejecting the usurpers who rule over human communities according to man-made laws. In this way, no human being is placed in a position of Lordship over other people. To proclaim God's authority and sovereignty means the elimination of all human kingship and to establish the rule of God, the Lord of the universe. In the words of the Qur'an: *"He alone is God in the heavens and God on earth."* (43: 84) *"All judgement rests with God alone. He has ordered that you should worship none but Him. That is the true faith, but most people do not know it."* (12: 40) *"Say: 'People of earlier revelations! Let us come to an agreement which is equitable between you and us: that we shall worship none but God, that we shall associate no partners with Him, and that we shall not take one another for lords beside God.' And if they turn away, then say: 'Bear witness that we have surrendered ourselves to God.' "* (3: 64)

Establishing the rule of God on earth does not mean that sovereignty is assigned to a particular group of people, as was the case when the Church wielded power in Christian Europe, or that certain men become spokesmen for the gods, as was the case under theocratic rule. God's rule is established when His law is enforced and all matters are judged according to His revealed law.

Nothing of all this is achieved through verbal advocacy of Islam. The problem is that the people in power who have usurped God's authority on earth will not relinquish their power at the mere explanation and advocacy of the true faith. Otherwise, it would have been very simple for God's messengers to establish the divine faith. History, however, tells us that the reverse was true throughout human life.

This universal declaration of the liberation of man on earth from every authority other than that of God, and the declaration that all sovereignty belongs to God alone as does Lordship over the universe, are not a theoretical, philosophical and passive proclamation. It is a positive, practical and dynamic message which seeks to bring about the implementation of God's law in human life, freeing people from servitude to anyone other than God alone. This cannot be achieved unless advocacy is complemented with a movement that confronts the existing human situation with adequate and competent means.

In actual life, Islam is always confronted with a host of obstacles placed in its way: some belong to the realm of beliefs and concepts, others are physical, in addition to political, social, economic, racial obstacles. Deviant beliefs and superstitions add further obstacles trying to impede Islam. All these interact to form a very complex mixture working against Islam and the liberation of man.

Verbal argument and advocacy face up to beliefs and ideas, while the movement confronts material obstacles, particularly political authority that rests on complex yet interrelated ideological, racial, class, social and economic systems. Thus, employing both verbal advocacy and its practical movement, Islam confronts the existing human situation in its totality with adequately effective methods. Both are necessary for the achievement of the liberation of all mankind throughout the world. This is a very important point that merits strong emphasis.

This religion of Islam is not a declaration for the liberation of the Arabs, nor is its message addressed to the Arabs in particular. It addresses itself to all humanity, considering the entire earth its field of work. God is not the Lord of the Arabs alone, nor is His Lordship limited to Muslims only. God is the Lord of all worlds. Hence, Islam wants to bring all mankind back to their true Lord, liberating them from servitude to anyone else. From the Islamic point of view, true servitude or worship, takes the form of people's submission to laws enacted by other human beings. It is such submission, or servitude, that is due to God alone, as Islam emphasizes. Anyone that serves anyone other than God in this sense takes himself out of Islam, no matter how strongly he declares himself to be a Muslim. The Prophet clearly states that adherence to law's and authorities was the type of worship which classified the Jews and Christians as unbelievers, disobeying God's orders to worship Him alone.

Al-Tirmidhi relates on the authority of ʿAdiy ibn Hatim that when the Prophet's message reached him, he fled to Syria. [He had earlier accepted Christianity.] However, his sister and a number of people from his tribe were taken prisoner by the Muslims. The Prophet [peace be upon him] treated his sister kindly and gave her gifts. She went back to her brother and encouraged him to adopt Islam, and to visit the Prophet. People were speaking about his expected arrival. When he came into the Prophet's presence, he was wearing a silver cross. As he entered, the Prophet was reciting the verse which says: *"They {i.e. the people of earlier revelations} have taken their rabbis and their monks, as well as the Christ, son of Mary, for their lords beside God."* (9: 31) ʿAdiy reports: "I said, 'They did not worship their priests.' God's Messenger replied, 'Yes they did. Their priests and rabbis forbade them what is lawful, and declared permissible what is unlawful, and they accepted that. This is how they worshipped them.' "

The explanation given by the Prophet is a clear statement that obedience to man-made laws and judgements constitutes worship that takes people out of Islam. It is indeed how some people take others for their lords. This is the very situation Islam aims to eradicate in order to ensure man's liberation.

When the realities of human life run contrary to the declaration of general human liberation, it becomes incumbent on Islam to take appropriate action, on both the advocacy and the movement fronts. It strikes hard against political regimes that rule over people according to laws other than that of God, or in other words, force people to serve beings other than God, and prevent them from listening to the message of Islam and accepting it freely if they so desire. Islam will also remove existing powers whether they take a purely political or racial form or operate class distinction within the same race. It then moves to establish a social, economic and political system that allows the liberation of man and man's unhindered movement.

It is never the intention of Islam to force its beliefs on people, but Islam is not merely a set of beliefs. Islam aims to make mankind free from servitude to other people. Hence, it strives to abolish all systems and regimes that are based on the servitude of one person to another. When Islam has thus freed people from all political pressure and enlightened their minds with its message, it gives them complete freedom to choose the faith they wish. However, this freedom does not mean that they can make their desires their gods, or that they choose to remain in servitude to people like them, or that some of them are elevated to the status of lordship over the rest. The system to be established in the world should be based on complete servitude to God al[...] [...] only. Within this system, every person is free to ad[...] This is the practical meaning of the principle that [...] Religion means submission, obedience, servitude a[...] God. According to Islam, the term 'religion' is much wider in scope than belief. Religion is actually a way of life, and in Islam this is based on belief. But in an Islamic system, it is possible that different groups live under it even though they may choose not to adopt Islamic beliefs. They will, however, abide by its laws based on the central principle of submission to God alone.

How defensive is *jihad*?

When we understand the nature of Islam, as it has already been explained, we realize the inevitability of *jihad*, or striving for God's cause, taking a military form in addition to its advocacy form. We will further recognize that *jihad* was never defensive, in the narrow sense that the term 'defensive war' generally denotes today. It is this narrow sense that is emphasized by the defeatists who succumb to the pressure of the present circumstances and to the Orientalists' wily attacks. Indeed the concept of striving, or *jihad*, for God's cause represents a positive movement that aims to liberate man throughout the world, employing appropriate means to face every situation at every stage.

If we must describe Islamic *jihad* as defensive, then we need to amend the meaning of the term 'defence' so that it means the defending of mankind against all factors that hinder their liberation and restrict their freedom. These may take the form of concepts and beliefs, as well as political regimes that create economic, class and racial distinctions. When Islam first came into existence, this world was full of such hindrances, some forms of which persist in present-day *jahiliyyah*.

When we give the term 'defence' such a broader meaning we can appreciate the motives for Islamic *jihad* all over the world, and we can understand the nature of Islam. Otherwise, any attempt to find defensive justification for *jihad*, within the contemporary narrow sense of defence, betrays a lack of understanding of the nature of Islam and its role in this world. Such attempts try to find any evidence to prove that early Muslims went on *jihad* to repel aggression by their neighbours against the Muslim land, which to some people is confined to the Arabian Peninsula. All this betrays stark defeatism.

Had Abu Bakr, ʿUmar and ʿUthman, the first three Caliphs, felt secure against any attack on Arabia by the Byzantine or the Persian Empires, would they have refrained from carrying the message of Islam to the rest of the world? How could they present Islam to the world when they had all types of material obstacles to contend with: political regimes, social, racial and class systems, as well as economic systems based on such social discrimination; and all these are guaranteed protection by the state?

Jihad is essential for the Islamic message, if it is to be taken seriously as a declaration of the liberation of man, because it cannot confine itself to theoretical and philosophical arguments. It must confront existing situations with effective means, whether the land of Islam is secure or under threat from neighbouring powers. As Islam works for peace, it is not satisfied with a cheap peace that applies only to the area where people of the Muslim faith happen to live. Islam aims to achieve the sort of peace which ensures that all submission is made to God alone. This means that all people submit themselves to God, and none of them takes others for their lords. We must form our view on the basis of the ultimate stage of the *jihad* movement, not on the early or middle stages of the Prophet's mission. All these stages led to the situation described by Imam Ibn al-Qayyim as follows:

> Thus, after the revelation of *Surah* 9, the unbelievers were in three different categories with regard to the Prophet's relations with them: combatants, or bound by a specified-term treaty, or loyal. The second category embraced Islam shortly thereafter, leaving the other two groups: combatants who feared him, and those who were loyal. Thus, all mankind were divided into three classes: Muslims who believed in the Prophet's message; those at peace with him who enjoyed security; and those who were hostile and feared him.[2]

Such is the attitude that is consistent with the nature of Islam and its objectives.

When Islam was still confined to Mecca, and in the early period of the Prophet's settlement in Medina, God restrained the Muslims from fighting. They were told: "*Hold back your hands {from fighting}, and attend regularly to prayer, and pay your* zakat." (4: 77) They were later permitted to fight, when they were told: "*Permission to fight is given to those against whom war is being wrongfully waged. Most certainly, God has the power to grant them victory. These are the ones who have been driven from their homelands against all right for no other reason than their saying, 'Our Lord is God!' Were it not that God repels some people by means of others, monasteries, churches, synagogues and mosques—in all of which God's name is abundantly extolled—would surely have been destroyed. God will most certainly succour him who succours God's cause. God is certainly most Powerful, Almighty. They are those who, if We firmly establish them on earth, attend regularly to their prayers, give in charity, enjoin the doing of what is right and forbid the doing of what is wrong. With God rests the final outcome of all events."* (22: 39–41) They were then required to fight those who fight them, but not other people: *"Fight for the cause of God those who wage war against you, but do not commit aggression."* (2: 190) But then they were ordered to fight against all idolaters: *"fight against the idolaters all together as they fight against you all together."* (9: 36) They were also told: *"Fight against those among the people of the scriptures who do not believe in God or the Last Day, and do not forbid what God and His Messenger have forbidden, and do not follow the religion of truth until they pay the submission tax with a willing hand and are utterly subdued."* (9: 29) This means, as Ibn al-Qayyim puts it, that "fighting was first forbidden, then permitted, then ordered against those who fight Muslims, and finally against all unbelievers who associate partners with God."

The seriousness that is characteristic of the Qur'anic texts and the Prophet's traditions on *jihad*, and the positive approach that is very clear in all events of *jihad* in the early Islamic periods and over many centuries make it impossible to accept the explanation concocted by defeatist writers. They have come up with such an explanation under pressure from the present weakness of the Muslim community and the unsavoury attacks on the concept of *jihad* by Orientalists.

When we listen to God's words and the Prophet's traditions on *jihad*, and follow the events of early Islamic *jihad*, we cannot imagine how anyone can consider it a temporary measure, subject to circumstances that may or may not come into play, or having the limited objective of securing national borders.

In the very first Qur'anic verse that gives Muslims permission to fight for His cause, God makes it clear to believers that the normal situation in this present life is that one group of people is checked by another so as to prevent the spread of corruption on earth: *"Permission to fight is given to those against whom war is being wrongfully waged. Most certainly, God has the power to grant them victory. These are the ones who have been driven from their homelands against all right for no other reason than their saying, 'Our Lord is God!' Were it not that God repels some people by means of others, monasteries, churches, synagogues and mosques—in all of which God's name is abundantly extolled—would surely have been destroyed."* (22: 39–40) We thus see that it is the permanent state of affairs for truth to be unable to co-exist with falsehood on earth. Hence, when Islam makes its declaration for the liberation of mankind on earth, so that they may only serve God alone, those who usurp God's authority try to silence it. They will never tolerate it or leave it in peace. Islam will not sit idle, either. It will move to deprive them of their power so that people can be freed of their shackles. This is the permanent state of affairs which necessitates the continuity of *jihad* until all submission is made to God alone.

A stage of no fighting

Holding back from fighting in Mecca, by divine order, was only a stage in a long-term strategy. The same was the case in the early days after the Prophet's migration to Medina. However, what made the Muslim community in Medina take its stance was not merely the need to defend Medina and make it secure against attack. This was certainly a primary objective, but it was by no means the ultimate one. Achieving this objective provided the means and the secure base from which to remove the obstacles that fettered man and deprived him of his freedom.

Besides, it is perfectly understandable that Muslims should refrain from taking up arms in Mecca. Advocacy of Islam was reasonably free. Assured of protection by his own clan, the Hashimites, the Prophet was able to declare his message, addressing it to individuals and groups and putting to them its clear principles and beliefs. There was no organized political power to stop him from doing so, or to stop individuals from listening to him. Hence, there was no need at this stage to resort to force. There were other reasons which we outlined in Volume III, pp. 234–236, when commenting on the verse that says: "*Are you not aware of those who have been told, 'Hold back your hands {from fighting}, and attend regularly to prayer, and pay your* zakat . . .?' " It may be useful to quote here a part of what we stated there:

1. One reason could be that the Meccan period was one of training, educating and preparing a particular group of people under certain conditions. One of the aims of such a programme is to discipline the Arab mind to persevere and endure personal and collective hardship as a means to transcend personal egos. One's own self and immediate community should no longer be the focus and prime movers in one's life. People needed to be taught restraint and self-control and how not to react with immediate rage and anger, as was their nature. They needed to learn to behave as members of an organized society with a central leadership to be consulted and obeyed in all matters, regardless of how different that was from their customs and traditions. This was the cornerstone in remodelling the Arab character to establish a civilized, orderly, non-tribal Muslim society that recognizes a governing leadership.

2. Another possible reason is that peaceful action was more effective in that particular Arab society of the Quraysh, which attached much importance to self-image and honour. The use of force in such a situation could only harden attitudes and result in fresh bloody grudges, reminiscent of the famous inter-Arab feuds of Dahis and al-Ghabra', and of al-Basus which raged for many years, wiping out complete tribes. Such a new conflict would always be associated in the Arab memory with Islam as the cause of vengeance and bloodshed rather than Islam as a universal Divine mission. The basic essence of Islam would, in that case, be forever obscured and obliterated.

3. There was also the need to avoid a bloodbath within every Arab household in Mecca since there was no organized authority perpetrating the persecution of Muslim converts. The harassment was unsystematic, following no specific order. Every household dealt with their converts as they saw fit. Prescription of armed confrontation in such circumstances would mean battles and massacres in every home for which Islam would be blamed. In fact, the Quraysh propaganda, spread during the pilgrimage and trading seasons, was already blaming Islam for family splits, feuds and divisions among the Arabs even before the use of force was eventually permitted.

4. Another reason for the delay in prescribing *jihad* by force of arms could be God's prior knowledge that many of the tormentors and perpetrators of maltreatment against the Muslims would, one day soon, themselves be converts and ardent defenders, indeed leaders, of Islam. "Was not 'Umar ibn al-Khattab one such person?

5. Another reason could be that Arab tribal chivalry was known to provoke

sympathy with the weak and the oppressed when they persevere in the face of adversity, especially if some of these hailed from the noble sections of society. This is borne out in several incidents including that whereby Ibn al-Dughunnah tried to persuade Abu Bakr, a noble man, not to leave Mecca and offered him protection, seeing it as a shame on all the Arabs that he should have to emigrate. Another incident was the repeal of the boycott on Hashim, Muhammad's clan, and the ending of their siege in the Hashimite quarters in Mecca, after an extended period of starvation and hardship. In other ancient civilizations, persecution might have led to the adulation of the oppressor and further humiliation for the oppressed, but not in Arab society.

6. It could have been due to the small number of Muslims at the time and their confinement in Mecca when Islam had not spread widely in Arabia, and the neutral stand that other Arab tribes would take in an internal conflict within Mecca. Confrontation could very well lead to the annihilation of the small band of Muslim converts, even if they were to kill twice as many as their own number, and the infidels would thus prevail. In this case, the religion of Islam, which was meant to be a universal way of life and a practical and realistic system, would no longer exist.

As for the early period in Medina, the treaty the Prophet agreed with the Jews and the Arab unbelievers in the city and the neighbouring areas was a suitable arrangement at this stage. Besides, there was an open opportunity for delivering God's message, with no political authority standing in opposition to it. All groups recognized the new Muslim state and the Prophet as its leader who conducted its political affairs. The treaty stipulated that no party or group could wage war against, or make peace or establish any relations with, any outside group without the express permission of the Prophet. Moreover, it was clear that real power in Medina was wielded by the Muslim leadership. Hence, God's message could be freely addressed to people and they could choose to accept it if they so wanted.

Moreover, the Prophet wanted to concentrate his efforts at this stage on the struggle against the Quraysh, whose relentless opposition to Islam constituted a hard obstacle preventing its spread to other tribes. Most Arabian tribes adopted a wait-and-see attitude to the struggle which they viewed as an internal conflict between the Quraysh and a group of its own members. Hence the Prophet started to send out expeditions, beginning in Ramadan, only seven months after his migration to Medina when his uncle Hamzah ibn ʿAbd al-Muttalib was the first commander.

Other expeditions followed, with the second taking place nine months after the Prophet's migration, and another after 13 months, and a fourth three months later on. Shortly after that the Prophet sent a small company commanded by ʿAbdullah ibn Jahsh, 17 months after his migration. It was on this particular expedition that fighting took place for the first time and one man was killed. This was in one of the four sacred months. In a comment on this incident the Qurʾan says: *"They ask you about fighting in the sacred month. Say, 'Fighting in it is a grave offence, but to turn people away from God's path, to disbelieve in Him and in the Sacred Mosque, and to expel its people from it—{all this} is far more grave in God's sight.' Religious persecution is worse than killing. They shall not cease to fight you until they force you to renounce your faith, if they can."* (2: 217)[3]

In Ramadan of the same year, the Battle of Badr took place, on which the present *surah* provides detailed commentary.

What justification for *jihad*?

When we review the situation with all its relevant circumstances, we realize that the argument that *jihad* is nothing more than a defensive war, in the narrow sense of the term, cannot hold. Those who try to find pure defensive reasons to justify the expansion of Islam find themselves cornered by Orientalists' attacks at a time when Muslims are powerless. Indeed Muslims today are far removed from Islam, except for a small minority who are determined to implement the Islamic declaration of man's liberation from all authority except that of God.

The spread of Islam does not need to find any justification other than those stated in the Qur'an: "*Let them fight in God's cause—all who are willing to barter the life of this world for the life to come. To him who fights in God's cause, whether he be slain or be victorious, We shall grant a rich reward. And why should you not fight in the cause of God and the utterly helpless men, women and children who are crying, 'Our Lord! Deliver us from this land whose people are oppressors, and send forth to us, out of Your grace, a protector, and send us one that will help us.' Those who believe fight in the cause of God, and those who reject the faith fight in the cause of evil. Fight, then, against the friends of Satan. Feeble indeed is the cunning of Satan.*" (4: 74–76)

"*Say to the unbelievers that if they desist, all that is past shall be forgiven them; but if they persist {in their erring ways}, let them remember what happened to the like of them in former times. Fight them until there is no more oppression, and all submission is made to God alone. If they desist, God is certainly aware of all they do. But if they turn away, know that God is your Lord Supreme. How splendid is this Lord Supreme, and how splendid is this giver of support.*" (8: 38–40)

"*Fight against those among the people of earlier revelations who do not believe in God or the Last Day, and do not forbid what God and His Messenger have forbidden, and do not follow the religion of truth until they pay the submission tax with a willing hand and are utterly subdued. The Jews say: 'Ezra is the son of God', while the Christians say: 'The Christ is the son of God.' Such are the assertions they utter with their mouths, echoing assertions made by the unbelievers of old. May God destroy them! How perverse they are! They make of their rabbis and their monks, and of the Christ, son of Mary, lords besides God. Yet they have been ordered to worship none but the One God, other than whom there is no deity. Exalted be He above those to whom they ascribe divinity. They seek to extinguish God's light with their mouths, but God will not allow anything to interfere with His will to bring His light to perfection, however hateful this may be to the unbelievers.*" (9: 29–32)

The justification carried in these verses is that of the need to establish the truth of Godhead on earth, and implement the way of life God has decreed in human life. Moreover, satanic forces and methods must be chased out and abolished; and the lordship of one man over others must be ended. Human beings are God's creatures and they serve Him alone. No one may be allowed to hold authority over them so as to make them his servants or enact arbitrary laws for them. This is sufficient justification, not forgetting at the same time the main principle that "*there shall be no compulsion in religion*" (2: 256) No one will ever be compelled or pressurized to adopt the Islamic faith after the liberation of all people and the acknowledgement that all submission must be to God alone, and that all authority belongs to Him.

It is sufficient to remember that Islam aims to free all mankind from servitude to creatures so that they may serve God alone to justify Islamic *jihad*. This was clearly in the minds of the early Muslims when they went out to fight the Byzantine and the Persian Empires. None of them justified their action by saying, 'We want to defend our country against external threats,' or, 'We want to repel Byzantine or Persian aggression,' or, 'We want to annex land and add to our wealth.' Their representatives, Rib'iy ibn

'Amir, Hudhayfah ibn Muhsin and al-Mughirah ibn Shu'bah, each met Rustam, the Persian army commander in the Battle of al-Qadisiyyah, alone on three successive days. In response to Rustam's question about their objectives, they all said the same thing: "It is God who has commanded us so that we may liberate anyone who wishes from servitude to human beings into the service of God alone, from the narrowness of this world into the expanse of this world and the hereafter, and from the injustices of different religions to the justice of Islam. God has sent His Messenger to deliver His message to His creatures. Whoever accepts it from us, we let him be, turn back and give him his land. We fight only those who rebel until we achieve martyrdom or victory."

The justification for *jihad* is inherent in the nature of this faith, its declaration of man's liberation, and its confrontation with existing human situations using adequate and effective means, suitably adapted and renewed for every stage. This justification exists in the first place, even though there may be no threat to the Muslim land or the Muslim community. It is of the essence of the Islamic approach and the nature of the practical obstacles that stand in its way in different communities. Islamic *jihad* cannot be linked merely to some limited and temporary defensive needs.

It is sufficient that a Muslim goes out on *jihad* laying down his life and sacrificing all his money, for God's cause, not for any considerations of any personal gain. Before going out on *jihad* a Muslim would have won the greater battle within himself, against his own desires, ambitions, personal and national interests and against any motive other than serving God and establishing His authority on earth after winning it back from rebellious usurpers.

People who try to justify Islamic *jihad* on the grounds of protecting or defending the Islamic homeland underrate the Islamic way of life, placing its importance below that of the homeland. Theirs is a new consideration that is alien to the Islamic outlook. The faith, the way of life based on it and the community that implements it are the considerations valued by Islam. The land in itself has no significance. It acquires its value when the Islamic way of life is implemented in it, so as to become the cradle of the faith, the practical model, the homeland of Islam, and the starting point for the liberation of mankind.

It is true that defending the homeland of Islam means protecting the faith, the way of life and the Muslim community, all at the same time; but this is not the ultimate objective of Islamic *jihad*. Defending the homeland of Islam is the means to establish God's authority within it, and to use it as the base from which to address all mankind. Islam is a message to all humanity, and the whole earth is its sphere of action.

As already stated, any effort that tries to spread the Islamic way of life is bound to meet obstacles created by the power of the state, the social system and the general environment. Islam aims to remove all these obstacles so that it can address people freely, appealing to their minds and consciences, after breaking their fetters so that they have genuine freedom of choice.

We must not be intimidated by the Orientalists' attacks on the concept of Islamic *jihad*, or allow the pressures of world political powers to weigh heavily on us, so as to seek justifications for *jihad* that do not fit with the nature of Islam.

When we look at historical events, we must not lose sight of the inherent factors in the nature of Islam, its universal declaration and practical way of life. We must not confuse these with temporary defensive needs. It was inevitable that Islam would defend itself against aggression, because its very existence, general objective, the movement it forms under a new leadership, and the birth of a new community which recognizes only God's sovereignty—all this is bound to provoke other societies, based on *jahiliyyah*, into trying to smash it in order to defend their own interests. It is inevitable that the new

Muslim community will also have to defend itself. This is an inescapable situation that arises with the advent of Islam in any society. There is no question that Islam wants to fight such a battle; it is imposed on it, and the struggle that follows is a natural one, between two systems that cannot co-exist for long. All this is undeniable. Hence, Islam has no choice but to defend itself against aggression.

A much more important fact, however, is that, by nature, Islam will take the initiative and move to save humanity and free people throughout the world from servitude to anyone other than God. It is not possible that Islam will confine itself to geographical boundaries, or racial limits, abandoning the rest of mankind and leaving them to suffer from evil, corruption and servitude to lords other than God Almighty.

A time may come when enemies of Islam may find it expedient not to try to suppress Islam if it is willing to leave them alone, practising within their national boundaries their own systems that allow some people to be lords over others. They may offer such a state of coexistence if Islam is willing not to extend its declaration of universal freedom to their people. But Islam will not accept such a truce, unless they are willing to acknowledge its authority in the form of paying the loyalty or submission tax, *jizyah*, to guarantee that the message of Islam may address their people freely, without putting any material obstacle in its way.

Such is the nature of Islam and its role of liberating all mankind from servitude to anyone other than God. The gulf is wide indeed between this understanding and confining Islam to a local status within national borders or racial limits, acting only to defend itself against outside aggression. To think of Islam in this light is to deprive it of its reasons for action.

The underlying reasons for *jihad* are clearly identified when we remember that Islam is the way of life God has given to man. It is not a system devised by an individual or a group of people, nor is it the ideology of a certain race. It is only when we begin to lose sight of this fundamental truth of God's absolute sovereignty and people's servitude to Him that we try to find external reasons to justify *jihad*. No one who is fully cognizant of this basic Islamic principle will need to look for any other justification for *jihad*.

The gulf may not seem too great between thinking that Islam had to fight a war imposed on it by the very fact of its existence alongside *jahiliyyah* societies, which were bound to attack it, and the recognition that Islam would have taken the initiative and embarked on its struggle. In both situations, Islam would have had to fight. But at the end the gulf between the two views is very wide indeed. It gives Islamic ideas and concepts a totally different colour. This is very serious indeed.

A gulf too wide!

Islam is a system given by God and it aims to establish the fundamental principle of God's sovereignty and people's servitude to Him alone. It gives practical implementation of this principle in the form of a human society where people are totally free from servitude to anyone other than God. Thus, people are governed only by God's law, demonstrating His authority, or, in other words, His Godhead. As such, Islam has the right to remove all obstacles in its way and address people freely, without any impediments such as a political system or social customs and traditions. Viewing Islam in this way is far removed from viewing it as a local system of a particular country or nationality, having the right to defend itself within its national borders.

The two views are worlds apart, even though in both cases Islam would have had to fight. However, the reasons, motives, objectives and results of *jihad* under the two concepts are widely different. Our understanding of these is part of our beliefs, strategies and aims.

It is the right of Islam to take the initiative. It is not the creed of a particular people or the system of a particular country. It is a system given by God for the entire world. As such, it has the right to take action to remove all obstacles that fetter man's freedom of choice. It is a faith that does not force itself on any individual; it only attacks situations and regimes in order to free individuals from deviant influences that corrupt human nature and restrict man's freedom.

It is right that Islam should liberate people from servitude to other individuals in order that they serve God alone. It thus puts into practice its universal declaration of God's Lordship over the entire universe and the liberation of all mankind. Servitude to God alone cannot be realized, from the Islamic point of view and in practice, except under the Islamic system. It is only under this system that God's law applies equally and in the same way to all people, rulers and ruled, white and black, rich and poor. Under all other systems, people serve other people who enact laws for them. Legislation is a most fundamental attribute of Godhead. Any human being who claims the right to decree laws of his own for a community of people actually and practically claims Godhead, even though he may not put such a claim in words. Anyone who recognizes such an authority as belonging to a human being admits that Godhead belongs to that human being, whether he calls it as such or not.

Islam is not a mere ideology to be explained to people by normal ways of communication. It is a way of life represented in a social set-up that takes the necessary action to liberate mankind. Other communities try to prevent it from addressing their individuals to convince them of adopting its way of life. Therefore, it becomes imperative that Islam should try to remove those regimes that impede the freedom of mankind. As stated earlier, this is the meaning of ensuring that all submission is made to God alone, so that no submission or obedience is given to any human being on account of his own position or status, as is the case with all other systems.

Defeated by the combined pressures of the present situation and Orientalists' attacks, some contemporary Muslim writers feel too embarrassed to state these facts. Orientalists have tried to paint a false picture of Islam, showing it to have been spread by the sword. These Orientalists know very well that this is absolutely false, but they deliberately try to distort the underlying reasons for Islamic *jihad*. In reply, some of our people try to disprove this charge by seeking defensive justifications for *jihad*, overlooking the nature of Islam, its role in human life and its right to take the initiative to liberate mankind. Such defeatist writers are heavily influenced by the Western outlook and how it views religion as a mere set of beliefs that have nothing to do with day-to-day life. Hence, to fight for a religious cause means fighting to compel people to adopt a particular faith.

But this is not the case with Islam, which is a way of life given by God for all mankind, ascribing Lordship and sovereignty to God alone, and providing a system for the conduct of all life affairs. To fight for Islam is to fight for the implementation of this way of life and its systems. Faith, on the other hand, is a matter for free personal conviction, after the removal of all pressures and obstacles. The whole issue thus appears in a totally different light.

Thus, whenever an Islamic community comes into existence and begins to implement the Islamic way of life, God gives it the right to move, take power and establish that system, guaranteeing total freedom of belief. The fact that God held back the early Muslim community from fighting at a particular stage is only a question of strategy, not a matter of principle.

When we have this fundamental principle clear in our minds, we can easily understand the different Qur'anic texts, applicable to different historical stages, without being confused as to their overall significance in relation to the constant Islamic approach.

A further point of view

Further explanation of the nature of *jihad* and the nature of Islam itself is given in a paper written by the great Muslim scholar, Abu'l A'la Mawdudi, which we will quote here at length.[4] This is very important for anyone who wishes to formulate a clear understanding of this issue which is central to the way of thinking of the Islamic movement.

> In common parlance the word '*jihad*' equates with holy war in English. For a considerable time now unfriendly interpreters have been adding spin to it as if it were nothing but pure zealotry—giving an image of a horde of religious fanatics surging forward, swords in hands, beards tucked under their lips, and chanting *Allahu Akbar* (God is great). To intensify this imagery, their eyes are shown as filled with blood. Wherever they see an infidel (non-Muslim) they lay their hand on him and force him to declare that there is no deity except God or face execution. The spin masters have thus painted us masterly with their tag: "This nation's history smells of blood."

Ironically, our picture makers are our old well wishers who have themselves been involved in an unholy war for the past many centuries against the poor and the wretched of the earth. History reveals a very ungainly picture of Westerners: equipped with all kinds of deadly weapons, they have thrown themselves on the peoples of the world establishing markets for their goods, searching for raw material resources, looking for lands to colonize, and minerals to exploit so that they can fuel their never-ending lust for other people's wealth. Their war is not for God but for greed to satisfy the demands of their baser selves. For them, it is enough of a reason for their bloodletting pursuits if others have resources to enrich them. Worse, they have annexed other people's lands where they have settled their surplus manpower. Some people even qualified themselves for such punitive action if their geographical areas provided access to a territory that they wanted to overpower.

What we, Muslims, have done is now history while the West's accomplishments are part of the contemporary scene witnessed by humanity every day. Asia, Africa, Europe, America—which part of the world is left unsoiled with the blood of the innocents owing to the West's unholy war? Horrible as it is, it redounds to their painting skills that they have brushed us in such exaggerated colours. Ghastly as it may be, they have succeeded in concealing their own ugly face behind ours. And so great is our naïvety that when we see our portrait thus made we are so terrified that we forget to see the faces of the painters behind it. Worse, we become apologetic, pleading: "Your Excellencies, we do not have anything to do with war; we are as peaceful a missionary as the Buddhists and the priests are. All we do is to refute a few beliefs and replace them with some others. Weapons are not our business. We do, however, admit that occasionally when someone comes to beat us we counter him against our will. But now we have discarded even our right to self-defence. To please your Excellencies we have officially proscribed weapon-wielding *jihad*. Now *jihad* is an effort waged with our mouths and pens. To fight with weapons is your prerogative."

Misgivings about jihad

Rhetoric aside, when we try to analyze the causes that have made *jihad* for God's sake an ungainly proposition for the non-Muslims as well as Muslims, we find two primary misconceptions behind it. The first lies in the fact that Islam has been misconceived as just another religion. The second centres around the fact that the Muslims are being viewed as a nation in the sense that this noun is generally perceived. Thus, two misconceptions have distorted not only the concept of *jihad* but have also damaged the whole complexion of Islam, giving Muslims a very bad image.

In common parlance, religion is nothing but a combination of a few articles of faith, and a few worship rituals. In this sense religion is doubtless a matter of private concern. One has the right to choose any faith one likes. One can also follow one's conscience in worshipping any deity one wants. And if one feels comfortable with it, one can even become part of the effort to spread it across the globe engaging others in polemics. This kind of faith does not need a sword for support. The proponents of traditional religion may rightly ask: "Do you want to beat people into embracing your faith?" This is a valid question that will inevitably be asked if one reduces Islam to a religion, in the common nuance of the word. In fact, once Islam is reduced to just another faith, then *jihad* invalidates itself in the overall scheme of Islam.

Likewise, what is a nation other than a homogeneous group of people which assumes distinction from other groups on account of its shared belief in some foundational values. In this sense a group having become a nation may rise in arms only for two reasons: when others attempt to deprive it of its legitimate rights or when it invades others to divest them of their rights. In the first situation, it has the moral ground to fight back; but even then some pacifists may disapprove. The second situation lacks moral content to justify armed invasion. None, other than a ruthless dictator, tries to justify such aggression. Indeed, intellectuals and statesmen of modern-day empires like France and Britain would not try to justify it.

The essence of jihad

Thus, if Islam is a religion and the Muslims are a nation, then *jihad* loses its most significant qualities that make it an important part of Islamic worship. Strictly speaking, Islam is neither a mere religion in the common sense, nor is the denomination "Muslim" the name of a nation.

So what is Islam? Islam is a revolutionary concept and a way of life, which seeks to change the prevalent social order and remould it according to its own vision. Based on this definition, the word 'Muslim' becomes the name of an international revolutionary party that Islam seeks to form in order to put its revolutionary programme into effect. *Jihad* signifies that revolutionary struggle involving the utmost use of resources that the Islamic party mobilizes in the service of its cause.

Like other revolutionary concepts, Islam avoids common words already in currency and opts for a more precise terminology so that its radical aspects stand distinct. As part of this special terminology, *jihad* serves a clear purpose. Islam deliberately discards words denoting war. Instead, it uses the word *jihad*, which is the equivalent of the English word "struggle". The Arabic word, however, is far more expressive and carries broader connotations, as it stands for exerting one's utmost endeavour to promote a cause.

One may ask why the old words were discarded and new expressions coined? The answer lies in the fact that the word 'war' has always been used for armed conflict between nations and empires aiming to achieve personal or national interests, devoid of any ideology or higher principles. Since Islam is not concerned with such mundane considerations, it dropped the old vocabulary altogether. Nor does Islam feel itself bound by a national concern. It has no interest in who occupies a particular piece of land. The only thing that matters for Islam is the well-being of humanity, for which it has its own particular perspective and action plan. Wherever there are governments opposed to its perspective, Islam aims to change them, regardless of where they function and the people they govern. Its ultimate objective is to establish its way of life and to put in place governments that implement its programme. Islam wants space—not a piece of the earth but the whole planet. It has no wish to monopolize resources for the benefit of a particular community; on the contrary, it wants to give all humanity spiritual and moral elevation through the implementation of its unique programme. To make it happen, it marshals every bit of manpower and material resource.

Islam gives the name *jihad* to such cumulative efforts. This includes efforts to change people through verbal advocacy. It also includes the possible armed struggle to end an oppressive system and establish justice. Spending money for the cause and physical exertion are also *jihad*.

For God's cause

Islamic *jihad* is not the mere exertion of effort; it has to be for God alone. Thus, it is imperative that *jihad* be undertaken only for God's cause, or to use the Arabic phrase, '*fi sabilillah*'. This is a special phrase that belongs to the particular repertoire of terminology that I have mentioned. Literally translated, it means 'in the way of God.' True as this translation is, some narrow-minded people imagine that coercing others to accept Islam falls under this heading. Such understanding only betrays their rigidly narrow concepts. The fact remains that in the Islamic lexicon it has much wider connotations and implications.

For example, any work that involves collective well-being with no worldly considerations is for God. That is why a charity dispensed by a person for a moral or material return is not altruistic. If, however, the intention is to please God by helping the poor, it will fall within the purview of *fi sabilillah*. Thus, this term is specific to those works that are unsoiled by selfish considerations, solely motivated by the desire to help improve the human situation. And that in doing so will please God the Exalted, who is the end-all of all human endeavours. This is the sole reason for adding the condition of *fi sabilillah*. Meaning thereby that when a person aims at replacing a system of life with Islam he should have no self-centred considerations. In other words, he should not seek to replace Caesar with another Caesar. Nor should his struggle for the mission bear even a shade of seeking wealth, fame, or honour for himself. Instead, his whole effort and sacrifice should be directed toward establishing a just system for humanity, and to please no one but God.

Says the Qur'an: "Those who believe fight in the cause of God, and those who reject the faith fight in the cause of evil. Fight, then, against the friends of Satan. Feeble indeed is the cunning of Satan." (4: 76)

The word *taghut* has its root in *tughyan*, which means crossing the limits. When a river swells outgrowing its banks, we say it is flooded. Likewise, when a person goes beyond his limits and uses power to become god over humanity or garners for himself monetary and other benefits then he follows the way of *taghut*. Opposed to this is fighting in the way of God to establish His laws of justice, and which calls for a sense of altruism not found elsewhere.

Thus says the Qur'an: "*As for that happy life in the hereafter, We grant it only to those who do not seek to exalt themselves on earth, nor yet to spread corruption. The future belongs to the God-fearing.*" (28: 83)

A *hadith* says that a person asked the Prophet "what does fighting in the way of God mean? One person fights for booty, another fights to prove his bravery; and a third fights for enmity toward someone or because he has a bias for his nation. Among them whose fight is in God's way?" The Prophet's reply was as follows: "Nobody's. The fight *fi sabilillah* is only of a person who has no other considerations but that the word of God prevails."

Another *hadith* says "if a person fought and had the intention to secure for himself even a camel's halter, he would lose his reward." God accepts only that deed which is performed solely for Him without any personal or group considerations. Thus, the conditionality of *fi sabilillah* is crucial from the Islamic viewpoint. For every living being (animal or human) is engaged in the *jihad* of survival with the full vigour of its existence.

Among the radical concepts of the revolutionary party named "Muslim" the most foundational is to engage every rebellious force that comes in Islam's way: fight them, muster everything possible to replace them. But make sure that you do not become rebellious instead. Your mandate is contingent on your cleansing the world of rebellion and wickedness and subjecting it to God's laws of justice and fair play.

After spelling out *jihad's* meaning and its link with *fi sabilillah*, I will now deal with Islam's revolutionary message so that you may understand the reason for waging *jihad* as a tool for the spread of Islam.

Islam's revolutionary message

One can summarize the Islamic message as follows: "*Mankind, worship your Lord who has created you and those who lived before you, so that you may become God-fearing.*" (2: 21) Islam does not address itself to the farm holders and the moneyed class of industrialists, or to the peasants and industrial workers, but rather to the whole of mankind. Its audiences are human beings (not classes): for if you are subservient to someone other than God, then you should give this up. If you crave to be a deity over humanity, then push this out of your mind for none has the right to exalt himself over others. You must all enter into God's servitude as equals. Thus, the Islamic call is universal, inviting a total change. It is to God alone that the right to rule belongs, and none else. Expressed differently, nobody has the authority to become the master of others, dictating to them what he thinks is right and wrong. To acknowledge anyone as such is to attribute Godhead to him, which undoubtedly complicates the human situation.

What causes distortion in the true human self and derails humans from the God-given straight path is that they lose sight of Him in their lives and thus forget their true nature. The result it formulates is equally disastrous. On the one hand, some people, class or group rise with claims to divinity and by virtue of their power reduce others into their servitude. On the other hand, because of this tendency to oust God from our lives and the consequent distortion of our true nature, a large number of people surrender themselves to the divinity of the powerful, accepting their right to decide for them. This, as I said, is the source of oppression in the world: Islam makes its first strike at this apparatus of divinity. It says loudly and clearly: "*Pay no heed to the counsel of those who are given to excesses—those who spread corruption on earth instead of setting things to rights.*" (26: 151–152) "*Contain yourself in patience with those who call on their Lord morning and evening, seeking His countenance. Let not your eyes pass beyond them in quest of the beauties of the life of this world. Pay no heed to any whose heart We have left to be negligent of all remembrance of Us because he had always followed his own desires, and whose case has gone beyond all bounds.*" (18: 28) "*Those {are the ones} who debar others from the path of God and would have it crooked, and who deny the life to come.*" (11: 18)

Islam asks people: do you want to continue with a servitude forced upon you by these small and petty multitude of deities or do you want one God who is all-powerful? If you refuse to return to the worship of one God, you will never liberate yourselves from the slavery of these hordes of self-made gods. They will overpower you one way or the other and cause disruption throughout human life. "*She said: 'Whenever kings enter a country, they corrupt it, and turn the noblest of its people into the most abject. This is the way they always behave.'* " (27: 34) "*Yet, no sooner does he turn his back than he strives to spread corruption in the world, destroying crops and progeny. God does not love corruption.*" (2: 205)

Without elaborating upon it further, I will be brief in presenting to you the fact that Islam's advocacy of God's oneness was not toward a religion, which invites people to certain articles of belief constituting a faith.

In fact, it was a social revolution that gave a direct blow to the stratified classes, which had institutionalized themselves into a priesthood, a kingship, moneylenders, feudal lords and cartel owners reducing people to bondage.

In some places they had even become gods unto themselves asking people in the name of their birth or class right to surrender themselves to their worship. In other places, while making use of the masses' ignorance, the ruling regime had carved for them artificial gods and built temples inducing them to accept their claims to divinity, under the patronage of those gods.

Thus, when Islam, opposed to idol worship and polytheism, invited humanity to worship one true God, the people in power and those who supported them and shared the privileges arising from power felt threatened. Hence why whenever a prophet raised the call of "My people, worship God alone, for you have no God other than Him," it triggered opposition towards him. The power elite along with the exploitative classes combined to crush the message, for they knew it was not merely a metaphysical proposition but a call for social change. In its very first reverberation they smelled rebellion of a political nature.

Characteristics of the call for an Islamic change

There is not a shadow of doubt that all the prophets were revolutionary leaders. And the most revolutionary among them was Muhammad (peace be upon him). However, what separated the prophets from the rest of the revolutionaries is their balanced approach towards life, their untainted sense of justice and equality. The non-prophet revolutionaries, despite their being well intentioned, had a tilted sense of justice and equality. [The problem being their relative backgrounds.]

Either such revolutionaries came from the oppressed classes or they rose with their support. Small wonder then that they viewed everything from a class perspective. Their vantage was coloured by their class bias and not by humanity considerations or impartiality. They swung between hatred for a particular class and their bias for the class that supported them. Hence why their solution for oppression was reactive, leading them to fall into the same trap and making them a new class of oppressors. For them to formulate a balanced collective system was an impossible proposition. Contrary to this, no matter how much the prophets and their companions were persecuted, their revolutionary movement remained free from resentment and bitterness. This was possible for they worked under the direct supervision of God, the Exalted, who does not suffer from any human weakness nor does He have a particular relation with any class of people or a grudge against anyone. This is why the prophets viewed things with justice. Their sole desire was to make sure that humanity's interests were served by bringing about a system in which people could exercise their due rights while living within legitimate means, and by creating a perfect balance between individual and societal interests. This perhaps explains why the prophet-led movements never turned into class warfare. Their reconstruction programme was not designed to impose one class over another. Rather, they followed the course of justice in a manner that people had equal space for their material and spiritual growth.

The need for jihad *and its objective*

In this short presentation it is difficult for me to spell out the entire socio-political order of Islam. Keeping within the constraints of my subject, I wish to emphasize the point that Islam is not merely the amalgamation of certain dogmas and rituals but rather a comprehensive code of life that seeks to blot out all oppressive modes of life and introduce its own programme for human welfare.

To meet this end, Islam seeks a wider audience by embracing humanity and not just a particular group. In fact, it even goes to the extent of inviting oppressors, including kings and the super rich, to come and live within the legitimate bounds fixed by their Creator. If they accept the truth, it says, they will have peace and security. Here, there is no enmity toward human beings. If there is hostility, it is towards oppression, social disorder, and immorality. In other words, it is towards those who by taking what is not theirs, transgress their natural limits.

Besides, whoever embraces this message no matter to what class, race, nation, and state he or she belongs, will have equal rights and status in the Islamic society, creating thus that universal revolutionary party which the Qur'an describes as *"Hizb Allah"* or what is also known as the "Islamic party" or "the Muslim *umma*".

The moment this party comes into being, it takes up *jihad* to pursue the objectives of its creation. This should not be surprising for it is logical to the demand of its existence em;that it will strive to replace paganism in human life with a balanced code of social reconstruction that the Qur'an alludes to as *kalimatullah*, or God's word.

Thus, sluggishness on its part to any change in the current administrative set-up aiming at substituting it with Islamic governance will deny it its justification to continue, for that is the sole purpose of its inception. Explaining the reason for its birth, the Qur'an says: *"You are the best community that has ever been raised for mankind; you enjoin the doing of what is right and forbid what is wrong, and you believe in God."* (3: 110)

It is not a party of preachers and missionaries but rather of divine enforcers. Its mission is to blot out, by force if necessary, oppression, moral anarchy, social disorder and exploitation so as to finish the so-called divine role of self-styled gods and replace evil with good. *"Fight them,"* the Qur'an says, *"until there is no more oppression, and all submission is made to God alone."* (Verse 39) *"Unless you do likewise, there will be oppression on earth and much corruption."* (Verse 73) *"He it is who has sent forth His Messenger with guidance and the religion of truth, to the end that He may cause it to prevail over all religions, however hateful this may be to those who associate partners with God."* (9: 33)

Thus, this Muslim party has no choice but to go for and control the power centres, for the simple reason that an oppressive immoral civilization derives its sustenance from an immoral governmental set-up. Likewise, a righteous state apparatus cannot be implemented unless the reins of government pass from the mischief-makers to the peacemakers.

That being the case, not to talk of reforming the world, this party will not be able to live up to its convictions if the ruling system is tied to some other mode of thought. For example, a person of a socialist bent will not be able to live by the norms of his preferred system if he resides under the capitalist systems of Britain and the United States. Likewise, if a Muslim seeks to live in a non-Islamic ambience, his desire to live a Muslim life will be hard to realize. This is due to the fact that the laws he considers defective, the taxes he considers wrong, the matters he considers illegitimate, the culture he considers ridden with immorality, the education system he considers horrible will be imposed upon him and his family, and he will not find a way out. Thus a person or a group who believes in a value system is forced by the logic of its truth to seek its establishment in place of the opposing value system. If he does not become part of the effort to change the situation, he will prove himself to be false in his faith. *"May God forgive you (Prophet)! Why did you grant them permission to stay behind before you had come to know who were speaking the truth and who were the liars? Those who believe in God and the Last Day will not ask you to exempt them from striving with their wealth and with their persons. God has full knowledge as to who are the God-fearing. Only those who do not truly believe in God and the Last Day ask for exemption. Their hearts are filled with doubt, and so do they waver."* (9: 43–45)

In the preceding words the Qur'an gives a clear verdict that an Islamic party must strive to make its value system reign supreme for that is the only touchstone to validate its sincerity. Should it accept the supremacy of the opposite value system, the falsity of its claim starts to unravel itself. That such a group will eventually lose even its alleged faith in Islam is only natural, though this happens in phases. It starts with the tacit acceptance of the reigning value system as a compulsive situation which is hard to change followed by an imperceptible shift of feeling from discomfort to ease with a non-Islamic situation. So much so that you will become part of the auxiliary forces supporting the system. You will give your wealth and your life in the cause of sustaining the reigning value system and opposing the call of Islam. At this point, there will hardly remain any difference between you and the unbelievers other than some hypocritical claims to belief in Islam. In a *hadith*, the Prophet clearly describes the consequence of such a state: "By Him who holds my soul in His hand, you will either call for goodness [to the people] and restrain them from evil and hold the hand of the evildoer and turn him toward the truth by force or God's natural law will move to its inexorable result: the evildoers will affect your hearts as well and like them you will become the accursed ones."

The universal revolution

The discussion so far should clarify the point that Islamic *jihad* seeks to replace the dominance of non-Islamic systems. This revolution is not territorial but international, though as a starter the members of the Muslim party, wherever they live, should focus on that place. Their eventual goal should, however, be a world revolution for the simple reason that any revolutionary ideology, which is humanity specific and seeking universal welfare, cannot reduce itself to a particular state or nation. It is innate in its nature to embrace the whole world, for the truth refuses to be confined to geography. For it, truth is indivisible: if it is truth on one side of a river, it is the same truth on the other side as well. No segment of humanity should be barred of its compassion. Whenever humans are oppressed, it must come to their rescue. Such is the dictate of its message. The Qur'an says the same: *"And why should you not fight in the cause of God and the utterly helpless men, women and children who are crying, 'Our Lord! Deliver us from this land whose people are oppressors, and send forth to us, out of Your grace, a protector, and send us one that will help us'"* (4: 75)

Besides, split as the peoples are into national confines, human relations are universal by their nature. In fact, no state can live up to its ideological moorings if neighbouring states do not share its vision of humanity. For the spread of the Muslim party's mission of improving the human situation, it is thus inevitable that the Islamic system should rise above the parochial outlook and embrace the universal. On the one hand, it should seek a global reach for its message inviting everyone to its fold for a better life. On the other hand, depending on its power resource, it should force non-Islamic governments to clean their stables or face the cleansing sweep of Islamic governance.

This was the policy that the Prophet [peace be upon him] and his successors followed. Arabia, the birthplace of the Muslim party, was Islamized first, and this was followed by extending the Islamic call to neighbouring states. It was only when they refused to accept the call and set on a direct course of opposing it that military action was taken against them. The Tabuk Expedition was the beginning of this policy. After the Prophet, his successor Abu Bakr engaged the non-Islamic empires of Rome and Persia. ʿUmar concluded the conquest. At first, the Egyptians and Syrians took the new event in history as an extension of Arabian imperialism. Looking for its parallel in the past, they thought that like previous nations which annexed other lands to enslave their populations, it wanted to tread the same path. For this very reason the Egyptians and Syrians came out to fight the Muslims under the banners of Caesar and Kisra. But when they came to know the revolutionary message of the Muslim party they could not believe it: the Muslims were not the bearers of an aggressive nationalism; they were above national interests and had come to deliver them from the inhuman yoke of their tyrant rulers. Those who were exploited thus felt themselves inclined toward the Muslim party and thus began a process of disenchantment in Caesar's and Kisra's camps. Where they were forced to fight the Muslims, they fought without any real zest, paving the way for those spectacular strings of victories in the early period of Muslim history. This is also because once the Islamic system was introduced and people saw it functioning they willingly joined the cadres of this international Muslim party and embraced its cause to facilitate its spread elsewhere.

The Battle of Badr

In the light of this exposition of the nature of Islam, the role of *jihad* and its importance, as well as the way of life Islam seeks to implement and its strategy of *jihad* and what it involves of progressive stages we can now consider the Battle of Badr and its importance. This was a battle which God describes as the Day of Distinction. We can also look at this *surah, al-Anfal*, which comments on this battle.

As stated earlier, the Battle of Badr was not the first action of Islamic *jihad*. Prior to it, a number of expeditions were sent out, but fighting took place during only one of these, involving the small company led by ʿAbdullah ibn Jahsh, 17 months after the Prophet's migration to Medina. All of these were in line with the fundamental principle underlying the concept of Islamic *jihad*, which I have fully discussed in this Prologue. They were all, it is true, directed against the Quraysh which drove the Prophet and his noble companions away from their homes, violating the sanctity of the Inviolable House of worship that was rightly observed under Islam and prior to its advent. But this was not the basis upon which the concept of Islamic *jihad* is founded. The basis is that Islam wants to liberate all mankind from servitude to any creature, so that they may serve only the Creator. It wants to establish Godhead as belonging to God alone, and remove all tyrannical authority that enslaves human beings. The Quraysh was the immediate tyrannical power which prevented people in Arabia from turning to the worship of God alone and acknowledging only His sovereignty. Hence, in line with its overall strategy, Islam had no option but to fight this tyrannical power. This had the added advantage of removing the injustice suffered by the noble companions of the Prophet in Mecca, and ensuring the security of the Muslim homeland in Medina against any possible aggression. However, when we state these immediate or local causes, we must not lose sight of the nature of Islam and its strategy that allows no power to usurp God's sovereignty, bringing people into servitude to anyone other than God.

We need to give a brief outline of the events of the Battle of Badr[5] before discussing this *surah* which comments on it. This will enable us to appreciate the general atmosphere prevailing at the time of its revelation, understand the meaning of its text, its practicality both in dealing with events and in explaining them. Qur'anic statements cannot be properly understood on the basis of their linguistic import alone. Their proper understanding requires, first and foremost, that we try to live in their historical atmosphere, appreciate their practical and positive approach to events and circumstances. Although their significance stretches well beyond the historical reality they deal with, Qur'anic statements do not reveal the full extent of their significance except in the light of such historical reality. Thus, they will continue to have their permanent significance and inspiration for those who work for the implementation of Islam, facing situations and circumstances that are not unlike those faced by the early Muslims. The Qur'an will never reveal its secrets to those who passively deal with its statements on the basis of their linguistic import alone.

> Muhammad ibn Ishaq[6] reports:
> Intelligence was brought to the Prophet (peace be upon him) that a large trade caravan, in which almost every household in the Quraysh had a share, was returning from Syria, led by Abu Sufyan ibn Harb, and travelling with 30 or 40 men from the Quraysh. He suggested to his Companions: "Here is a caravan of the Quraysh, with much of their wealth. If you intercept it, God may reward you with it." People began to get ready, while others did not. No one thought that the Prophet would have to fight a battle.

In *Zad al-Ma'ad* and in *Imta' al-Asma'* it is mentioned that the Prophet only ordered those whose mounts were ready to move immediately to march, without giving too much importance to numbers. Ibn al-Qayyim states:

> The total number of Muslims to take part in Badr was 317 men, 86 of them were from the Muhajirin, 61 from the Aws and 170 from the Khazraj. The number of the Aws people was much less than the Khazraj, despite the fact that the Aws were the stronger fighters and more steadfast, because their quarters were further away from the city, and the call to get ready came as a surprise. The Prophet said that he wanted only those who were ready to move, and had their mounts available. Some people who lived in the outskirts requested him to wait until they got their mounts, but he refused. Indeed, there was no intention to fight a battle, and no preparations were taken for such an eventuality, but God caused them to meet their enemy when they were totally unprepared.[7]

As Abu Sufyan drew near the Hijaz, he tried to obtain intelligence, seeking information from any traveller he met on his way. He was worried for the safety of people's property he carried with him. Some travellers told him that Muhammad had mobilized his followers to intercept his caravan. Abu Sufyan hired Damdam ibn 'Amr al-Ghifari, sending him to Mecca to alert its people to the need to defend their property and to tell them that Muhammad and his Companions were about to intercept the caravan. Damdam moved very fast towards Mecca. Al-Maqrizi reports:

The people of Mecca were alarmed to hear Damdam shouting: "People of the Quraysh! Descendants of Lu'ayy ibn Ghalib! A tragedy! A disaster! Your property with Abu Sufyan is being intercepted by Muhammad and his Companions. I doubt whether you can save the caravan. Help! Help!" To indicate the gravity of his message Damdam cut his camel's ears, and tore his own shirt. The Quraysh immediately started to mobilize all their resources, getting ready in three days, and in only two days according to some reports. The strong among them helped those who were weak. Suhayl ibn ʿAmr, Zamʿah ibn al-Aswad, Tuʿaymah ibn ʿAdiy, Hanzalah ibn Abi Sufyan and ʿAmr ibn Abi Sufyan were all urging people to join the Quraysh army. Suhayl said to his people: "Are you going to allow Muhammad and the apostates from Yathrib to confiscate your property and caravan? Whoever needs money or power, he may have these." Umayyah ibn Abi al-Salt praised him in a short poem.

Nawfal ibn Muʿawiyah al-Dili spoke to a number of rich people urging them to make financial contributions so as to provide mounts for people to join the army, who did not have their own. ʿAbdullah ibn Abi Rabiʿah gave him 500 Dinar [a gold currency] to spend in the way he wished in strengthening the army. He also received 200 Dinars from Huwaytib ibn ʿAbd al-ʿUzza, and a further 300 Dinars to buy arms and mounts. Tuʿaymah ibn ʿAdiy provided 20 camels and undertook to look after the fighters' families. Anyone who did not wish to join the army in person sent someone in his place. They spoke to Abu Lahab, but he refused to join or send anyone in his place, but it is also reported that he sent in his place al-ʿAsi ibn Hisham ibn al-Mughirah, who owed money to him, saying to him that he would write off his debt if he went in his place, which he did.

ʿAddas,[8] a Christian slave, tried hard to dissuade his masters, ʿUtbah and Shaybah, sons of Rabiʿah, as well as al-ʿAs ibn Munabbih from joining. Umayyah ibn Khalaf, on the other hand, decided not to join the army, but ʿUqbah ibn Abi Muʿayt and Abu Jahl rebuked him severely. He said to them: "Buy me the best camel in this valley." They bought him a camel for 300 Dirhams [a silver currency], but it was part of the spoils of war taken by the Muslims.

None was less enthusiastic to go than al-Harith ibn ʿAmir. Damdam ibn ʿAmr had seen the valley of Mecca with blood running from both of its two ends. ʿAtikah bint ʿAbd al-Muttalib, the Prophet's aunt, had seen in her dream, warning of death and blood in every home. Hence, people known for sound judgement were disinclined to march for war. They began to exchange views. Among those unwilling to go were al-Harith ibn ʿAmir, Umayyah ibn Khalaf, ʿUtbah ibn Rabiʿah, Shaybah ibn Rabiʿah, Hakim ibn Hizam, Abu al-Bakhtari ibn Hisham, ʿAli ibn Umayyah ibn Khalaf, and al-ʿAs ibn Munabbih, but Abu Jahl rebuked them all, aided in this task by ʿUqbah ibn Abi Muʿayt and al-Nadr ibn al-Harith ibn Kildah. Thus the Quraysh settled for marching to meet the Muslims.

The Quraysh army left in a festive mood, with singers and music playing, and feeding themselves well. Their army was 950 men strong, with 100 horses mounted by 100 heavily armoured soldiers, and a large number of body armour for those who were walking. They had 700 camels. They were most aptly described in the Qur'an: *"Do not be like those who left their homes full of self-conceit, seeking to be seen and praised by others. They debar others from the path of God; but God has knowledge of all that they do."* (Verse 47)

As they marched, they were nursing great hatred against the Prophet and his Companions because of their intention to intercept their trade caravan. The Muslims had earlier killed ʿAmr ibn al-Hadrami and took the small caravan he was leading.[9] Abu Sufyan was leading the caravan accompanied by 70 men,[10] among whom were Makhramah ibn Nawfal and ʿAmr ibn al-ʿAs. The caravan had no less than 1000 camels, loaded with merchandise. When they were near to Medina, they were extremely alarmed, particularly because they felt that Damdam ibn ʿAmr and the help from the Quraysh were slow in coming. As Abu Sufyan arrived in Badr at the head of the caravan, he was worried lest he should be detected. Therefore, he changed route and took his caravan closer to the sea, leaving Badr to his left and marching with speed.

Meanwhile, the Quraysh army was marching at leisure, feeding anyone who caught up with them and slaughtering many camels for food. Then Qays ibn Imriʾ al-Qays came to them with a message from Abu Sufyan advising them to go back "so that you do not leave yourselves liable to be killed by the people of Yathrib [i.e. the old name of Medina]. You have only marched to protect your trade caravan and your property. Now that it is safe by God's help, you have no further purpose." He tried to persuade the Quraysh to go back, but they refused. Abu Jahl said: "We will not go back, but we shall march on to Badr, where we shall stay for three days to celebrate. We shall slaughter camels for food, feed whoever cares to come to us, drink wine in abundance and be entertained by singers and dancers. The whole of Arabia shall hear about us and hold us in awe for the rest of time."[11]

Qays went back to Abu Sufyan and told him that the Quraysh army marched on. He said: "Woe to my people! This is all the work of ʿAmr ibn Hisham [i.e. Abu Jahl]. He does not want to go back because he assumed leadership and went too far. Excess spells a bad omen. If Muhammad gets the upper hand, we will be humiliated."[12]

Muhammad ibn Ishaq reports:

Al-Akhnas ibn Shariq, who was an ally of the Zuhrah clan, said to his people: "God has saved your property and spared your tribesman, Makhramah ibn Nawfal. You have mobilized to save him and his property. Put the blame on me if you are accused of cowardice, and let us go back. There is no need for you to go on a fighting course for nothing. Do not listen to what this man [meaning Abu Jahl] says." They accepted his advice and went back home. Not a single man from Zuhrah took part in the Battle of Badr. The rest of the Quraysh clans succumbed to the pressure and had some of their men participating, except for the clan of ʿAdiy ibn Kaʿb. Moreover, Talib ibn Abi Talib was with the Quraysh army, but some people said to him: "We know you, the Hashimites, well. Even though you may come with us, your sympathy is with Muhammad." Therefore, he went back home without continuing with the marchers.

Meanwhile, the Prophet marched with his Companions in the month of Ramadan. They had only 70 camels which they rode in turns. The Prophet, ʿAli ibn Abi Talib and Marthad al-Ghanawi shared one camel. Hamzah ibn ʿAbd al-Muttalib, Zayd ibn Harithah, and the two servants of the Prophet, Abu Kabshah and Anasah had one camel to share, while Abu Bakr, ʿUmar and ʿAbd al-Rahman ibn ʿAwf shared another.[13]

In *Imtaʿ al-Asmaʿ*, al-Maqrizi reports:

The Prophet marched on until he approached Badr when he received intelligence of the march of the Quraysh army. He consulted his Companions. Abu Bakr was the first to speak, and his words were reassuring to the Prophet. ʿUmar was next, and he spoke in the same vein, before adding: "Messenger of God! It is indeed the Quraysh defending its honour. They have never been humiliated since they achieved their present honourable position, and they have never believed ever since they sunk into disbelief. By God, they would never compromise their position of honour and they will most certainly fight you. Hence, you had better be prepared."

Al-Miqdad ibn ʿAmr, the next to speak, said: "Messenger of God! Go ahead and do whatever you feel is best. We will never say to you as the Israelites said to Moses: 'Go with your Lord and fight the enemy while we stay behind!' What we will say is: 'Go with your Lord and fight the enemy and we will fight alongside you.' By Him who has sent you with the message of truth, if you ask us to march with you to Bark al-Ghimad [a remote place in Yemen] we will fight with you anyone who stands in your way until you have got there." The Prophet thanked him and prayed for him.

But the prophet continued to say to his Companions: "Give me your advice." He particularly wanted to hear from the *Ansar*, because he felt they might think that they were only bound to defend him against those who attacked him in Medina when they pledged to protect him as they protected their women and children.[14] Saʿd ibn Muʿadh stood up and said: "I will answer for the *Ansar*. You seem to want to know our opinion, Messenger of God?" When the Prophet indicated that it was so, Saʿd said: "It seems to me that you might have set out for a certain objective and then you received revelations concerning something different! We have declared our faith in you and accepted your message as the message of truth. We have made firm pledges to you that we will always do as you tell us. Go ahead, therefore, Messenger of God, and do whatever you wish, and we go with you. By Him who has sent you with the message of truth, if you take us right to the sea, we will ride with you. None of us shall stay behind. Make peace with whomever you will and cut relations with whomever you will, and take from our wealth and property what you may. Whatever you take is better placed than what you leave. By Him who holds my soul in His hand, I have never come this way, and I do not know it. Yet we have no qualms about encountering our enemy tomorrow. We fight hard and with strong determination when war breaks out. We pray to God to enable us to show you what would please you. You march, then with God's blessings."

Another report mentions that Saʿd said to the Prophet: "We have left behind some of our people who love and obey you as much as we do; but they did not turn up because they thought it was only the trade caravan. Shall we erect for you a shed to stay in, and we will have your mount ready? We will then fight our enemy. If we win by God's grace, then that is what we want. If it is the other eventuality, then you will ride your horse to join the rest of our people." The Prophet said some kind words to him and added: "Or God may will something better."

The Prophet then said to his Companions: "March on, with God's blessings. God has promised me one of the two hosts. By God, it is as if I can see the place where some of them will be killed." As they heard these words, the Prophet's Companions realized that they would be involved in a battle, and that the trade caravan would manage to escape. As they heard the Prophet's words, they hoped for victory. The Prophet assigned banners to three people, one he gave to Musʿab ibn ʿUmayr, and two black ones were given to ʿAli and a man from the *Ansar*, [said to be Saʿd ibn Muʿadh]. He put out the weapons. When the Prophet left Medina, he had no banner holder.

The Prophet arrived at the bottom of the Badr plain on Friday night, 17 Ramadan.

He later sent 'Ali, al-Zubayr, Sa'd ibn Abi Waqqas and Basbas ibn 'Amr to gather intelligence around water wells. He pointed out a knoll and said: "You may get some news there." They found there a number of camels for carrying water, belonging to the Quraysh. Most of the men with the camels fled. One of them called 'Ujayr shouted to the Quraysh: "Your man [meaning the Prophet] has taken your water carriers. This sent an air of disturbance among them. Rain was pouring over them. That night, they took with them Abu Yasar, a slave belonging to 'Ubaydah ibn Sa'id ibn al-'As, Aslam who belonged to Munabbih ibn al-Hajjaj and Abu Rafi' who belonged to Umayyah ibn Khalaf. All three were brought to the Prophet when he was praying. They declared that they were responsible for fetching water to the Quraysh, but the Prophet's Companions disliked that and beat them. So, they said that they were travelling with Abu Sufyan and his caravan. So they left them and waited. As the Prophet finished his prayer, he said to his Companions: "If they tell you the truth, you beat them; and if they lie, you leave them alone!" He then asked the captives about the Quraysh, and they told him that they were beyond the hill, and that they slaughtered nine or ten camels every day for food, and named some of those who were in the army. The Prophet said: "The host is between 900 and 1,000 strong. Mecca has sent you its dearest children."

The Prophet consulted his Companions about the place to encamp. Al-Hubab ibn al-Mundhir ibn al-Jamuh said: "Take us forward, right to the nearest well to the enemy. I know this place and its wells. One of its wells is plentiful in fine water, where we can encamp, make a basin and throw in our containers. We will thus have water to drink when we fight. We will also close the rest of the wells." The Prophet said to him: "You have given good counsel."[15] He rose and marched on to encamp at the well indicated by al-Hubab.

The Prophet spent that night, Friday 17 Ramadan, praying with his face turned towards the stem of a felled tree. There was a rainfall, but it was light where the Muslims were, making the ground firm but not difficult to walk on, but the rain was much heavier where the Quraysh were, although the two hosts were not far apart. Indeed the rain was a blessing for the believers and a real adversity for the unbelievers. That night the Muslims experienced deep slumber, so much so that a man might have his head on his chest and not feel it until he fell to one side. A young man, Rifa'ah ibn Rafi'ibn Malik had a wet dream and managed to bathe before the night was out. The Prophet sent 'Ammar ibn Yasir and 'Abdullah ibn Mas'ud to go around the place where the Quraysh encamped. When they came back, they told him that the unbelievers were in fear and it was pouring with rain.

A shed was erected for the Prophet near the well, and Sa'd ibn Mu'adh stood at the door with his sword in his hand. The Prophet went around the area where the battle was to take place, and pointed out certain places to his Companions, saying this person will be killed here and that person will be killed there. None of the ones he named was killed beyond the place the Prophet indicated. The Prophet marshalled his Companions and went back to the shed with Abu Bakr.[16]

Rejecting wise counsel

Ibn Ishaq reports:

The Quraysh marched on in the morning to draw near to the Muslims. When the Prophet saw them coming into the valley, he said: "My Lord, this is the Quraysh demonstrating all its conceit to contend against You and call Your Messenger a liar.

My Lord, grant me the victory You have promised me. My Lord, destroy them today." The Prophet saw 'Utbah ibn Rabi'ah riding a red camel, and said: "If any of these people has some wisdom, it is the man with the red camel. If they obey him, they will follow good counsel."

Khufaf ibn Ayma' ibn Rahdah al-Ghifari, or his father, sent to the Quraysh some slaughtered animals he had prepared for them as a gift as they passed close to his quarters. He also sent them a message that he was ready to support them with men and arms. They sent him a message of thanks, and added: "You have done more than your duty. If we are fighting men like us, we are more than a match for them, but if we are fighting God, as Muhammad says, then no one can stand up to God."

When the Quraysh encamped, some of their men, including Hakim ibn Hizam, came up to the Prophet's basin and the Prophet ordered his Companions to let them do what they wanted. Every one of them who drank from the basin was killed in Badr, except for Hakim ibn Hizam who later became a good Muslim. Subsequently, if he wished to swear very firmly, he would say: "By Him who saved me on Badr day."

When the Quraysh had encamped, they sent 'Umayr ibn Wahb of Jumah to make a good guess at the number of Muslim troops. He went around the troops on his horse before returning to his people to say: "They are three hundred, give or take a few. But hold on a while and I will see if they have any hidden support." He went far into the valley, but found nothing. He came back with this report: "I have found no hidden support, but I can see a catastrophe and much killing. They simply have no protection apart from their swords. I think that we will not kill any one of them without him killing one of us first. Should they be able to kill their number from our side, life would not be worth living. You make your own decision."

When Hakim ibn Hizam heard that, he went to 'Utbah ibn Rabi'ah and said to him: "You are the honourable man of the Quraysh and its obeyed master. Shall I tell you something which would bring you high praise for the rest of time?" When 'Utbah showed his interest, Hakim said: "Tell the Quraysh to go back and you will pay the indemnity for the death of Ibn al-Hadrami, for he was your ally. You also bear the loss of his looted caravan." Recognizing the great advantages of this course of action 'Utbah immediately accepted and asked Hakim to act as his witness. He also said to him: "Go to Ibn al-Hanzaliyyah [meaning Abu Jahl], because I fear that he is the only one to oppose that."

'Utbah then stood up and addressed the Quraysh, saying: "Take it from me and do not fight this man [meaning the Prophet] and his Companions. You will gain nothing by fighting them. Should you win, many a man among us will look around and see the killer of his father or brother. This will lead to much enmity and hostility in our ranks. Go back and leave Muhammad to the rest of the Arabs. If they kill him, they will have done what you want. If they do not, you will meet him without having such barrier of enmity."

Hakim reports: "I went up to Abu Jahl and I found him preparing a spear. I said to him: 'Abu al-Hakam, 'Utbah has sent me with this message to you.' And I told him what 'Utbah said. He said: 'His cowardice has surfaced now that he has seen Muhammad and his Companions. We shall not go back until God has judged between our two parties. 'Utbah does not believe what he says. It is simply that having seen that they are few in number and that his son is among them, he fears that his son may be killed.' "

Abu Jahl also sent a message to 'Amir ibn al-Hadrami, saying: "Your ally is trying to take the people back now that you have the chance to get your revenge. Stand up and appeal to the Quraysh by your brother's blood to get your revenge." 'Amir did that and shouted, 'Woe to 'Amr'. Thus, the air was one of war, and people were more determined to fight. Abu Jahl frustrated the good counsel 'Utbah had given. When 'Utbah was told what Abu Jahl had said, he answered: "This woman-like person will soon know whose cowardice has surfaced: mine or his."

As the army moved, one of its number, al-Aswad ibn 'Abd al-Asad of the Makhzum clan, a vulgar ill-bred man, sprang out from the ranks, saying: "I pledge to God to drink from their reservoir, or I will pull it down, or I will die in my attempt." Hamzah ibn 'Abd al-Muttalib, the Prophet's uncle struck him with his sword, chopping off his leg. Al-Aswad, however, continued to crawl towards the reservoir and Hamzah followed him until he killed him at the reservoir.

'Utbah ibn Rabi'ah, his brother Shaybah and his son al-Walid came out of the Quraysh army and offered a six-man duel. Three young men from the *Ansar*, 'Awf ibn al-Harith and his brother Mu'awwadh and a third man said to be 'Abdullah ibn Rawahah, answered the challenge. The challengers asked them who they were, and when they told them that they were from the *Ansar*, they said that they had no business with them. It is said that 'Utbah said to them: "You are honourable equals, but we only want some of our own people." One of them shouted: "Muhammad, let our equals come out for a duel." The Prophet sent out three of his own relatives: Hamzah, his uncle, and his two cousins 'Ali and 'Ubaydah ibn al-Harith. 'Ubaydah, the eldest of the three fought 'Utbah, Hamzah fought Shaybah and 'Ali fought al-Walid. In no time, Hamzah and 'Ali succeeded in killing their two opponents, while 'Utbah and 'Ubaydah struck each other at the same time. Both fell to the ground wounded. Hamzah and 'Ali then made sure that 'Utbah was killed, and carried 'Ubaydah with them to the Prophet.

The two armies began to draw near to each other. The Prophet ordered his companions not to move forward until he had given them the order. "When they approach, try to repel them with your arrows." He then marshalled them and went to his shed with Abu Bakr. His prayers included: "My Lord, I appeal to you for the fulfilment of Your promise to me. Should this company of believers be overrun, You will not be worshipped again on earth." Abu Bakr said to him: "Messenger of God! Not so hard with your appeal to Your Lord. He will surely grant you what He has promised you."[17]

Al-Maqrizi mentions in *Imta' al-Asma'*:

'Abdullah ibn Rawahah said to the Prophet: "Messenger of God! I counsel you—knowing that God's Messenger is far greater and more knowledgeable than to need counsel—that God is too great in His majesty to be appealed to for the fulfilment of His promise." The Prophet said to him: "Should I not appeal to God to fulfil His promise? God never fails to fulfil a promise."[18]

Ibn Ishaq continues:

The Prophet was momentarily overtaken by sleep. When he woke up he was markedly cheerful. He said to his companion: "Rejoice, Abu Bakr. Victory is certainly coming from God. This is the Angel Gabriel holding the rein of his horse with dust all over it."

Mahja', a slave belonging to 'Umar ibn al-Khattab, was killed when he was hit by an arrow, and thus he was the first casualty among the Muslims. Harithah ibn

Suraqah, from the Najjar clan was also hit in his neck by an arrow as he was drinking from the reservoir, and he died.

The Prophet went on encouraging his Companions, saying: "By Him who holds Muhammad's soul in his hand, anyone who is killed fighting these people, dedicating his life for the cause of God, moving forward not backward, shall be admitted by God into heaven." On hearing this, ʿUmayr ibn al-Hamam from the Salamah clan, said as he held a few dates in his hand and was eating them: "Well, Well! All that separates me from heaven is that these people should kill me!"

ʿAwf ibn al-Harith asked the Prophet: "What would make God smile at a servant of His?" The Prophet said: "His determined fight without protection." He took off his body armour and threw it away, picking up his sword and fighting until he was killed.

As the two armies drew closer, Abu Jahl said: "Lord! Let the side which severs relations of kinship, and invents falsehood, be destroyed today." His was a prayer to ensure his own ruin.

The Prophet took a handful of dust and said: "Let these faces be hung down." He then blew the dust at the Quraysh. He then ordered his Companions to fight hard, and they did to ensure the defeat of the Quraysh. God caused the killing and capture of so many of the Quraysh's nobility.

When the Muslims started to take enemy prisoners, the Prophet, who was in his shed with Saʿd ibn Muʿadh and a group of the *Ansar* standing at the door, swords in hands, guarding him, the Prophet noticed that Saʿd looked displeased. He said to him: "You do not seem to be pleased with what our people are doing?" He said: "Indeed. This is the first defeat God has inflicted on the idolaters. I would have preferred killing their men rather than sparing them."

At one point the Prophet said to his Companions: "I have come to know that a few men from the Hashim clan and others have been made to join the army against their will. They have no quarrel with us. Any one of you who meets any Hashimite should not kill him. If you come across Abu al-Bakhtari ibn Hisham, do not kill him. If you meet al-ʿAbbas ibn ʿAbd al-Muttalib, do not kill him. He came out against his will." Abu Hudhayfah ibn ʿUtbah ibn Rabiʿah said on hearing this: "Are we to kill our fathers, sons, brothers and tribesmen and let al-ʿAbbas alone? By God, if I see him, I will certainly hit him with my sword." The Prophet said to ʿUmar ibn al-Khattab: "Abu Hafs![19] Is God's Messenger's uncle to be hit with the sword in his face?" ʿUmar said: "Messenger of God! Allow me to kill him, for he is a hypocrite."[20] Abu Hudhayfah used to say afterwards: "I am always worried about what I said that day, and fear that it may condemn me, unless it is atoned if I gain martyrdom." He was to die a martyr in the Battle of al-Yamamah.

The Prophet singled out Abu al-Bakhtari ibn Hisham, ordering that he should not be killed, because he was the most moderate among the Quraysh in his attitude towards the Prophet. Never did he try to harm the Prophet, or say something against him. Besides, he was one of the five men who successfully mounted the campaign to end the three-year boycott of the Prophet's clan by the rest of the Quraysh.[21]

ʿAbd al-Rahman ibn ʿAwf reports: "Umayyah ibn Khalaf was a friend of mine when we were in Mecca. My name at the time was ʿAbd ʿAmr, but when I became a Muslim, I changed my name to ʿAbd al-Rahman. He said to me once when we were still in Mecca: 'ʿAbd ʿAmr! Do you reject a name given to you by your father?' I confirmed that. He said: 'I do not know who is al-Rahman. Let us agree on a name I call you by, so that you do not reply to me if I call you by your original name and I do not call you by what I do not know.' Afterwards, if he called me ʿAbd ʿAmr, I would not reply. Then I said to him: 'Abu 'Ali, you choose whatever you are comfortable with.' He said: 'I will call you 'Abd al-Ilah [another name of God].' I agreed. After that, when I passed by him, he would call me 'Abd al-Ilah, and I would respond and have some conversation with him.

On the Day of Badr, I passed by him as he was standing with his son 'Ali, holding his hand. I was carrying some body armour which I had looted. When he saw me, he called me 'Abd 'Amr, and I did not respond. He called me again 'Abd al-Ilah and I responded. He said: 'Would you rather have me, for I am a better gain for you than this body armour.' I agreed and told him to come with me, and threw the body armour away. I took him and his son prisoners and walked away. He said: 'I have never seen a day like this! Do you not need milk?'[22] I proceeded leading them away.

Umayyah asked me as I walked between him and his son, holding both their hands: ''Abd al-Ilah, who is the man in your host who has an ostrich feather on his chest?' I told him that he was Hamzah ibn 'Abd al-Muttalib. He said: 'He is the one who has done us a great deal of harm.' Then, as I was leading them away, Bilal saw him with me. It was Umayyah who used to torture Bilal in Mecca to force him to abandon Islam. He would take him out to the sandy area when it was extremely hot, and cause him to lie back on the sand, and place a large rock on his chest, telling him that he would remain so until he abandoned Muhammad's faith. Bilal's reply was always: 'He is One! He is One!' Now, when Bilal saw him, he shouted: 'Umayyah, head of idolatry, may I perish if he survives!' I said to him: 'Bilal! Would you kill my two prisoners?' He said: 'May I perish if he survives.' I said: 'Do you hear me, you son of a black woman!' He repeated his words. Bilal appealed to the *Ansar*: 'Supporters of God's cause! Here is Umayyah, head of idolatry. May I perish if he survives.' A group of the *Ansar* surrounded us forming a circle and I was trying to defend him, but one of the men struck Umayyah's son's leg and he fell down. Umayyah uttered a loud cry, the like of which I never heard before. I said to him: 'Try to escape, but there seems to be no escape for you. By God, I cannot defend you.' They soon killed both of them." 'Abd al-Rahman used to say afterwards: 'May God forgive Bilal! I lost my loot and he killed my two prisoners.'[23]

Ibn Ishaq later adds:

When the battle was over, the Prophet instructed some people to look for Abu Jahl among the dead. The first man to meet Abu Jahl in the battle was Mua'dh ibn 'Amr ibn al-Jamuh of the Salamah clan. He reports: "I noticed a group of men standing around him like a siege, saying to one another: 'Abu al-Hakam[24] shall not be reached.' When I heard them saying that, I resolved to get to him. I made a determined attack towards him and when he was within my reach I struck him with my sword once, which was enough to send half his leg high into the air, as a date stone flies from underneath the date-stone crusher. His son, 'Ikrimah, struck back at me and cut off my arm, which remained attached to my body by a thin piece of my skin. I was prevented by the raging battle from coming back on him. I, however, kept on fighting for the rest of the day, pulling my arm behind me. When it became too troublesome I bent down and put my hand under my foot and stood up to cut off my arm."

As Abu Jahl was wounded, Mu'awwadh ibn al-Harith passed by him and hit him hard until he could not get up. He then left him, not quite dead. Mu'awwadh went on fighting until he was killed.

When the Prophet ordered a search for Abu Jahl among the dead, 'Abdullah ibn

Mas'ud found him. The Prophet had told his Companions: 'If you cannot identify him among the dead, look for a cut on his knee. When we were young, he and I pushed each other when we were attending a banquet held by 'Abdullah ibn Jud'an. I was a little thinner than him. When I pushed him, he fell on his knees, badly injuring one of them.' 'Abdullah ibn Mas'ud reports: "I found him at his last breath. When I recognized him, I put my foot over his neck. Once in Mecca he had attacked and hurt me. Now I said to him: 'You enemy of God, haven't you been humiliated?' He said: 'How? Am I not a man of merit you have killed? Tell me, who is victorious today?' I said: 'God and His Messenger.' " Some people from Abu Jahl's clan of Makhzum later claimed that Ibn Mas'ud mentioned that Abu Jahl said to him as he put his foot over his neck: 'You have climbed high, you little shepherd.'[25] 'Abdullah ibn Mas'ud continues his report: "I chopped off his head and took it to the Prophet and said: 'Messenger of God! This is the head of Abu Jahl, God's enemy.' He said: 'God is One. There is no deity other than Him.' I put his head before the Prophet and he praised God."[26]

Ibn Hisham says:

It is reported that 'Umar ibn al-Khattab said to Sa'id ibn al-'As when he passed by him: 'I see that you harbour some feelings and that you may think that I killed your father. Had I killed him, I would not apologize to you; but I killed my uncle al-'As ibn Hisham ibn al-Mughirah. As for your father, I passed by him as he was searching like a bull with his horns and I sidestepped him. His cousin 'Ali went to him and killed him.'[27]

Ibn Ishaq reports on the authority of 'A'ishah, the Prophet's wife:

When the Prophet ordered that the killed be buried, they were all buried in one grave except for Umayyah ibn Khalaf, whose body swelled inside his armour. When they tried to remove it, his flesh was cut. So, they left it on him and buried him. When they were all buried, the Prophet stood at the grave and said to them: 'People in the grave! Have you found out that what your Lord has promised you to be true? I have found that His promise to me has come true.' Some of his Companions asked him: 'Messenger of God! Do you speak to dead people?' He said: 'They have known that what God has promised is true.' Some people mention that he said, 'They hear what I say to them.' But the Prophet only said, 'They have known.' " . . .

When the Prophet ordered that they should be buried, the body of 'Utbah ibn Rabi'ah was drawn towards the grave. The Prophet looked at his son Abu Hudhayfah and saw that he was sad. He asked him: "Abu Hudhayfah! You may be experiencing some misgivings concerning what happened to your father." He said: "No, Messenger of God. I have no doubt about my father and his death. But I knew him to be a sagacious and honourable man and I hoped that this would guide him to accept Islam. When I saw what happened to him and remembered that he died an unbeliever, I felt sad." The Prophet prayed for Abu Hudhayfah and said some kind words . . .

The Prophet then ordered that all the booty picked up by the Muslims be collected together. As it was collected, people differed concerning it. Those who picked up the booty claimed it, while those who were fighting and chasing the enemy said to them: "Had it not been for us, you would not have picked it up. We kept the people preoccupied while you took it away." A third group providing a guard to the

Prophet said: "You do not have a claim stronger than ours. We had the booty close to us, and we could have picked it up, but we feared that the enemy would attack the Prophet and kept guarding him."

Asked about *Surah al-Anfal*, or The Spoils of War, 'Ubadah ibn al-Samit answered: "It was revealed concerning us, the people of Badr, when we disputed about the booty and were impolite about it. God removed it from us and gave it up to His Messenger who divided it equally among the Muslims." . . .

When the Prophet arrived in Medina, he assigned the prisoners to various groups of his Companions and said to them: "Look after the prisoners well." Among the prisoners was Abu 'Aziz ibn 'Umayr ibn Hashim. He reports that his brother, Mus'ab passed by him as he was being taken captive by a man from the *Ansar*. Mus'ab said to the *Ansari* man: "Hold tight to him. His mother is rich and she might give a good ransom for him." Abu 'Aziz says: "I was assigned to a group of the *Ansar*. When they laid out their lunch or dinner, they would give me the bread while they themselves ate dates without bread.[28] This was because of the Prophet's instructions to them. Every time any one of them had a piece of bread he would give it to me. Sometimes I felt embarrassed by their hospitality and I gave the bread to any one of them who was around. He would return it without taking a single bite."

Ibn Hisham explains: Abu 'Aziz was the holder of the banner of the unbelievers in Badr, next to al-Nadr ibn al-Harith. When his brother Mus'ab ibn 'Umayr said this to Abu al-Yusr, the man who held him captive took hold of him tightly, whilst Abu 'Aziz remonstrated with him: "Is this what you recommend about me?" Mus'ab said: "He is my brother, ahead of you." His mother asked what the highest ransom paid for a man from the Quraysh was, and she was told that it was 4000 dirhams. She sent that amount as his ransom. Then the Quraysh sent ransom for other prisoners.[29]

Qur'anic comments

It was in comment on the Battle of Badr, of which we have given a brief outline, that this *surah* was revealed. It portrays the obvious events of this battle, and also shows the ultimate power behind the events and how God determined the sequence of events. Beyond that, it shows the line followed throughout human history. It describes all this in the unique language of the Qur'an and its inimitable style. We will speak about all these in detail as we discuss the text. Here we will only highlight the main lines of the *surah*.

A particular event reported by Ibn Ishaq on the authority of 'Ubadah ibn al-Samit, the Prophet's Companion who says in reference to this *surah*: "It was revealed concerning us, the people of Badr, when we disputed about the booty and were impolite about it. God removed it from us and gave it up to His Messenger who divided it equally among the Muslims."

This event sheds ample light on the opening of the *surah* and the line it takes. The Prophet's Companions disputed over the little booty they gained in a battle that God considered a landmark in human history for the rest of time. But God wanted to teach them, and all humanity in succeeding generations, some highly important facts.

The first thing He wanted them to understand was that this battle was far more important than the spoils of war over which they were in dispute. Therefore, He called the day that witnessed it *"the day when the true was distinguished from the false, the day when the two hosts met in battle."* (Verse 41)

He also wanted them to know that this greatly important event was accomplished by God's will and planning, in every step and every move. He had a purpose which He wished to accomplish. This means that they had nothing to do with the planning and accomplishment of this great victory or with its outcome and consequences. Both its small booty and great consequences were the result of God's will and design. He only put the believers, by His grace, through a fair test of His own making.

He wanted to show them the great gulf between what they wished for themselves, which was to take the caravan, and what He wanted for them, and for all humanity, through the escape of the caravan and the encounter with the Quraysh army.

The *surah* starts with recording their questions about the spoils of war, and explains God's ruling concerning them. It gives the spoils of war to God and His Messenger, calling on the believers to remain God-fearing and set to right their internal relations, after they were impolite concerning the booty, as ʿUbadah ibn al-Samit, the Prophet's Companion describes. They are further called upon to obey God and His Messenger, reminding them of their faith which requires them to be so obedient. Furthermore, right at the outset, the *surah* paints a highly inspiring and awesome picture of the believers: *"They ask you about the spoils of war. Say: The spoils of war belong to God and the Messenger. So, have fear of God and set to right your internal relations. Obey God and His Messenger, if you are true believers. True believers are only those whose hearts are filled with awe whenever God is mentioned, and whose faith is strengthened whenever His revelations are recited to them. In their Lord do they place their trust. They attend regularly to their prayers and spend on others some of what We have provided them with. It is those who are truly believers. They shall be given high ranks with their Lord, and forgiveness of sins and generous provisions."* (Verses 1–4)

This is followed by a reminder of what they wished and hoped for themselves and what God wanted for them. It describes what they see of what is happening on earth and God's unlimited power beyond them and the events they see. (Verses 5–8) This is followed by a further reminder of the support God had given them, the victory He facilitated for them, and the reward He has, by His grace, set for them. (Verses 9–14)

Thus the *surah* proceeds, recording that the whole battle was fought by God's will and under His direction, with His help and support. It is all by His will, and for His sake and to serve His cause. Thus, the fighters have no claim to the spoils of war, as they belong to God and His Messenger. Thus, when God gives them back the spoils of war, this becomes an act of His grace. They must be purged of any desire to gain such booty, so that their *jihad* and struggle is undertaken purely for God's sake. (Verses 17–18, 26, 41–44)

Why believers fight

Since every battle believers fight is of God's own planning, under His command and for His cause, the *surah* mentions time and again the need to remain steadfast, prepare well for it remembering that God's support is certain to come, guard against the lure that keeps believers away from it, including property and offspring. They have to observe all values related to it, and guard against any element of showing off. The Prophet is ordered to encourage the believers to fight it. (Verses 15–16, 24, 27–28, 45–47, 60, 65)

While orders are given to remain steadfast and stand firm in battle, the *surah* provides clarifications of different aspects of the Islamic faith, strengthening its roots, making it the source of every commandment and every judgement. Thus, orders are not left as individual and unrelated items; they are seen to be stemming from the same clear, consistent and profound source.

1. On the question of the spoils of war, the believers are reminded of the need to remain God-fearing, to feel their hearts filled with awe when He is mentioned,

and of the close and permanent manifestation of faith by obedience to God and His Messenger: *"They ask you about the spoils of war. Say: The spoils of war belong to God and the Messenger. So, have fear of God and set to right your internal relations. Obey God and His Messenger, if you are true believers. True believers are only those whose hearts are filled with awe whenever God is mentioned, and whose faith is strengthened whenever His revelations are recited to them. In their Lord do they place their trust. They attend regularly to their prayers and spend on others some of what We have provided them with. It is those who are truly believers. They shall be given high ranks with their Lord, and forgiveness of sins and generous provisions."* (Verses 1–4)

2. On the battle strategy, they are reminded of God's will, power and planning. It is He who intervened to direct every stage: *"{Remember the day} when you were at the near end of the valley and they were at the farthest end, with the caravan down below you. If you had made prior arrangements to meet there, you would have differed on the exact timing and location. But it was all brought about so that God might accomplish something He willed to be done."* (Verse 42)

3. On the events and results of the battle, they are reminded of God's leadership, help and support: *"It was not you who slew them, but it was God who slew them. When you threw {a handful of dust}, it was not your act, but God's, so that He might put the believers through a fair test of His own making."* (Verse 17)

4. When the order is given to the believers to remain steadfast, they are reminded of the fact that God wants them to have a true and worthy life, and that He is able to stand between a man and his heart. It is He who guarantees victory to those who place their trust in Him alone: *"Believers, respond to the call of God and the Messenger when he calls you to that which will give you life, and know that God comes in between a man and his heart, and that to Him you shall all be gathered."* (Verse 24) *"Believers, when you meet an enemy force, be firm, and remember God often, so that you may be successful."* (Verse 45)

5. Defining the ultimate objective of the battle, God commands: *"Fight them until there is no more oppression, and all submission is made to God alone."* (Verse 39) *"It does not behove a Prophet to have captives unless he has battled strenuously in the land."* (Verse 67) *"God promised you that one of the two hosts would fall to you. It was your wish that the one which was not powerful to be yours, but it was God's will to establish the truth in accordance with His words and to wipe out the unbelievers. Thus He would certainly establish the truth firmly and show falsehood to be false, however hateful this might be to the evildoers."* (Verses 7–8)

6. On the organization of the Muslim community's international relations, faith is seen as the basis of the community and its distinctive character. It is faith values that determine position and loyalty. (Verses 72–75)

In this *surah*, the line that is seen to be clearly prominent, side by side with the line of faith, is that of *jihad*. It is given its high value both in concept and in strategy. It is also purged of all personal elements. Its essential justification is clarified so that it is well understood by all those who fight for God's cause at any time. They reiterate this justification with confidence, reassurance and pride. Overall, the *surah* gives this impression, but we may refer to some verses that are particularly relevant and will elaborate upon it when we discuss them. These are verses 15–16, 55–57, 60, 65, 67, 74.

The *surah* also sets the Muslim community's international relations on the basis of faith, as we have already stated. It outlines the rules that form the basis of such relations with other communities in times of war and peace, up to the time when this *surah* was revealed. It details rulings on the distribution of the spoils of war; and also on international treaties, providing fundamental principles that govern all these areas. (Verses 1, 15–16, 20–21, 24, 27, 38–39, 41, 45–47, 55–62, 64–71, 72–75)

To sum up

Such are the main lines of the *surah*. When we remember that it was revealed to comment on the Battle of Badr, we can appreciate some aspects of the method the Qur'an follows in the education of the Muslim community, preparing it for the leadership of humanity. We can also recognize how Islam looks at what happens on earth and in human life, in order to give Muslims the right perception.

Badr was the first major battle when the Muslims inflicted a very heavy defeat on their idolater enemies. But the Muslims did not leave their homes for this purpose or with this intention. They only marched to intercept a trade caravan belonging to the Quraysh, the tribe that confiscated all their homes and property. They wanted to regain some of their losses, but God wanted something else. He wanted the caravan to escape and the Muslims to meet in battle their most hardened enemies who were able to place Islam under siege in Mecca. They further plotted to kill God's Messenger [peace be upon him] after they had mounted an uncompromising campaign of persecution against his companions.

God willed that this battle would be the criterion that separates the truth from falsehood, and that it be a landmark in the line of Islamic history and, consequently in human history. He willed that this battle should show the great gulf between what people may plan for themselves, believing it to serve their best interests, and what God chooses for them, even though they may think little of it at first sight. He wanted the emerging Muslim community to properly learn the factors that bring victory and those that bring defeat, receiving these directly in the battlefield, from none other than God, their Lord and protector.

The *surah* includes highly inspiring directives pointing to these highly important issues, as well as much of the rules that govern states of peace and war, captives and booty, treaties and pacts, and what ensures victory or defeat. All these are given in the most enlightening and instructive style of the Qur'an which begins by expounding the faith and its main concepts, making it the prime mover in all human activity. This is characteristic of the Qur'anic method of looking at events and evaluating them.

The *surah* also portrays scenes of the battles and images of thoughts and feelings before, during and after the battle. These scenes and images are so vivid and lifelike that they enable the reader and the listener to interact with them.

At times, the *surah* gives glimpses of the life the Prophet and his companions lived in Mecca, when they were few in number, weak, fearing that others may do away with them. Now when they remember what their life was like then, they will realize the extent of God's grace in giving them this great victory. They know that they can only achieve victory with God's help, and by following the faith they preferred to their own life and property. The *surah* also portrays some images of the life of the unbelievers before and after the Prophet's migration to Medina, as well as images of the doom suffered by earlier unbelievers such as Pharaoh and his people. These are given in order to establish the law that never fails, which gives victory to believers and defeat to God's enemies.

The second half of the *surah* mirrors the first, beginning with a definitive ruling on the sharing out of the spoils of war, coupled with a call to believe in God and His revelations. It expounds on God's planning in this battle that gave the Muslims such spoils of war, portraying images of what actually took place in the battle. We clearly see that the believers were only a means through which God accomplished His purpose. Believers are then urged to always remain steadfast when they meet their enemy in battle, remembering to glorify God, obey Him and His Messenger, and steer away from internal conflict, lest they weaken and be defeated. They must also guard against showing off and against being deceived by Satan's wicked schemes. They must always place their full trust in God who alone can bring them victory. It tells them of the rule God has established in punishing unbelievers for their sins.

In the first half, the *surah* mentioned how the angels were ordered to support the believers and strike the unbelievers' necks and hands. Here in the second half, we see them striking the unbelievers on their faces and backs. The description of the unbelievers as the worst of all animals which occurs in the first half is repeated in the second in the context of their violation of every treaty or promise they make. This leads to the rules defined by God for the conduct of international relations by the Muslim community, both with those who take a hostile attitude and those who wish to live in peace with it. Some of these rules are provisional and some final.

Up to this point, the nature and sequence of issues discussed in the second half of the *surah* mirror the first half, with some more details on rules governing relations with other communities. As the *surah* draws to its close, it adds certain issues and rules to complete the picture.

God reminds His Messenger and the believers of His favour of bringing about unity of their hearts, which could not have been accomplished except through God's will and grace. The Prophet and the believers are also reassured that God will protect them. God then commands His messenger to encourage his followers to fight, making it clear that, with their faith and if they remain steadfast, they are a good match to a force of unbelievers ten times their number, because the unbelievers are devoid of understanding, since they do not believe. When they are at their weakest, the believers are equal to twice their number, provided they remain steadfast. God is sure to support those who are steadfast in the defence of His cause.

God then takes issue with the believers because of their taking ransom from their prisoners of war, in return for their release, when the Muslims had not yet fought hard to irretrievably weaken their enemy and establish their own authority. Thus the policy of the Islamic movement in different stages and conditions is established and shown to be flexible, looking at every stage and what responses are suitable for it. The *surah* tells the believers how to treat prisoners of war, and how to present the Islamic faith to them in a fair manner to encourage them to embrace it. God makes it clear to the prisoners of war that to resort to treachery again is futile. It was God who gave the believers mastery over them when they played false to Him by refusing to believe in Him and His Messenger. Should they try to play false to the Prophet, God will most certainly hand them over to him.

The final passage in the *surah* organizes internal relations within the Muslim community, and its relations with groups that embrace Islam but remain away from the land of Islam. It also regulates relations between the Muslim community and unbelievers in certain cases, and in general. These rules clearly show the nature of the Muslim community and the Islamic approach to its relations with others. It is absolutely manifest that Islam will always exist in a positive, forward-looking and proactive community. All the rules governing its internal and external relations are based on this fact. It is simply not possible to separate the faith and the law from the positive, proactive approach and the sound structure of the Muslim community.

5   The basis of inter-communal relations

Overview

This opening passage was revealed later than the rest of the *surah*. We have explained in earlier volumes that the final ordering of the verses in each *surah* followed instructions given by the Prophet himself. This means that such ordering is final and done on the basis of instructions received by the Prophet from on high.

This passage terminates treaties and agreements that were in force at the time between the Muslims and the unbelievers. A notice of four months is given to those who have treaties running indefinitely, or those who have violated their treaties. Others who have treaties running for a specified term and have honoured their obligations under those treaties, without ever backing or aiding anyone against the Muslims, are promised to have their treaties honoured by the Muslims to the end of their specified terms. Thus, the final outcome is the termination of all treaties with unbelievers in the Arabian Peninsula, and an end to the very concept of having a treaty with idolaters. This takes the form of a disavowal of all obligations towards idolaters and questioning the very idea of idolaters having a treaty or covenant with God and His Messenger.

The passage also includes a ban on idolaters from doing the *tawaf*, which is the ritual walk around the Ka'bah, or visiting it for worship in any way or form. This abrogates the earlier mutual pledges of security between the Prophet and the idolaters ensuring the safety of all people in the Ka'bah and during the sacred months.

When we review the events that took place during the Prophet's lifetime so as to draw an outline of the historical progress and nature of the proactive approach of Islam, its progressive stages and ultimate goals, we see very clearly that this decisive step was taken at its most appropriate time. It was now possible to reorganize relations between the Islamic community and other camps, whether idolaters or people of earlier revelations.

Stage after stage and event after event, it was practically demonstrated that it was impossible to achieve coexistence between two diametrically opposed ways of life with such deep-rooted and fundamental differences that affect every detail of concepts, beliefs, moral values, social behaviour, as well as social, economic and political structures. Such fundamental differences were bound to surface as a result of the differences in beliefs and concepts. We have one way of life based entirely on submission of all mankind to God alone who has no partners, and another that makes people submit to other human beings and false deities. The two are bound to be in conflict at every step and in every aspect of life.

It was not just a coincidence that the Quraysh should take such a permanently hostile attitude to the Islamic call which raised the banner that "there is no deity other than God, and Muhammad is God's Messenger." Its hostility continued throughout the period when the Prophet was in Mecca and sought to crush it in open warfare after he migrated to Medina. Nor was it by coincidence that the Jews in Medina should stand up in opposition to the Islamic message or that they should join forces with the idolaters, in spite of the Scriptures in which they professed to believe. Both the Quraysh and the Jews tried to forge an alliance grouping all Arab tribes in an all-out effort to exterminate the whole Muslim community. They felt that the establishment of the Muslim state in Medina on the basis of faith and its implementation of the divine way of life represented a danger that threatened them and which they felt they had to remove.

We will learn presently that the same can be said for the Christians' attitude towards the Islamic message despite the fact they also had divine Scriptures. This was the case in Yemen, Syria and beyond both these areas, and at all times. It is all in the nature of things.

Those who adopt other creeds and philosophies know that it is in the nature of the Islamic approach to insist on the establishment of a state based on belief in God. It aims to liberate all mankind from submission to other creatures so that they may submit to God alone, and to remove all physical and material impediments that prevent human beings from exercising their right to freedom of choice. It is also natural that those who follow other creeds try to crush the divine way of life in which they see a real threat to their very existence, their systems and social set-ups. Such a polarization is, then, inevitable.

Such hostility, inevitable as it certainly is, surfaced in a variety of forms, time after time, and served to emphasize the need for this final step announced in this *surah*. The immediate causes mentioned in some reports were only episodes in a long chain of events that had been going on ever since the early days of the Islamic message.

When we adopt such a broad perspective and try to delve into the root causes dictating attitudes and actions, we can properly understand the need for this final step. We must not overlook the immediate causes because these, in turn, were only episodes in a long series of events.

In his commentary on the Qur'an, Imam al-Baghawi quotes earlier commentators as saying: "When the Prophet set out on his expedition to Tabuk, the hypocrites started to spread rumours while the idolaters began to violate the treaties they had with the Muslims. God then revealed this verse which is applicable to the latter group. He gave them four months' notice if their treaties were of shorter duration, and announced the termination of longer-lasting treaties after four months."

Reviewing the views of other commentators, Imam al-Tabari says:

> As for the notice given by God permitting idolaters with a treaty to '*go freely in the land for four months,*' perhaps the more accurate view is to say that this notice is given by God to those idolaters who, despite having peace treaties, collaborated with others against the Prophet and the Muslim community violating their treaties before they ran out. As for those who fulfilled their obligations under such treaties and refrained from collaborating with others, God – limitless is He in His glory – ordered His Messenger to honour his treaty with them until their term had been completed. This is clear in the Qur'anic statement: "*Except for those idolaters with whom you have made a treaty and who have honoured their obligations {under the treaty} in every detail, and have not aided anyone against you. To these fulfil your obligations until their treaties have run their term. God loves those who are righteous.*" (Verse 4)[1]

Al-Tabari also quotes Mujahid as saying:

> In the statement, '*Disavowal by God and His Messenger {is hereby announced} to those of the idolaters with whom you have made a treaty,*' the reference here is made to the tribe of

Mudlij and the Arabs bound by a treaty with the Muslims and all other peoples with similar treaties. It is reported that when the Prophet returned from Tabuk, he wanted to go on pilgrimage. He then thought, 'the Ka'bah is visited by idolaters who do the *tawaf* naked. I would rather delay my pilgrimage until such a practice is stopped.' He sent Abu Bakr and 'Ali who went to see people at Dhu'l-Majaz and other markets, as well as their encampments in pilgrimage. They gave notice to all people who had treaties with the Prophet that they would have four months of peace. When those four consecutive months, beginning with the twenty days remaining of Dhu'l-Hijjah to the tenth day of Rabi'II, were over, the treaties would come to an end. All people in Arabia would then be in a state of war with the Muslims unless they believed in God and His Messenger. The whole Arab population of Arabia became Muslims and none continued with their old religion.[2]

A number of immediate causes were naturally a factor in taking this final and decisive step. Nevertheless they were only links in a long chain which arises from the basic conflict between the two ways of life which cannot coexist except for short periods and which are bound to come to an end sooner or later.

Peace or no peace

The late Shaikh Muhammad Rashid Rida, a leading scholar of the late nineteenth and early twentieth centuries, tries to identify these links in the chain right from the early days of the Islamic message. However, he does not try to outline the basic and permanent conflict which gives rise to the whole episode, leading eventually to the natural result outlined in this *surah*. In his commentary, *al-Manar*, he writes:

An indisputable fact known to all people is that God sent His Messenger, Muhammad, the last of all prophets, with the message of Islam that provides a complete and final version of the divine faith. His greatest proof is the Qur'an, which defies human beings with a multifaceted challenge that we have outlined in our commentary on Verse 3 of *Surah* 2. The essence of advocacy of the divine message is based on irrefutable rational and scientific evidence.[3] He has also established clearly that compulsion could in no way be adopted as a means of spreading the faith. This has been outlined in our commentary on verse 256 of *Surah* 2.

The idolaters took an attitude of resistance, subjecting the believers to a campaign of persecution and torture to force them to turn away from Islam. They also tried to forcibly prevent the Prophet from conveying his message to people. No one who accepted the new faith and believed in the Prophet's message felt safe or secure from death and torture unless he enjoyed the protection of an ally or a relative. Hence they had to migrate time after time.

Then they escalated their campaign against the Prophet. They considered arresting him permanently, and they also thought of banishing him, and they also considered killing him openly in their meeting place. They finally opted to murder him. God then ordered him to emigrate, as we have explained when commenting on verse 30 of *Surah* 8.[4] The Prophet emigrated with those of his Companions who were able to do so. They settled in Medina where they found support by the *Ansar* who were believers in God and His Messenger, showing their love of those who migrated to settle in their land, and extended to them fine hospitality and a most generous treatment.

The conditions that prevailed between them and the idolaters of Mecca and other areas in Arabia were naturally war conditions, as would have been expected at the time. The Prophet entered into a peace treaty with the Jews in Medina and the surrounding area. But they violated their treaty and forged an alliance with the idolaters, supporting them in their campaigns against the Prophet and Islam. We have outlined all this in commenting on *Surah* 8.

At al-Hudaybiyah, the Prophet entered into a peace treaty with the idolaters which provided for peace and security for ten years. He accepted conditions which were most favourable to the idolaters, but this was an act of magnanimity, not weakness. He wanted peace to prevail so that he could ensure the propagation of his faith through clear argument and irrefutable evidence.[5] The tribe of Khuzaʿah entered into a treaty with the Prophet, while the tribe of Bakr joined an alliance with the Quraysh. The latter launched an aggression against the former and they were helped in this by the Quraysh who supported them with arms, thus violating their treaty with the Prophet.

This was the cause for ending the peace and returning to a situation of war which resulted in the Prophet's campaign that ended with Mecca falling peacefully to Islam. This was an event that considerably weakened and humiliated the idolaters. However, they continued to fight against the Prophet whenever they felt strong enough to do so. Experience had shown that they could never be relied upon to honour their pledges, whether their position was one of strength or weakness. We will presently see, in Verse 7, the exclamation, *"How can there be a treaty with God and His Messenger . . ."* leading to the instruction in Verse 12: *"Fight these archetypes of faithlessness who have no {respect for a} binding pledge, so that they may desist."* This means that they will never honour their pledges or fulfil their obligations. What the *surah* emphasizes here is that Muslims cannot coexist with them under the provisions of their treaties, in order to ensure peace and security, while they remain idolaters, observing no well-defined law which would have committed them to fulfil the conditions of their treaty. Indeed, the people of earlier Scriptures, who should have demonstrated a greater degree of integrity and honour, were even quicker to violate their covenants and breach their treaties.[6]

This is the basis of the provisions outlined in this *surah* which abrogated their open-ended treaties, and allowed other treaties to run their course, provided they remained faithful to such treaties. The reason for this was to remove idolatry from the Arabian Peninsula so that it became wholly and purely for the Muslims. All this is done while observing at the same time and as far as possible the earlier rules, such as *'Fight for the cause of God those who wage war against you, but do not commit aggression,'* (2: 190), and *'If they incline to peace, then incline you to it as well.'* (8: 61) Nevertheless, many scholars are of the view that this latter verse has been abrogated by the verse instructing the Muslims to abrogate treaties with the idolaters and to fight them.[7]

It is clear from this presentation and the subsequent comments, as well as what follows in Shaikh Muhammad Rashid Rida's commentary that he properly defines the real cause of this long series of treacherous actions by the idolaters who were always on the look-out for an opportunity to suppress Islam and overpower its advocates. Nevertheless, he does not dig deep enough to see how outstretched the roots behind this attitude were. Nor does he visualize the fundamental quality in the nature of this religion and its method of action, or the nature of radical differences between the divine way of life and those devised by God's creatures. Such differences make a meeting between the two practically impossible. Hence, there can be no permanent peaceful coexistence between a community implementing God's law and other communities.

Under strong pressure

By contrast, in his book, *al-Tafsir al-Hadith*, Muhammad ʿIzzat Darwazah goes far beyond the root causes on which the Islamic attitude to other communities is based. Like other contemporary authors writing under oppressive pressures of the miserable conditions of today's Muslims and the all-too-visible strength of contemporary idolaters, atheists and followers of other religions, he has a clear purpose in mind. Hence, he tries hard to prove that Islam is a religion of peace, aiming at nothing more than to live within its borders in peace. Wherever it is possible to make a peace treaty, Islam should be keen to put it in place, making it its clear objective.

Hence, Muhammad ʿIzzat Darwazah finds no reason for these new and final provisions, included in this present *surah*, other than the violation by some idolaters of their treaties. As for those who honoured their treaties, whether these were of limited or indefinite duration, the *surah* gives instructions to the Muslims to honour them. Indeed, he claims that new treaties may be concluded with them after the expiry of their present ones. The same applies, in his view, to the violaters of their present treaties. He considers the verses giving provisional rulings to prevail over the principles given in the final verses.

In his discussion of the first passage of the *surah* he identifies the following verses: *"except for those idolaters with whom you have made a treaty and who have honoured their obligations {under the treaty} in every detail, and have not aided anyone against you. To these fulfil your obligations until their treaties have run their term. God loves those who are righteous. When these months of grace are over, slay the idolaters wherever you find them, and take them captive, besiege them, and lie in wait for them at every conceivable place. Yet if they should repent, take to prayer and pay the* zakat, *let them go their way. For God is Much-forgiving, Merciful."* (Verses 4–5) He then says:

> In these two verses and the ones preceding them we have scenes of life towards the end of the Medina period at the time of the Prophet. We note from these verses that there were peace agreements between Muslims and unbelievers which were in force after the fall of Mecca to Islam, and perhaps were signed before that event. We note that some idolaters honoured their agreements while others violated them, or contemplated such violations.
>
> We stated earlier that commentators describe the second of these two verses as 'the verse of the sword', and treat it as abrogating every previous verse which gives instructions to adopt a reconciliatory attitude towards the idolaters and allowing them time to make their position clear, and to forbear and let matters take their course. They consider this verse to order fighting them as the proper attitude. Some commentators make an exception in the case of those who have a treaty allowing such treaties to run to the end of their terms. Others do not make such exceptions, saying that their only option after the revelation of this verse is that they must embrace Islam. We also made it clear that such an explanation is too extreme and contradicts a number of definitive rulings that prohibit fighting anyone other than enemies and orders fair and kindly treatment of those who adopt a peaceful attitude.
>
> When discussing this verse, commentators repeatedly quote reports attributed to the earliest commentators on the Qurʾan. Ibn Kathir, for example, quotes Ibn ʿAbbas's view that the verse contains an order to the Prophet to take up arms against those with whom he had a treaty until they have embraced Islam. He is further ordered to terminate the conditions he approved when negotiating such treaties. The same commentator quotes a singular view attributed to Sulayman ibn ʿUyaynah which groups these verses together with other verses in this and other *surahs* that do

not refer to fighting and calls these verses, the swords. He claims that the Prophet sent his cousin ʿAli ibn Abi Talib to convey these verses to people on the day of the greater pilgrimage. These included this verse which he describes as a sword on the Arab idolaters. Another sword was against the hypocrites, and it is included in the later verse: "*Fight against those who – despite having been given Scriptures – do not truly believe in God and the Last Day, and do not treat as forbidden that which God and His Messenger have forbidden, and do not follow the religion of truth, till they {agree to} pay the submission tax with a willing hand, after they have been humbled.*" (Verse 29) A third sword against the hypocrites is included in this verse: "*Prophet, strive hard against the unbelievers and the hypocrites, and press on them. Their ultimate abode is hell, and how vile a journey's end.*" (Verse 73) A fourth sword is levelled against rebels, which is included in *Surah* 49: "*If two groups of believers fall to fighting, make peace between them. But then, if one of the two goes on acting wrongfully towards the other, fight against the one that acts wrongfully until it reverts to God's commandment.*" (49: 9) What is most singular is that al-Tabari expresses the view that this present verse (i.e. Verse 5) applies equally to those who are bound by a treaty and those with no treaty. Yet he himself takes a different view when commenting on the following verse: "*For such of the unbelievers as do not fight against you on account of your faith, and neither drive you forth from your homelands, God does not forbid you to show them kindness and to behave towards them with full equity. Surely God loves those who act equitably.*" (60: 8) He says that this last verse is definitive, making clear that God does not forbid extending kindly and fair treatment to those who adopt an attitude of peaceful coexistence and neutrality, whatever their faith may be. These may not even be bound by a treaty.

All this when it is clear that the verse refers, in context and import, to fighting only the idolaters who violate their treaties. It is reasonable to say that considering it a sword pointed at all idolaters, regardless of their position and attitude, is to impose on it an interpretation it cannot admit. The same may be said about the claim that it abrogates several earlier statements given in a form of definitive principles, such as the prohibition of compulsion in matters of religion and faith, the advocacy of the divine message with wisdom, kindly admonition and fair argument, the order to extend kindly and fair treatment to those who do not fight against the Muslims and not to drive them out of their homeland. A few verses on, the *surah* also includes a clear order to all Muslims to remain faithful to their commitments towards people with whom they have concluded treaties in the vicinity of the Sacred Mosque, as long as the latter continue to honour their obligations. This last verse gives clear support to our view.

Two points may be raised concerning the rulings included in the two verses quoted above. The first refers to the exception made in the first verse in respect of the completion of the term of a treaty. The question asked here is whether the idolaters who have such a treaty will be included in the disavowal declared by God and His Messenger, and in this case must they be fought? Commentators generally seem to answer this question in the affirmative. We for our part have not seen any authentic report attributed to the Prophet on this particular point. Hence, what commentators say may be questioned if they treat it as universally applicable. The whole matter requires clarification.

Those unbelievers who are party to a treaty with the Muslims could have been prior to the treaty either enemies who fought the Muslims in war and then negotiated a peace treaty with them, as was the case with the Quraysh when they signed the al-Hudaybiyah peace treaty, or else they might have wished to have such a peace treaty without ever having been at war against the Muslims. Consider this following verse: *"Except in the case of those of them who have ties with people to whom you yourselves are bound by a covenant, or those who come to you because their hearts shrink from the thought of fighting you or fighting their own people. Had God so willed, He would have given them power over you, and they would have fought you. Therefore, if they leave you alone, and do not make war on you, and offer you peace, God has given you no way against them."* (4: 90) We believe that this verse speaks of a true situation.

In the Prophet's history we have several examples, such as the report by Ibn Saʿd to the effect that the Prophet made an agreement with the Sakhr clan of the Kinanah tribe that neither party would raid the other, and that they would never aid any party against the Prophet and his Companions. All this was put in a written agreement. There is nothing in this verse, or indeed in any other verse, to prevent the renewal of the treaty or extending its term, should the other party desire that, without having ever given any indication of violating their commitments. Muslims may not refuse such an extension because they are ordered to fight only those who wage war or launch an aggression against them. A later verse in the *surah* includes an express order to the Muslims to remain true to their treaties with idolaters as long as those idolaters continue to honour such treaties. This supports our view.

The second point concerns the last part of the second verse which makes releasing the idolaters and stopping the fight against them that resulted from their treaty violations conditional upon a fundamental change indicated by turning away from idolatry, attending regularly to prayer and paying the obligatory charity, i.e. *zakat*.

What appears to me is that by violating their original treaties and fighting the Muslims, the idolaters actually forfeited their right to have a new treaty. It is right that the Muslims should now impose the condition that guarantees their safety and security, which is that they should accept Islam and fulfil its worship requirements, ritual and financial. This does not constitute any compulsion to force them to become Muslims. Suffice it to say that idolatry represents a very low ebb to which humanity may sink when it allows its reason to be subservient to ideas and forces that have no trace of truth or logic. Besides, idolatry is an ignorant system governed by oppressive tradition and bizarre habits. When they embrace Islam, they are certain to rid themselves of all that and rise to a position of respectability in thought, morality, faith, belief, worship and daily practices. Besides, we do not see any reason to prevent the renewal of treaties with those whom the Muslims have fought for violating their original treaties, should the interests of the Muslim community require such renewal.

These paragraphs and many similar ones in the author's commentary make it clear that he does not even consider that Islam has an inalienable and absolute right to move forward to liberate mankind from the evil of submission to other human beings so that people may submit themselves to God alone. Islam does so whenever it is feasible, regardless of whether the Muslim community is under attack or not. This concept, which is the basis of *jihad* in Islam, does not figure at all in this author's thinking. Without it Islam is denied its right to remove physical obstacles impeding its progress, and it loses its serious, practical approach which requires facing obstacles with suitable and adequate means. It will have to confront physical powers with verbal advocacy. This is far from satisfactory.[8]

It is also clear that this author does not pay sufficient attention to the method of action Islam adopts, which requires that any situation should be faced with adequate means. He attaches final rulings to provisional texts and rulings which were given earlier. In so doing, he does not take into consideration the fact that the earlier rulings dealt with practical situations different from the ones that prevailed at the time of the revelation of the final verses. It is true that the earlier rulings are not abrogated in the sense that makes them inapplicable to any situation. They remain in force but only to face new situations that are largely similar to the ones they originally addressed. However, these earlier rulings do not restrict the Muslims should they face situations similar to the ones that prevailed at the time when the final rulings were revealed. The whole question requires broader knowledge, and a good understanding of the nature of Islam and its method of action.

The nature of Islamic international relations

At the beginning of our commentary we said: "When we review the events that took place during the Prophet's lifetime so as to draw an outline of the historical progress and nature of the proactive approach of Islam, its progressive stages and ultimate goals, we see very clearly that this decisive step was taken at its most appropriate time. It was now possible to reorganize relations between the Islamic community and other camps, whether idolaters or people of earlier revelations."

One experience after another had revealed the nature of the law that governs relations between Islamic society which attributes Godhead, Lordship, sovereignty and the authority to legislate to God alone, and ignorant or, to use the Islamic term, *jahiliyyah* societies which assign all this to some beings other than God, or claim that God has partners sharing with Him all these attributes. This law is essentially one of conflict, which is expressed in God's statements in the Qur'an: *"Were it not that God repels some people by means of others, monasteries, churches, synagogues and mosques – in all of which God's name is abundantly extolled – would have been destroyed."* (22: 40) *"Had it not been for the fact that God repels one group of people by another, the earth would have been utterly corrupted."* (2:251)

The practical results of this essential law were manifested in two practical phenomena. The first was that Islam moved from one step, expedition and stage to the next following the divine approach and conveying God's message to one area and tribe after another. This was a necessary step towards conveying the message to all mankind and removing all material obstacles that prevented the divine message from reaching all people. This continued to be the case until Mecca fell to Islam and the Quraysh tribe, the major obstacle in the face of the Islamic march, was vanquished. The large tribes of Hawazin and Thaqif, which were akin to the Quraysh in strength, also surrendered to the Muslim state. Islam had then enough power to strike fear in the hearts of its enemies. It was thus able to take the final and decisive step in the Arabian Peninsula, in preparation for taking the same step across the rest of the world, as and when circumstances allowed. The ultimate aim being that there should be no strife on earth and all submission be made to God alone.

The other phenomenon was the violation of treaties and covenants which were made with the Muslims in different circumstances, whenever a chance presented itself to violate such treaties with impunity. At the first suggestion that the Muslims were going through some difficulty which made the idolaters, and even the people of earlier revelations, feel they could safely violate their treaties, such violations were certain to come. The treaties were not made in the first place as a result of any keen desire to live in peace with the Muslims. The enemies of Islam were compelled, by force of circumstance, to go into such treaties to serve their own interests. *Jahiliyyah*, which is the name Islam gives to any society that rejects God's law, does not like to see Islam establishing its solid presence when it contradicts the very basis of its existence and every detail of the programmes of such societies. *Jahiliyyah* knows that by virtue of the active nature of

Islam, and its instinctive desire to stamp out tyranny from human life, it will work hard to bring people back to the worship of God alone.

It is to emphasize this last phenomenon that God says with reference to the unbelievers: *"They shall not cease to fight you until they force you to renounce your faith, if they can."* (2: 217) He also says about the people of earlier revelations; *"Many among the people of earlier revelations would love to lead you back to unbelief, now that you have embraced the faith. This they do out of deep-seated envy, after the truth has become manifest to them."* (2: 109) Concerning them He also says: *"Never will the Jews nor yet the Christians be pleased with you unless you follow their faith."* (2: 120) In all these categorical statements God makes it clear that all those in the camp of *jahiliyyah* have the same objectives when it comes to dealing with Islam and Muslims. They pursue their goals with clear persistence that never fades with the passage of time, nor does it change as a result of changing circumstances.

Unless we understand this essential law that is inherent in the nature of the relationship between the Muslim community and the camp of *jahiliyyah*, we cannot understand the nature of Islamic *jihad*, or the motives for that long struggle between the two. Nor can we, without such understanding of this law, comprehend the motives of the early Muslims, or the secrets of Islamic conquests, or the war that has been waged against Islam by hostile forces over the 14 centuries of Islamic history. It continues to be waged against the children of Muslim communities, despite the fact that these have sadly abandoned true Islam, with its holistic approach to life, and are content to keep it in name only. The war continues to be waged against those latter-day Muslim communities, even those living in the midst of hostile creeds such as communism and idolatry of all forms, whether in Russia, China, Yugoslavia, Albania, India, Kashmir, Ethiopia, Zanzibar, Cyprus, Kenya, South Africa or the United States. All this comes on top of the brutal attempts to exterminate the advocates of Islamic revival in the Muslim World, or more accurately, the world which used to be Muslim. Communism, idolatry, and other world powers collaborate with, and give active support to, the regimes that undertake such extermination efforts against the advocates of Islamic revival. They pour their aid on these governments to the extent that they practically give them every type of help to ensure that they stay in power. Their support often takes the form of tacit or silent approval of what they are doing to those noble believers who seek to persuade people to believe in God and implement His law.

Such understanding of all these aspects can only be achieved when we understand the essential law we have talked about and the phenomena it brings into our life. This law demonstrated itself in the period leading to the conquest of Mecca, in the two phenomena we have outlined. At that time, it appeared clearly that a decisive step must be taken in the Arabian Peninsula, against the idolaters, which we will discuss presently, and against the people of earlier revelations which we will discuss in Chapters 2 and 3.

Crystallizing attitudes

The need for such a decisive step might have been very clear for the Islamic leadership at the time, but that did not necessarily mean that it was similarly clear to all groups in the Muslim community, particularly the newcomers to Islam and those who were only on friendly terms with the Muslims.

Some people in the Muslim community, perhaps among the noblest and most dedicated Muslims, might have felt uneasy about the termination of all treaties with the unbelievers on the terms outlined in the *surah*: after four months for those who violated their treaties, and those with treaties that did not specify a term, and those whose treaties ended in less than four months and those who had no treaties and were not at war with the Muslims. Those who had treaties with specified terms and continued to honour their obligations would have their treaties respected and observed for the remainder of their terms. Such conscientious Muslims might have understood that the treaties with the violators and those from whom violation was expected should be terminated, as was clear in the provisional instructions given to the Prophet in the previous *surah*: "*if you fear treachery from any folk, cast {your treaty with them} back to them in a fair manner. God does not love the treacherous.*" (8: 58) However, the termination of treaties after four months or after their term was over might have appeared to those people contrary to the familiar practice of maintaining peaceful relations with those who did not adopt any hostile attitude. God, on the other hand, had a far greater objective than maintaining what was familiar practice.

Other people in the Muslim community, perhaps also among the noblest and most dedicated Muslims, might have felt that there was no longer any need to fight the idolaters generally after Islam had attained supremacy in Arabia, leaving only scattered pockets of resistance which represented no threat whatsoever. On the contrary, they were expected to change their attitude to Islam gradually after peace would have been maintained for sometime in Arabia. Such Muslims might have felt particularly uneasy about fighting against relatives and friends as well as people with whom they might have had social and economic relations. After all there was still hope that such people would still see the light of Islam without resorting to such a drastic measure. But God wanted faith to be the basic bond that united people in a cohesive community. He also wanted the Arabian Peninsula to be a secure base for Islam, as He was aware of the plots the Byzantines were preparing against the Muslim state. This will be explained later.

Yet others in the Muslim community, some of whom might have been among the noblest and most dedicated Muslims, might have feared economic depression ensuing from the disruption to business transactions in Arabia as a result of declaring war against all Arabian idolaters. That was bound to affect the pilgrimage season, particularly after it had been announced that no idolater would be allowed to go on pilgrimage after that year, and that idolaters would not be allowed to enter into mosques and places of worship. Such people's fears were made even greater by the fact that such a step was not particularly necessary. Its outcome could have been reached in a slower but more peaceful way. But, as we have said, God wanted the basic bond to unite people in the Muslim community to be the bond of faith, so that faith should be felt to have far greater weight than blood relationships, friendships and economic interests. He also wanted the Muslims to realize that He alone gave them all the provisions they had and was their only provider. The means they might have had to earn their living were not the only ones He could have granted them.

There were others in the Muslim community who lacked strength of faith, or were hesitant, or who were hypocrites, or who might have been among the large numbers who embraced Islam but had not yet fully absorbed its truth. Most of these feared the possibility of open warfare with the idolaters, the economic depression that might result from war, the lack of security for trade and travel, the disruption of contacts and transport and worried about the likely costs of mounting a *jihad* campaign. Such people might have not reckoned with such a prospect of full-scale war. They might have been encouraged to embrace Islam by the fact that it appeared victorious, and that it would have enjoyed security and stability. To them, embracing Islam might have seemed the best alternative that allowed them to gain much for a little outlay. Newcomers to Islam as they were, they felt ill at ease with what was required of them. God, on the other hand, wanted to test people's intentions and their commitment and determination. He says to the believers: "*Do you think that you will be left alone, unless God takes cognizance of those of you who strive hard for His cause and establish close association with none other than God, His Messenger and the believers? God is well aware of what you do.*" (Verse 16)

All these aspects made it necessary to give a detailed account which employs various modes of expression and produces varied effects which are calculated to remove the traces of weakness in people's hearts and remove whatever doubts they might be entertaining. Hence the *surah* opens with a general announcement of disavowal by God and His Messenger of all dealings with the idolaters. The same disavowal is repeated another time, with similar forcefulness and clarity after only one verse in the *surah* so that no believer will entertain any thought of maintaining relations with such people when God and His Messenger are acquitting themselves of any dealings with them. "*Disavowal by God and His Messenger (is hereby announced) to those of the idolaters with whom you have made a treaty.*" (Verse 1) "*And a proclamation from God and His Messenger is hereby made to all mankind on this day of the greater pilgrimage: God is free from obligation to the idolaters, and so is His Messenger.*" (Verse 3)

The believers are also reassured while the unbelievers are threatened with misery and humiliation. Those who turn away are warned that they cannot escape God's judgement: "*You may go freely in the land for four months, but you must realize that you can never escape God's judgement, and that God shall bring disgrace upon the unbelievers.*" (Verse 2) "*If you repent, it shall be for your own good; and if you turn away, then know that you can never escape God's judgement. Give the unbelievers the news of grievous suffering.*" (Verse 3)

The very idea that idolaters may have a treaty with God and His Messenger is questioned, except for those who had shown true commitment in observing their treaty with honesty. With these the existing treaties were to be honoured for the rest of their terms, as long as the unbelievers remained faithful to them. The believers are warned, however, that the idolaters would try to do them harm whenever they could as also feeling that they would escape punishment. "*How can there be a treaty with God and His Messenger for the idolaters, unless it be those of them with whom you have made a treaty at the Sacred Mosque? So long as they are true to you, be true to them; for God loves those who are God-fearing. How {else could it be} when, should they prevail over you, they will respect neither agreement made with you, nor obligation of honour towards you? They try to please you with what they say, while at heart they remain adamantly hostile. Most of them are transgressors. They barter away God's revelations for a paltry price and debar others from His path. Evil indeed is what they do. They respect neither agreement nor obligation of honour with regard to any believer. Those indeed are the aggressors.*" (Verses 7–10)

The believers are further reminded of their own bitter experiences with them, and their feelings of happiness at the crushing of their enemy by God's might. "*Will you not fight against people who have broken their solemn pledges and set out to drive out the Messenger, and who were the first to attack you? Do you fear them? It is God alone whom you should fear, if you are true believers. Fight them: God will punish them at your hands, and will bring disgrace upon them; and will grant you victory over them and will grant heart-felt satisfaction to those who are believers, removing all angry feelings from their hearts. God will turn in His mercy to whom He wills. God is All-knowing and Wise.*" (Verses 13–15)

They are told that they must cut themselves off, as far as family relations with the unbelievers were concerned. They are required to weaken the effects of their family ties with the unbelievers. They are told to choose between those ties of blood and friendship on the one hand and God and His Messenger on the other. "*Believers, do not take your fathers and brothers for allies if they choose unbelief in preference to faith. Those of you who take them for allies are indeed wrongdoers. Say: 'If your fathers, your sons, your brothers, your spouses, your clan, and the property you have acquired, and the business in which you fear a decline, and the dwellings in which you take pleasure, are dearer to you than God and His Messenger and the struggle in His cause, then wait until God shall make manifest His will. God does not provide guidance to the evildoers.'* " (Verses 23–24)

They are also reminded of the numerous victories they achieved with God's help, the most recent of which was the Battle of Hunayn. They were able to achieve victory only when God provided them with His help and gave reassurance to His Messenger who remained steadfast: *"God has granted you His support on many a battlefield, and also in the Battle of Hunayn, when you took pride in your numerical strength, but it availed you nothing. For all its vastness, the earth seemed too narrow for you, and you turned back in flight. God then bestowed from on high an air of inner peace on His Messenger and on the believers, and He sent down forces whom you could not see, and punished those who disbelieved. Such is the reward for the unbelievers."* (Verses 25–26)

They are also reassured about their provisions, and that they should not fear any loss of trade or lack of business. What they get is subject to God's will, not to the apparent causes people associate with profitable business: *"Believers, know that the idolaters are certainly impure. So, let them not come near to the Sacred Mosque after this year is ended. If you fear poverty, then in time God will enrich you with His own bounty, if He so wills. Truly, God is All-knowing, Wise."* (Verse 28)

All these concerns which required reassurance and clear judgement are indicative of the situation that prevailed in the Muslim state in Medina. Had it not been for the fact that the Muslim community in Medina was firm in its belief, stable and enlightened, these conditions might have represented a serious threat to it, and to the very existence of Islam itself.

Having given this detailed preview, we now begin to discuss the verses of this passage in more detail.

An announcement is made

> *Disavowal by God and His Messenger {is hereby announced} to those of the idolaters with whom you have made a treaty. (Announce to them:) You may go freely in the land for four months, but you must realize that you can never escape God's judgement, and that God shall bring disgrace upon the unbelievers. And a proclamation from God and His Messenger is hereby made to all mankind on this day of the greater pilgrimage: God is free from obligation to the idolaters, and so is His Messenger. If you repent, it shall be for your own good; and if you turn away, then know that you can never escape God's judgement. Give the unbelievers the news of grievous suffering, except for those idolaters with whom you have made a treaty and who have honoured their obligations {under the treaty} in every detail, and have not aided anyone against you. To these fulfil your obligations until their treaties have run their term. God loves those who are righteous. When these months of grace are over, slay the idolaters wherever you find them, and take them captive, besiege them, and lie in wait for them at every conceivable place. Yet if they should repent, take to prayer and pay the* zakat, *let them go their way. For God is Much-Forgiving, Merciful. If any of the idolaters seeks asylum with you, grant him protection, so that he may hear the word of God, and then convey him to his place of safety. That is because the idolaters are people who lack knowledge.* (Verses 1–6)

These verses and the following ones, up to verse 28, provide a framework demarcating relations between the Muslim community, now well established in Medina and the Arabian Peninsula generally, and the unbelievers in Arabia who chose not to accept Islam. Relations were thus regulated with those Arabs who had violated their treaties with the Prophet when they felt that the Muslims were about to meet their match from the Byzantines at Tabuk. Relations were also put on a proper footing with those Arabs without a treaty but who maintained good relations with the Muslims, and those who had a treaty which they continued to observe, entertaining no thoughts of treachery.

The style employed in these verses takes the form of a general declaration coupled with high resonance to ensure perfect harmony between the subject matter, the general atmosphere surrounding the whole issue and the mode of expression.

Several reports speak of the general conditions prevailing at the time when this declaration was made, as well as the method and the person chosen for its announcement. Perhaps the most accurate and more fitting with the prevailing situation of the Muslim community and the nature of the Islamic approach is the one chosen by Ibn Jarir al-Tabari, an early commentator on the Qur'an. We will quote here some of his comments on the various reports which support our view of the event and how it took place. The following report he attributes to Mujahid:

> In the statement, '*Disavowal by God and His Messenger {is hereby announced} to those of the idolaters with whom you have made a treaty*,' the reference is made to the tribe of Mudlij and the Arabs bound by a treaty with the Muslims and all other peoples with similar treaties. It is reported that when the Prophet returned from Tabuk, he wanted to go on pilgrimage. He then thought, 'the Ka'bah is visited by idolaters who do the *tawaf* naked. I would rather delay my pilgrimage until such a practice is stopped.' He sent Abu Bakr and 'Ali who went to see people at Dhu'l-Majaz and other markets, as well as their encampments in pilgrimage. They gave notice to all peoples who had treaties with the Prophet that they would have four months of peace. When those four consecutive months, beginning with the twenty days remaining of Dhu'l-Hijjah to the tenth day of Rabi'II, were over, the treaties would come to an end. All people in Arabia would then be in a state of war with the Muslims unless they believed in God and His Messenger. All the population of Arabia became Muslims and none continued with their old religion.[9]

Examining the views of other commentators, Imam al-Tabari says:

> As for the notice given by God permitting idolaters with a treaty to '*go freely in the land for four months*,' perhaps the more accurate view is to say that this notice is given by God to those idolaters who, despite having peace treaties, collaborated with others against the Prophet and the Muslim community violating their treaties before they ran out. As for those who fulfilled their obligations under such treaties and refrained from collaborating with others, God – limitless is He in His glory – ordered His Messenger to honour his treaty with them until their term had been completed. This is clear in the Qur'anic statement: "*Except for those idolaters with whom you have made a treaty and who have honoured their obligations {under that treaty} in every detail, and have not aided anyone against you. To these fulfil your obligations until their treaties have run their term. God loves those who are righteous.*" (Verse 4)
>
> Some people may feel differently, taking the order to mean that once the truce was over, the Muslims were meant to kill all unbelievers. They may quote in support of their view the next verse which states: '*When these months of grace are over, slay the idolaters wherever you find them.*' (Verse 5) But this view is wrong. Verse 7 confirms our view and shows the opposite as wrong: '*How can there be a treaty with God and His Messenger for the idolaters, unless it be those of them with whom you have made a treaty at the Sacred Mosque? So long as they are true to you, be true to them; for God loves those who are God-fearing.*' Those people to whom this verse refers are idolaters, and God

commands the Prophet and the believers to remain faithful to their treaty with them as long as they kept their part and fulfilled their obligations.

Numerous are the reports which confirm that when the Prophet sent ʿAli to declare the disavowal of treaties to people, he also commanded him to make it clear that "whoever had a treaty with the Prophet, that treaty continued until its specified expiration date." This provides the clearest support of our view. God did not order the Prophet to terminate a treaty with any group of people who remained faithful to it. He only put on four-month notice those who had violated their treaties and those whose treaties had no specified term. The treaties which ran for a specific term and were observed properly by the other side were to remain in force until their term was over. The Prophet sent his Companions to announce this during the pilgrimage, for this would ensure the announcement was well publicized.[10]

In another comment on the various reports concerning treaties, al-Tabari says:

The four-month notice was made to those whom we have mentioned. As for those whose treaties specified a term of expiry, God did not allow the Prophet and the believers to terminate such treaty in any way. Hence, the Prophet fulfilled God's order and honoured his commitments under these treaties to their final dates. This is clearly stated in God's revelations, and confirmed by many reports attributed to the Prophet.[11]

If we discard the reports which are doubtful and overlook those which might have been coloured by the political differences between the Shiʾa and the Sunnis, we may say with confidence that the Prophet sent Abu Bakr as the leader of pilgrimage that year. The reason for that was that the Prophet did not like to perform the pilgrimage when the idolaters continued with their abominable practice of doing the *tawaf*, or the ritual walk around the Kaʿbah in the nude. After Abu Bakr had left for pilgrimage, the opening passage of this *surah*, Repentance, was revealed. The Prophet despatched ʿAli to join Abu Bakr and make the declaration. He did this outlining all its final provisions at the gathering which ensured that all people in Arabia would be aware of them. Among these provisions was the one which made it clear that no idolater would be allowed in Mecca to do the *tawaf* or the pilgrimage.

Al-Tirmidhi relates a report which quotes ʿAli as saying: "God's Messenger sent me after the revelation of the *surah* Repentance to announce four points: no one may do the *tawaf* naked, and no idolater may come near the Sacred Mosque after that year, and whoever had a treaty with God's Messenger, their treaty would be observed until it had expired, and that no one may enter heaven except one who submits totally to God." This report is the most authentic in this connection.

The principles of international relations

"Disavowal by God and His Messenger {is hereby announced} to those of the idolaters with whom you have made a treaty." (Verse 1) This is a general declaration, carrying a sharp rhythm, which outlines the basic principles that governed relations between the Muslims and the idolaters at the time, throughout the Arabian Peninsula. The treaties to which it refers were those that the Prophet had concluded with the idolaters in Arabia. The disavowal of these treaties by God and His Messenger defines the attitude of every Muslim. It generates a very strong impression on Muslim minds to leave no room whatsoever for hesitation or second thought.

This general statement is followed by qualifications and explanations: "*{Announce to them:} You may go freely in the land for four months, but you must realize that you can never escape God's judgement, and that God shall bring disgrace upon the unbelievers.*" (Verse 2) This statement clarifies the terms now given to the unbelievers: they are given a period of four months during which they can move about freely to carry out business transactions, fulfil their commitments and modify their situations in peace. Those were four months when they would be sure that their treaties would be scrupulously honoured. That included even those idolaters who were quick to violate their treaties, when they felt that the Prophet and his followers would never return from their expedition to Tabuk, but would instead be taken captive by the Byzantines. That was also the eventuality expected by the hypocrites in Medina.

It is pertinent to ask here: when was this notice outlining this period of truce and security given? It followed a long period of treaty violations by the unbelievers, whenever they felt that they could get away with it and remain immune from punishment. It came after a long series of events which showed clearly that the idolaters would continue to fight the Muslims until they had turned them away from their faith, if they could. At what period in history was it announced? It was at a time when humanity was governed by the law of the jungle. What dictated relations between communities was merely the ability to invade others: no notice was given, no hint was dropped, no commitment was considered binding. Once the opportunity was there, it was taken mercilessly.

Islam maintains the same position it adopted at the outset, when it was first revealed. Its constitution is outlined by God and its principles and foundations are not meant to be influenced or modified by the passage of time. Time allows human beings to develop and improve their conditions within the framework of Islamic principles. Islam deals with changing human conditions using appropriate methods.

With this four-month notice period, the idolaters are reminded of God's will which in turn sends fear into their hearts. They are meant to open their eyes to the fact that they can never escape God's judgement. They cannot seek refuge against what God has determined for them, which was certain disgrace and humiliation: "*You must realize that you can never escape God's judgement, and that God shall bring disgrace upon the unbelievers.*" (Verse 2) How could they escape God's judgement and what refuge could they seek when they, and the whole world, were in His grasp? He has predetermined to inflict misery and disgrace on the unbelievers. No power can ever stop God's will.

This is followed by specifying the time when this disavowal was to be announced to the unbelievers, so that they would be fully aware of the time limits it included: "*And a proclamation from God and His Messenger is hereby made to all mankind on this day of the greater pilgrimage: God is free from obligation to the idolaters, and so is His Messenger. If you repent, it shall be for your own good; and if you turn away, then know that you can never escape God's judgement. Give the unbelievers the news of grievous suffering.*" (Verse 3)

Reports vary on which is the day of the greater pilgrimage: the day of ʿArafat or the day of sacrifice? It is perhaps more accurate to say that it is the day of sacrifice. The Arabic term used in this passage for 'proclamation' signifies an assurance that those to whom the proclamation is made have received it. This properly took place during the pilgrimage, when the disavowal by God and His Messenger of all treaties with all idolaters was made. An exception was then added in the next verse which allowed certain treaties to run their term. This is most appropriate. First the general principle is outlined because it is the one which constitutes the permanent situation. Then the exception is made because it applied to specific cases that would end once the term specified had been reached.

With the termination of all treaties and the proclamation of absolute disavowal, the unbelievers are encouraged once again to seek and follow divine guidance and warned against the consequences of remaining in error: "*If you repent, it shall be for your own good; and if you turn away, then know that you can never escape God's judgement. Give the unbelievers the news of grievous suffering.*" (Verse 3)

This warning and encouragement to the unbelievers to mend their ways, coming as they do in this particular context of disavowal of treaties, are indicative of the Islamic approach. It is first and foremost an approach seeking to give guidance to people. The idolaters are given this four-month grace period not only because Islam does not like to take them by surprise but also because it does not want to inflict oil them unnecessary humiliation. These have always been the essence of power relations, except under Islam. The truce also gives the idolaters a chance to reflect and reconsider their options. Hence they are encouraged to choose divine guidance and turn back to God in submission. They are warned against turning away and shown that it will inevitably lead them to a position of grievous suffering in the hereafter, which compounds their humiliation in this life.

At the same time it provides reassurance to the Muslims which removes any lingering worries or fears of what may happen. The whole matter has been determined by God Himself. The eventual outcome has been sealed.

Honouring commitments

The exception is then made in the case of treaties specifying a term of validity. These were allowed to remain in force for the rest of their term: "*Except for those idolaters with whom you have made a treaty and who have honoured their obligations {under the treaty} in every detail, and have not aided anyone against you. To these fulfil your obligations until their treaties have run their term. God loves those who are righteous.*" (Verse 4)

Perhaps the most accurate report concerning the identity of those people who benefited by this exception is that they were a clan of Bakr, named the Khuzaymah ibn ʿAmir clan of the Bakr ibn Kinanah tribe. They were party to the Treaty of al-Hudaybiyah which the Prophet had concluded with the Quraysh and their allies. This clan did not take part in the attack made by the Bakr against the Khuzaʿah tribe. That aggression, in which the Bakr were aided by the Quraysh, violated the al-Hudaybiyah peace treaty. Thus, that treaty which was to last for ten years, was treacherously breached after only two years. This Khuzaymah clan continued to observe the terms of their agreement while other unbelievers did not. The Prophet is here instructed to honour his obligations under the treaty to those people for the rest of the term agreed.

This report which we endorse is related by Muhammad ibn ʿAbbad ibn Jaʿfar, who quotes al-Suddi as saying: "These were two clans of Kinanah known as Damrah and Mudlij." Mujahid, an authoritative early scholar says: "The tribes of Mudlij and Khuzaʿah had entered into treaties and these were the ones meant in the instruction: "*To these fulfil your obligations until their treaties have run their term. God loves those who are righteous.*" (Verse 4) It should be noted, however, that the Khuzaʿah tribe embraced Islam after the conquest of Mecca, but this statement of exception applied to the idolaters who did not accept Islam.

Our view is confirmed by a statement that follows: "*How can there be a treaty with God and His Messenger for the idolaters, unless it be those of them with whom you have made a treaty at the Sacred Mosque? So long as they are true to you, be true to them; for God loves those who are God-fearing.*" (Verse 7) These two clans from Kinanah were among those who were party to the peace treaty at al-Hudaybiyah. They did not violate their treaty and were true to their obligations under it, aiding no party against the Muslims. It is to these, then, that the exception applies, as confirmed by early scholars and commentators on the Qur'an, and by Shaikh Muhammad Rashid Rida.

Muhammad 'Izzat Darwazah, however, expresses his opinion that the phrase, '*with whom you have made a treaty at the Sacred Mosque,*' refers to a group of people other than those mentioned in the first exception. This is in line with his view which permits the negotiating and concluding of permanent treaties with idolaters. Relying on the instruction, "*so long as they are true to you, be true to them,*" he concludes that Islam does not object to the negotiation of treaties with unbelievers. This view seems extremely odd and does not fit with the nature of the Islamic method of operation and general attitudes.

Islam has honoured its obligations to those who were true to theirs. It did not give them notice of termination, as it did with all others. It allowed their treaties to run their term in recognition of their faithful observance of their obligations. This was the Islamic attitude, although Islam was in urgent need of eradicating all idolatry from the whole of Arabia, so that the Peninsula could become its safe base. The enemies of Islam in neighbouring countries were alerted to the danger to themselves that Islam represented. They began to make preparations for an eventual encounter with the Muslims, as we will explain in our discussion of the Tabuk Expedition. Indeed, the earlier Battle of Mu'tah served as a warning of the preparations the Byzantines had started for a battle with Islam. Moreover, they were in alliance with the Persians in Yemen, in southern Arabia.

Subsequent events, as mentioned by Ibn al-Qayyim, witnessed that all those in whose favour the exception was made and with whom treaties were to be observed embraced Islam before their treaties expired. Indeed the others who were keen to violate their treaties as well as the rest of those put on four-month notice also opted for acceptance of Islam. No one remained an idolater for the rest of the four-month notice.

As He determined the path of the Islamic message and the various steps it would take in practical matters, God was aware that it was time for this decisive step which represented a final attack at the roots of idolatry. Suitable preparations were made for such a decisive step, which took place in accordance with God's design for the progress of His message.

It is important to reflect on the comment which concludes the verse that requires the Muslims to remain true to their obligations: "*To these fulfil your obligations until their treaties have run their term. God loves those who are righteous.*" (Verse 4) It relates the fulfilment of obligations to righteousness and to God's love of the righteous. Thus, God makes the fulfilment of obligations to people an act of worship addressed to Him and an aspect of the righteousness He loves. This is the basis of Islamic ethics. Islam does not act on the basis of gain and interest, or on the basis of constantly changing traditions. All Islamic ethics are based on worshipping God and fearing Him, which is the essence of righteousness. A Muslim brings his behaviour in line with that which he knows to please God. His aim is to win God's pleasure and to ensure that He is not displeased with him. This is the essence of the strong hold Islamic ethics have on Muslims. These ethics also serve people's interests and work for their benefit. They establish a society in which friction and contradiction are reduced as much as possible. They also help human beings in their continuous march to a higher standard of humanity.

When the period of grace is over

Thus the opening verses of the *surah* make it clear that God and His Messenger would have no dealings whatsoever with the idolaters, whether or not they had a treaty with the Prophet. They were given a four-month period of grace in which they were safe. When this period was over, treaties would continue to be observed to the end of their terms, but only with those who were true to their obligations under those treaties, and did not collaborate with any enemy of the Muslims. Now the *surah* mentions what the Muslims were to do when the four-month grace period was over.

The Qur'anic instruction is very clear. A state of all-out war was then to be declared: "*When these months of grace are over, slay the idolaters wherever you find them, and take them captive, besiege them, and lie in wait for them at every conceivable place. Yet if they should repent, take to prayer and pay the* zakat, *let them go their way. For God is Much-forgiving, Merciful.*" (Verse 5)

The word which is used here to describe those four months in the Qur'anic text is '*hurum*' which is the one that describes the four months when fighting is not allowed except to repel aggression. These form two periods every year when people can go freely, secure from any danger of war. Because of the same usage scholars have disagreed in their interpretations of this statement here, on whether the four months meant the same ones observed annually, i.e. Dhu'l-Qaʿdah, Dhu'l-Hijjah, Muharram and Rajab. In that case, the remaining period of grace given after the declaration of the termination of treaties would only be the rest of Dhu'l-Hijjah and Muharram, i.e. 50 days. Or were these four months, when fighting was forbidden, to start on the day of sacrifice and to end on 10 Rabiʿ II? A third point of view suggests that the first interpretation applies in the case of those who had violated their treaties and the second applies to those who did not lave any treaty and those who had treaties with an unspecified duration.

The correct interpretation, in our view, is that the four months meant here are different from the four sacred months observed annually. The same description is given to both because fighting during them is forbidden. This new period of grace also applied to all, except in the case of those who had treaties lasting for a specified length of time, in which case such treaties were to be honoured in full. Since God has said to them: "*You may go freely in the land for four months,*" then the four months must start from the day when the announcement was made to them. This fits with the nature of this announcement.

God's instructions to the Muslims were clear: when the four months were over, they were to kill any idolater wherever he was found, or they were to take him captive, or besiege him if he was in a fortified place, or lie in wait for him so that he could not escape without punishment, except for those to whom obligations were to be observed for as long as their treaties remained in force. Indeed the idolaters were given enough notice, which meant that they were not taken by surprise. Nor did they fall victim to any treachery. Their treaties were terminated publicly and they were made fully aware of what was to be done with them.

Moreover, this was not meant as a campaign of vengeance or extermination, but rather as a warning which provided a motive for them to accept Islam. "*If they should repent, take to prayer and pay the* zakat, *let them go their way. For God is Much-Forgiving, Merciful.*" (Verse 5) For 22 years they had been listening to the message of Islam put to them in the clearest possible way. For 22 years they were, nevertheless, trying to suppress the message of Islam by persecution, open warfare and forging alliances to destroy the Islamic state. This was a long history that contrasted with the never failing tolerance of Islam, as demonstrated by God's Messenger and his Companions. Nevertheless, Islam was now opening its arms to them. Instructions are here issued to the Prophet and the Muslims, the very victims of persecution who were driven out of their homeland and suffered a war of aggression, to extend a hand of welcome to those idolaters should they turn to God in repentance. Such repentance should be genuine, confirmed by their observance of the main duties of Islam. That is because God never rejects anyone who turns to Him in sincere repentance, no matter how great his sins are: "*For God is Much-forgiving, Merciful.*" (Verse 5)

We do not here want to go into any of the arguments which are frequently found in books of commentary on the Qur'an or Islamic jurisprudence, i.e. *fiqh*, concerning the proviso mentioned in this verse: *"If they should repent, take to prayer and pay the* zakat, *let them go their way."* (Verse 5) These arguments discuss whether these are the essential conditions of being a Muslim, in the sense that a person who does not observe them is considered an unbeliever. They also discuss whether these are sufficient for the acceptance of anyone who declares repentance without going into the other basic duties of Islam. We do not feel this verse is concerned with any such argument. Rather, it simply tackles a real situation involving the idolaters in Arabia at the time. None of these would have declared their repentance, prayed regularly and paid the *zakat* without the full intention of submitting themselves to God and being Muslims in the full sense of the word. Hence the Qur'anic verse specifies the declaration of repentance, regular prayers and *zakat* payment as a mark of the acceptance of Islam in full with all its conditions and significance. The first of these is naturally the submission to God by declaring one's belief that there is no deity other than God and belief in the Prophet Muhammad's message by declaring that Muhammad is God's Messenger. This verse is not, then, about making any rulings on legal matters, but it outlines practical steps to deal with a particular situation where certain circumstances applied.

Asylum for the enemy

Yet despite the declaration of war against all the idolaters after the four months are over, Islam continues to demonstrate its grace as well as its serious and realistic approach. It does not seek to exterminate all idolaters. On the contrary, it also declares a campaign of guidance whenever that is possible. Individual idolaters who are not part of a hostile and belligerent community are guaranteed safety in the land of Islam. God instructs His Messenger to give them asylum so that they may listen to God's word and become aware of the nature of the Islamic message before they are given safe conduct to their own domiciles. All this, even though they are still idolaters: *"If any of the idolaters seeks asylum with you, grant him protection, so that he may hear the word of God, and then convey him to his place of safety. That is because the idolaters are people who lack knowledge."* (Verse 6)

This shows how Islam was keen to reach out to every heart with its guidance. No single case was to be taken lightly. Whoever appeals for protection shall be granted it. Anyone who seeks such asylum cannot at the same time try to join a hostile force seeking to undermine the Muslim community. Hence granting protection to such a person provides him with the opportunity to listen to the Qur'an and to get to know the true nature of the Islamic faith. When God's word is heard in such an atmosphere, hearts may well respond positively. Even, if they do not, the Muslims are still required to ensure the safety of anyone who appeals for their help until he is returned to a place where he feels secure.

This is one of the sublime heights to which Islam raises its community. Protection is provided for an idolater, an enemy who might have participated in persecution of the Muslims themselves. Now they are required to give him safe conduct until he has reached a place where he feels secure outside the Muslim state. This is a mark of the Islamic method of action. It is a method of guidance, and guidance remains its ultimate goal even when its efforts are concentrated on the protection of the land of Islam.

Yet some people claim that the purpose of Islamic *jihad* was to compel people to accept Islam. There are others who try to defend Islam against such a charge by claiming that *jihad* was merely a war of self defence within national borders. Both need to look at this great instruction given to the Prophet and the Muslim community: *"If any of the idolaters seeks asylum with you, grant him protection, so that he may hear the word of God, and then convey him to his place of safety. That is because the idolaters are people who lack knowledge."* (Verse 6)

This religion seeks to provide knowledge to those who lack such knowledge, and to give protection to whoever appeals for protection, even though they may belong to the enemy camp and who might have fought to suppress the Islamic message. It resorts to the use of force only to destroy physical forces that prevent people from listening to God's word and stop them from knowing what He has revealed. Such forces deprive them of the chance to follow God's guidance and force them into submission to beings other than God. When such physical forces have been destroyed and impediments have been removed, individuals are given protection, despite choosing to remain unbelievers. Islam only informs them of God's word without subjecting them to fear or pressure, and grants them protection and security, the fact that they continue to reject God's message notwithstanding.

There are countless regimes extant today where the dissenter has no sense of security for his life, property, honour or human rights. Yet people who see this taking place in front of their own eyes try to defend Islam against this false charge by distorting the image of the divine message. They try to portray Islam as nothing more than a passive message that confronts swords and guns with nothing more than words, whether in our own time or at any other time.

This is, then, an outline of the final rulings that determine the relations between the Muslim community and the remaining idolaters in Arabia. They mean an end to the state based on peace agreements with all idolaters, after four months in some cases and at the end of their specified terms in others. The eventual outcome of these rulings is that there will only be one of two situations: either repentance, mending of ways, attending to prayers and payment of *zakat*, which in essence means the acceptance of Islam, or fighting idolaters, taking them captive and chasing them out of their hiding places.

This termination of the state of peace based on treaties and agreements is followed by a rhetorical question stating that it is just not possible that idolaters should have such covenants with God and His Messenger. The very principle of having such agreements is rejected outright: *"How can there be a treaty with God and His Messenger for the idolaters?"* (Verse 7)

This outright denunciation, coming as it does in the verses that follow the opening ones, may be understood to abrogate the first rulings which allowed the continued observance of treaties with those who fulfilled their obligations under those rulings and did not provide any assistance to any group hostile to the Muslim community. In order to dispel any such misunderstanding, the ruling is restated once more: *"Unless it be those of them with whom you have made a treaty at the Sacred Mosque? So long as they are true to you, be true to them; far God loves those who are God-fearing."* (Verse 7)

This restatement adds a new provision. The first instruction required the Muslims to honour their obligations to those who had shown their true commitment to their peace agreements and fulfilled their own obligations under such agreements. Now the instruction to keep faith with them is qualified, making it clear that the Muslims were to honour their obligations to them for as long as they themselves continued to observe their treaties in full, as they did in the past. Here we note the careful phraseology of texts relating to dealings, transactions and relations with others. Implicit understanding is not sufficient. It is followed by a clear statement.

Considering the different aspects that prevailed in the Muslim community at the time and the way this decisive step was likely to be received by the Muslim community, the *surah* reminds the Muslims of the true nature of the idolaters, their feelings, intentions and attitudes towards the Muslims. We are told by God Himself that the idolaters will never respect an agreement or honour an obligation or observe a moral value or a tradition once they are sure they can get away with such treachery. Hence, they cannot be trusted to honour their obligations. The only way is for them to accept Islam and show their commitment to it.

No peace possible

"How can there be a treaty with God and His Messenger for the idolaters?" (Verse 7) The idolaters do not submit themselves truly to God, nor do they acknowledge His Messenger or the message he conveys to them. How could they, then, have a treaty with God and His Messenger? They do not simply deny a creature like themselves, or a constitution devised by human beings. Rather, they deny the One who has created them and continues to provide them with sustenance to preserve their lives. By so doing they place themselves in opposition to God and His Messenger. How is it conceivable, then, that they should have a treaty with them? The rhetorical question posed by the *surah* addresses the very principle of having such a treaty. It is not concerned with any particular application of the principle.

It may be said here that some of the idolaters had such treaties and God ordered that some of these treaties must be honoured. There were also treaties concluded after the establishment of the Muslim state in Medina, some of which were with the idolaters and some with the Jews. Moreover, the peace agreement of al-Hudaybiyah was signed in the sixth year of the Islamic calendar. Earlier *surahs* included verses that clearly permitted such treaties, although they also permitted the termination of such treaties in case of surmised or actual treachery. So if it is the very principle of having agreements that is condemned here, how was it possible that such treaties were permitted and concluded?

Such an argument does not stand when we understand the nature of the Islamic method of operation, which we discussed in the introductions to this *surah* and the preceding one, The Spoils of War. These treaties dealt with existing situations with adequate means. The final ruling, however, is that the idolaters should not have any treaty with God and His Messenger. These treaties were made under provisional rulings. Otherwise, the ultimate goal of the movement which aims to establish Islam is that there should not be any idolatry on the face of the earth. All submission must be to God alone. Islam has declared this ultimate goal from the very first day, deceiving no one. The prevailing circumstances in a certain period made it necessary to conclude a peace agreement with those who wanted peace so that it could deal with those hostile forces trying to suppress its message. Islam does not lose sight of its ultimate goal. It does not overlook the fact that the idolaters themselves looked at those agreements as only temporary. They were bound to launch new aggressions against the Muslim community. They would not leave the Muslims alone when they were aware of the aim of Islam. They would not remain at peace with the Muslim community for long when they had completed their preparations for a new confrontation. God said to the believers right at the beginning: *"They shall not cease to fight you until they force you to renounce your faith, if they can."* (2: 217) This continues to be their attitude at all times. The verse describes a permanent situation, not one that applies in certain circumstances.

Although the principle itself is denounced, God has permitted the honouring of treaties with those who continued to honour their obligations. He only made the proviso that this should be reciprocated, which means that treaties were to be honoured by the Muslims as long as the idolaters continued to honour them: *"Unless it be those of them with whom you have made a treaty at the Sacred Mosque? So long as they are true to you, be true to them; for God loves those who are God-fearing.*" (Verse 7)

Unlike what some contemporary commentators have understood, those people who had a treaty signed at the Sacred Mosque were the same group as they to whom reference was made earlier in the *surah*: "*Except for those idolaters with whom you have made a treaty and who have honoured their obligations (under the treaty) in every detail, and have not aided anyone against you. To these fulfil your obligations until their treaties have run their term. God loves those who are righteous.*" (Verse 4) The two verses refer to the same group. However, the first reference makes an exception in their case as opposed to all those whose treaties are terminated. They are mentioned again in verse 7, in connection with the denunciation of the principle of making peace agreements with idolaters. Their second mention is necessary to make it clear that there is no abrogation of the first ruling in their favour. The righteous and the God-fearing are mentioned on both occasions, using the same Arabic word for both, and highlighting the fact that God loves those who are righteous and God-fearing, to indicate that the subject matter is the same. The second statement completes the conditions stated earlier. In the first, their past attitude of honouring their obligations is mentioned, and in the second the condition of their continued observance of these obligations is made clear. The careful phraseology requires that both statements are taken together to grasp the meaning in full.

The principle of making peace with the idolaters is then denounced on historical and practical grounds, after it had been denounced on grounds of faith. Both sets of reasons are grouped together in the verses that follow: "*How (else could it be) when, should they prevail over you, they will respect neither agreement made with you, nor obligation of honour towards you? They try to please you with what they say, while at heart they remain adamantly hostile. Most of them are transgressors. They barter away God's revelations for a paltry price and debar others from His path. Evil indeed is what they do. They respect neither agreement nor obligation of honour with regard to any believer. Those indeed are the aggressors.*" (Verses 8–10)

How is it conceivable that the idolaters should have a covenant with God and His Messenger when they do not make any agreement with you unless they are unable to overcome you? Should they prevail over you, they would subject you to their wrath, observing no agreement, honouring no commitment and heeding no moral or ethical value. They would respect no pledge and allow no limit in the punishment they would inflict on you if only they could prevail against you in war. They would not even respect the values of their own society, risking any criticism they might incur for not abiding by these limits. No matter what agreements they may have with you, their blind hatred of you causes them to trespass all limits and violate all commitments, if only they can prevail over you. What prevents them from doing that now is not the sort of agreements they have with you. They are only prevented by the fact that they cannot achieve victory over you in battle. Now that you are too strong for them, they try to please you with what they say and by showing that they are true to their commitments. But in truth, their hearts are full of grudges against you. With such heart-burning animosity, they will always wish you ill. They have no desire to be in a relation of friendship with you and they harbour no good intention towards you.

No obligation honoured

"*Most of them are transgressors. They barter away God's revelations for a paltry price and debar others from His path. Evil indeed is what they do.*" (Verses 8–9) There is a basic reason for their treacherous attitude: that they are transgressors who have deviated widely from God's guidance. They have bartered away God's revelations for a paltry price in the shape of fleeting pleasures and temporary comforts. They fear that adopting Islam will deny them some or all of these interests or that it may involve some financial cost. Hence they do not merely refuse to accept Islam, but they also try to debar others from its path. This is, then, the result of the deal they made when they exchanged God's message for a paltry price. Hence, they turn away from God's path and debar others from following it. What they do is evil indeed, as God Himself states: "*Evil indeed is what they do.*" (Verse 9)

The grudge they harbour is not directed against you personally, nor are their evil actions levelled at you as individuals or a particular group. Their grudge is against every believer, and their evil deeds shall always be levelled against every Muslim. It is an animosity directed at the very quality of faith, or indeed against faith itself. This has always been the case with the enemies of faith, in all periods of history. Thus said the sorcerers to Pharaoh when he threatened them with torture, vengeance and a woeful doom: "*You want to take vengeance on us only because we have believed in the signs of our Lord when they were shown to us.*" (7: 126) The same was said by the Prophet, on God's instructions, to the people of earlier revelations who opposed him: "*Say: People of earlier revelations! Do you find fault with us for any reason other than we believe in God alone?*" (5: 59) In reference to the People of the Pit who in former times burned the believers with their women and children, God says: "*They took vengeance on them for no reason other than that they believed in God, the Almighty, the Praised One.*" (85: 8)

Faith is then the cause of all their hatred for the believers. Hence their ill-will and atrocities are directed against every believer: "*They respect neither agreement nor obligation of honour with regard to any believer. Those indeed are the aggressors.*" (Verse 10) It is in their nature that they are aggressors. Their aggression begins with their hatred of the divine faith and their rejection of its message. It is their aggression that leads them to stand in opposition to faith and adopt a hostile attitude to the believers, respecting no treaty or obligation of honour. Hence, should they prevail and feel that they can get away with what they want, they will resort to any atrocity without limit.

God then gives His instructions on how the believers should react to this state of affairs: "*Yet, if they repent, take to prayers and pay the* zakat, *they are your brethren in faith. Clear do We make Our revelations to people of knowledge. But if they break their pledges after having concluded a treaty with you, and revile your religion, then fight these archetypes of faithlessness who have no {respect for a} binding pledge, so teat they may desist.*" (Verses 11–12)

In view of such a long history as well as the nature of the inevitable battle between God's message, which seeks to free mankind from subjugation by other creatures in order that they submit to God alone, and *jahiliyyah* systems which seek to make some people tyrannize over others, God gives a very clear and decisive directive to the Muslims: "*Yet, if they repent, take to prayers and pay the* zakat, *they are your brethren in faith. Clear do We make Our revelations to people of knowledge. But if they break their pledges after having concluded a treaty with you, and revile your religion, then fight these archetypes of faithlessness who have no respect for a binding pledge, so that they may desist.*" (Verses 11–12)

The choice before them, then, is clear. They may accept what the Muslims have accepted and repent of whatever aggression and transgression they have committed. In this case, the Muslims will forgive them for whatever they might have committed against them in the past. A new relationship will then be established which makes these new Muslims brothers of the older Muslims and the past is forgiven and forgotten altogether: "*Clear do We make Our revelations to people of knowledge.*" (Verse 11) These rulings are best appreciated and acted upon by the people of knowledge who are the believers.

Having made pledges and concluded a treaty with the believers, the other choice they had was to violate their pledges and speak ill of the Islamic faith. In such a situation they would assume the leadership of disbelief and faithlessness. No treaty would be valid in their favour and no obligation to them need be respected. The Muslims are required then to fight them, for they may, perchance, reflect on their situation and see the truth for what it is. As we have already said, the strength of the Islamic camp and its success in *jihad* may influence people to recognize its truth. They would thus see that the truth is triumphant because of its being the truth and because it relies on God's power and support. They would recognize that the Prophet (peace be upon him) was only saying the truth when he told them that God, and His Messenger, are overpowering. That should lead them to repentance for their past misdeeds and a resolve to follow divine guidance, not by force and compulsion, but through conviction that often comes as a result of seeing the truth triumphant.

An attitude confirmed by history

It is now pertinent to ask: to what stages of history and to what communities do these statements apply? What sort of historical and social dimensions apply to them? Are they valid only in the case of Arabia at the time of revelation? Or do they extend to other times and places? These verses reflect a situation that prevailed at the time in Arabia between the Muslims and the camp of idolatry. There is no doubt that the rulings they outline deal with that situation; the idolaters they mention are those in Arabia at that particular time. All this is true; but how far are they applicable and in which situations? In order to answer these questions, we need to review the attitudes idolaters have adopted towards the believers throughout history.

As for the Arabian stage, the events that took place during the lifetime of the Prophet are sufficient to give us a clear answer. In our commentary on this *surah* alone we have enough information to describe the attitude of the idolaters towards this religion and its followers ever since its early days in Mecca up to the time of the revelation of these verses. It is true that the later and much longer-lasting conflict was between Islam on the one hand and the Jews and Christians on the other, rather than between Islam and idolatry. Nevertheless, the idolaters have always adopted the same attitude towards Muslims as described in these verses: *"How {else could it be} when, should they prevail over you, they will respect neither agreement made with you, nor obligation of honour towards you? They try to please you with what they say, while at heart they remain adamantly hostile. Most of them are transgressors. They barter away God's revelations for a paltry price and debar others from His path. Evil indeed is what they do. They respect neither agreement nor obligation of honour with regard to any believer. Those indeed are the aggressors."* (Verses 8–10) As for the people of earlier revelations, i.e. the Jews and Christians, and their attitude towards the Muslims, this will be discussed at length in Chapter 2 of this volume. We need to reflect now on the history of the idolaters with the Muslims.

If we consider that Islam, which is the faith based on the principle of submission to God alone, concluded, rather than started, with the message of the Prophet Muhammad, we are bound to recognize that the attitude of idolaters towards every one of God's Messengers and to divine messages reflects the attitude of idolatry towards faith. This should place matters in the right perspective. We see this attitude for what it is in reality, as truthfully described in these Qur'anic verses. It is an attitude that we recognize in all periods of history.

What did the idolaters do to those noble prophets and messengers: Noah, Hud, Salih, Abraham, Shu'ayb, Moses, Jesus, (peace be upon them all), each in his own time? And what did they do to the Prophet Muhammad and his followers? They certainly respected no agreement or obligation of honour, until they had been overcome. Again, what did the idolaters do to the Muslims in the second great campaign mounted against Islam, when the banner of idolatry was this time hoisted by the Tartars? Even today, fourteen centuries after the revelation of these verses, what is being done to the Muslims by the idolaters and the atheists everywhere? They simply do what the Qur'an states: *"They respect neither agreement nor obligation of honour with regard to any believer."* (Verse 10)

When the Tartars won victory over the Muslims in Baghdad, an unprecedented massacre took place. We will mention here only a brief account of what is recorded by the historian Ibn Kathir in his book, *al-Bidayah wa 'l-Nihayah*, as he describes the events of the year 656 H. (1258 CE):

> When the Tartars descended on the city of Baghdad, they killed whomever they met of men, women and children, young and old. Many people tried to hide in wells, rubbish dumps and sewers, where they stayed for several days. Some people locked themselves in inns and guesthouses, but the Tartars broke into every such house, and chased the people they found there to the roofs where they killed them. Gutters and alleys were overflowing with blood, and so were mosques and other places of worship. The only survivors were the Jews and the Christians in the city and those who sought refuge with them, and those who were given shelter in the house of Ibn al-'Alqami, the Shi'ite minister. A group of businessmen were also spared and given safety after they had paid large sums of money for the purpose. Baghdad, which used to be the most friendly and peaceful of cities, was totally in ruin, inhabited only by a small portion of its original population, and even these were living in fear, hunger and humiliation.
>
> Reports on the number of the Muslims killed in Baghdad in this battle vary, with some estimating the dead to be eight hundred thousands, while other reports suggest the dead numbered a million, and still others putting the estimate at two million people. We can only say what Muslims are recommended to say at the time of a calamity: *"To God we belong and to Him do we return . . . All power belongs to God, the Most High, the Almighty."*
>
> The Tartars entered Baghdad towards the end of the month of Muharram, and continued the killing of its population for forty days. The Caliph, Al-Musta'sim Billah, was killed on Wednesday, 14 Safar and his grave was erased. On the day of his death he was 46 years of age and 4 months. His reign lasted for 15 years, 8 months and a few days. His eldest son, Ahmad Abu al-'Abbas, was killed at the same time at the age of 25, while his middle son, 'Abd al-Rahman, who was 23, was killed a short while later. His youngest son, Mubarak, and his three sisters, Fatimah, Khadijah and Maryam, were taken prisoner.
>
> The most prominent scholar in Baghdad, Shaikh Yusuf ibn Shaikh Abu al-Faraj ibn al-Jawzi, who was hostile to the Minister, was killed together with his three sons, 'Abdullah, 'Abd al-Rahman and 'Abd al-Karim. All the nobility in the city were killed one by one. Prominent among these were Mujahid al-Din Aybak, and Shihab al-Din Sulayman Shah and many others. Anyone who belonged to the 'Abbas ruling family might be called out, and he would have to go with his women and children to al-Khallal graveyard, where he would be slaughtered like a sheep. The Tartars might choose some of his daughters or other women in his household to keep as prisoners. The most prominent and eldest scholar in Baghdad, 'Ali ibn al-Nayyar, who had educated the Caliph when he was young, was also killed as well as most imams and scholars in the city. Mosques were abandoned and no congregational or Friday prayer was held in any mosque for several months in Baghdad.
>
> After forty days, when the massacre was over, Baghdad was in total ruin, with only the odd person walking about. Dead bodies were placed in heaps in the streets. Rain

had changed their colour and their bodies had begun to rot. The smell in the city was most awful and there were outbreaks of several diseases which moved far and wide, reaching as far as Syria. People were then facing scarcity of necessary commodities, an unabating massacre, as well as epidemics. Those were indeed hard times.

When safety was announced for the survivors, those who were hiding in holes and graveyards came out. They looked so pale as though they were brought back from the dead. They were practically unrecognizable, to the extent that a father might not recognize his son, and brothers might not recognize each other. They were vulnerable to any disease and many of them soon died. . . .[12]

Hostility unabated

Such were the facts of history when the idolaters overpowered the Muslims. They respected no provision of any treaty, nor any obligation of honour. The question to be asked here is whether this was an isolated episode of ancient history, typical only of the Tartars at that particular period of time?

The answer is certainly a negative one. In modern history we find examples of similarly ghastly atrocities. What the Indian idolaters did at the time of the partition of India is by no means less hideous or appalling than what the Tartars of old did. Eight million Muslims decided to migrate to Pakistan when they were in fear of their lives as a result of the barbaric attacks launched against those Muslims who decided to stay in India. Only three million of them managed to reach the Pakistani borders. The other five million were killed on the way. They were attacked by well organized Hindu militia. These were well known to the Indian government, and indeed were controlled by some highly placed officials in the Indian government itself. Those five million Muslims were slaughtered like sheep. Their bodies were left along the roads after many of them were disfigured in a way which was no less horrendous than what the Tartars of old did in Baghdad.

The most horrible single incident was that involving the train which carried no less than 50,000 Muslim employees from different parts of India on their way to Pakistan. It was agreed at the time when the partition agreement was made that any government official who wanted to migrate to Pakistan would be allowed to do so. The train carried all those thousands of employees. It had to travel through a tunnel at the Khaybar Pass close to the borders, but when the train came out of the tunnel, it carried no living soul. Its cargo was nothing other than the dead bodies of all its passengers, having been torn to pieces. What happened was that those same Hindu militia stopped the train inside the tunnel and killed all its passengers. The train was allowed to proceed only when this most ghastly massacre was over. God certainly tells the truth as He says: "*Should they prevail over you, they will respect neither agreement made with you, nor obligation of honour towards you?*" (Verse 8) Such massacres continue to be committed in a variety of ways.

We then ask what have Communist Russia and China done to their Muslim populations? Within a quarter of a century they exterminated 26 million of them, with an average of one million a year. The policy of exterminating the Muslims is still going on. This is not to say anything about the horrible methods of torture that have become common practice in those countries. Only this year,[13] the Chinese sector of Muslim Turkmanistan witnessed events that outbid all the Tartars' atrocities. A leading figure of the Muslim community was placed in a hole specially dug for him in the middle of the road. Members of his community were forced to bring their stools, which were normally used by the state in the manufacture of fertilizers, and throw them on their leader standing in his hole. This continued for three days until the man slowly suffocated and died.

Communist Yugoslavia has also been guilty of similar atrocities against its Muslim population. One million Muslim people have been killed there since the Communist takeover in that country at the end of the Second World War. Muslim men and women were thrown into meat mincers to come out as a minced whole. This is only an example of the continuing massacres and torture being committed there.

The same sort of evil tactics are employed by all Communist and pagan countries, even today in the twentieth century. True indeed is God's statement: *"Should they prevail over you, they will respect neither agreement made with you, nor obligation of honour towards you."* (Verse 8) *"They respect neither agreement nor obligation of honour with regard to any believer. Those indeed are the aggressors."* (Verse 10)

God's description of the unbelievers' attitude towards the Muslims is not limited to a special situation that prevailed in Arabia at a particular period of history. Nor was what happened in Baghdad at the hands of the Tartars an isolated case. Indeed that statement describes a typical attitude that we meet everywhere, whenever a community of believers who submit themselves to God alone are confronted by idolaters or atheists who submit to beings other than God.

Hence, although these statements were meant to deal with a particular situation in the Arabian Peninsula, and outlined a framework for dealing with the idolaters in Arabia, they have far greater significance. They, in fact, address any similar situation, wherever it takes place. They are to be acted upon whenever their implementation is possible as was the case in Arabia. It is the Muslims' ability to put them into effect that counts, not the particular circumstances that led to their revelation.

Doubts dispelled

Will you not fight against people who have broken their solemn pledges and set out to drive out the Messenger, and who were the first to attack you? Do you fear them? It is God alone whom you should fear, if you are true believers. Fight them: God will punish them at your hands, and will bring disgrace upon them; and will grant you victory over them and will grant heart-felt satisfaction to those who are believers, removing all angry feelings from their hearts. God will turn in His mercy to whom He wills. God is All-knowing and Wise. Do you think that you will be left alone, unless God takes cognizance of those of you who strive hard for His cause and establish close association with none other than God, His Messenger and the believers? God is well aware of what you do. (Verses 13–16)

These verses come immediately after questions have been raised over the very principle of a treaty or a covenant being granted to the idolaters by God and His Messenger. In the same verses the idolaters were given the choice either to accept the faith based on submission to God alone or open warfare, except for the person who may seek refuge with the Muslims. Such a person is given shelter and made to listen to God's revelations before he is given safe conduct to his place of security. The reason for questioning the principle itself is that the idolaters will never respect any agreement or obligation of honour with regard to any believer when they prevail over the Muslims.

These verses are given here to answer any doubts felt within the Muslim community, at all levels, and the reluctance of some of the believers to take such drastic action by terminating existing treaties. It also responds to the desire felt on the part of some believers that the remaining idolaters in Arabia would eventually come round to recognize the truth of the Islamic message and accept it without the need to fight them, with all that a war involves of risk to life and property.

The Qur'an answers all these feelings and fears by reminding the Muslims of their own experiences of the idolaters' attitude to their treaties with the believers. It reminds them of the time when the idolaters tried to expel God's Messenger from Mecca before he left to settle in Medina. It also reminds them that it was the idolaters who were the aggressors when they first attacked the Muslims in Medina. It then arouses their sense of shame if they fear confronting the idolaters on the battlefield. If they are true believers, then they should fear God alone. It encourages them to fight the unbelievers, so that God may inflict punishment on them at their hands. This means that the believers would be the means to accomplish God's will when He determines to punish His enemies and bring about their humiliation, giving at the same time satisfaction to the believers who have suffered at their hands. These verses also answer the excuses that are made to justify a reluctance to fight those idolaters, including the hope that those unbelievers might eventually accept Islam without the need to fight them. The Muslims are told that true hope should be pinned on the victory of the Muslims in the war against them. When the idolaters are defeated by God's will, some of them may turn to God in repentance and accept Islam. Finally, these verses draw the attentions of the believers to the fact that it is only God's will that He tests believers with such duties so that they may prove themselves. Such laws which God has set in operation will continue to apply as long as human life on earth remains.

"Will you not fight against people who have broken their solemn pledges and set out to drive out the Messenger, and who were the first to attack you? Do you fear them? It is God alone whom you should fear, if you are true believers." (Verse 13) The whole history of the idolaters with the believers is one of violating solemn pledges and breaching agreements. The most recent example was the violation of the peace treaty concluded at al-Hudaybiyah. Acting on instructions from his Lord, the Prophet accepted in that agreement their conditions which were felt by some of his best Companions to be totally unfair to the Muslims. He fulfilled his obligations under that agreement as meticulously as possible. For their part, the idolaters did not respect their agreement, nor did they fulfil their obligations. Within two years, and at the first opportunity, they committed a flagrant breach of their obligations, extending active support to their allies who launched a treacherous attack against the Prophet's allies.

Moreover, it was the idolaters who tried to expel the Prophet from Mecca, and who were determined finally to kill him. This was before he migrated to Medina. It was in the Sacred Mosque, the Inviolable House of Worship, where even a murderer was sure to be unharmed. Anyone might meet there someone who had killed his father or brother and he would not lift a finger against him. In the case of Muhammad, God's Messenger who advocated submission to God alone and the following of His guidance, they did not respect even that obligation of honour. They did not even respect their traditions which they observed even with vengeance killers. They went as far as plotting to kill him in the Sacred Mosque itself.

It was also the idolaters who tried to fight the Muslims in Medina. Under Abu Jahl's leadership, they insisted on fighting the Muslims after their trade caravan had been able to escape. They went on the offensive in the Battles of Uhud and the Moat, and they mobilized other tribes against the believers in the Battle of Hunayn. All these encounters and events were still fresh in the memories of the believers. They all confirm the persistent attitude of the idolaters which is described by God in the Qur'an: *"They shall not cease to fight you until they force you to renounce your faith, if they can."* (2:217) This is clear in the nature of the relationship between the camp which worships all sorts of deities and the one which worships God alone.

After this reminder, God asks them: *"Do you fear them?"* (Verse 13) They should not refrain from fighting the idolaters, after this long history of treachery, unless they were afraid of them. But this question is followed by a statement which stirs new feelings of determination and courage: *"It is God alone whom you should fear, if you are true believers."* (Verse 13) A true believer fears no creature whatsoever, because he only fears God. So they should examine their true feelings, because if they are true believers they will fear no one other than God.

An order to fight

The feelings of those early Muslims were heightened when they were reminded of those events: how the idolaters plotted to assassinate the Prophet, and how they repeatedly violated their agreements with the Muslims and launched a treacherous attack against them, taking them by surprise whenever a chance presented itself. They also remembered how the idolaters, in their despotic insolence, were the first to attack them. With their feelings so heightened, they are encouraged to fight the idolaters and are promised victory over them: *"Fight them: God will punish them at your hands, and will bring disgrace upon them; and will grant you victory over them and will grant heart-felt satisfaction to those who are believers, removing all angry feelings from their hearts."* (Verses 14–15)

When you fight them, God will make you the means of the execution of His will, and He will bring about their punishment by your hands, causing them to be defeated and humiliated after they have arrogantly been demonstrating their power. With the victory He will grant you, God will make the believers who had been at the receiving end of the idolaters' repression and persecution happy. This happiness will come about as a result of the complete victory of the truth and the defeat of falsehood and its advocates.

But this is not all. There is more good news and more reward for certain people: *"God will turn in His mercy to whom He wills."* (Verse 15) When the Muslims achieve victory some of the idolaters may open their hearts to the truth. They may be able to recognize that this victory was achieved with the help of a power that is totally superior to all that human beings can muster. They may appreciate the effects faith brings about in the outlook and behaviour of the believers and feel that faith makes its followers better people. All this takes place in reality. Hence the believers receive the reward for their *jihad* and struggle against disbelief, and they are rewarded for enabling unbelievers to see the truth of faith. Islam will gain in strength as a result of those who join its ranks after the victory of the believers: *"God is All-knowing and Wise."* (Verse 15) He knows the outcome of events before they even take place, and in His wisdom, He is aware of the results and effects of forthcoming actions and moves.

The emergence of the power of Islam and its establishment as a force to be reckoned with will inevitably attract the hearts and minds of people who may prefer to turn away from Islam when it is weak or when its power and influence are not clearly demonstrated. The advocates of Islam will have a much easier task in trying to make the truth of Islam clear to people when they have the sort of power which causes their community to be held in awe by others. It must be remembered, however, that when God educated the small, persecuted Muslim community in Mecca, implanting the Qur'anic principles in their hearts, He promised them only one thing, which was heaven, and He made only one requirement of them, which was perseverance. When they demonstrated their perseverance and sought the prize of admittance into heaven and nothing else, God granted them victory and encouraged them to achieve it so that it would soothe their hearts and bring them full satisfaction. In such circumstances, victory is not granted to the Muslim community as individuals or as a community; it is granted to God's message. The Muslims are only the means for the execution of His will.

It was also necessary that the Muslims should launch their struggle against all the idolaters as one camp, and that all treaties with all the idolaters should be terminated at the same time, and that the Muslims would form a solid, united camp against all idolaters. Thus, those who had harboured different intentions and sought excuses of business, blood relations or other interests to justify their continued dealings with the idolaters should make their true position clear, free of all ambiguity. All such excuses had to be tested so that those who make of them a means to maintain close relations with the idolaters, in preference to their association with God, His Messenger and the believers should be known. If such excuses could be made in the past when relations between different camps had not crystallized, there was no room for any ambiguity now: *"Do you think that you will be left alone, unless God takes cognizance of those of you who strive hard for His cause and establish close association with none other than God, His Messenger and the believers? God is well aware of what you do."* (Verse 16)

As happens in all communities, there was a group among the Muslims that was skilled in manoeuvres, climbing over fences and making plausible excuses. Making use of the fluid situation when relations between the different camps had not crystallized, such people continued to make contacts with the enemy behind the backs of the Muslim community, seeking to serve only their own interests. Now that the situation was finally outlined, with each camp making its standpoint very clear, all such loopholes and back doors were finally and firmly closed.

It is certainly in the interest of the Muslim community and the interest of the Islamic faith to make the situation clear and to lay all intentions bare, so that those who strive hard for no reason other than earning God's pleasure are distinguished by their sincerity. Similarly those who have different intentions, and those who try to circumvent Islamic rules in order to pursue their own interests with the unbelievers are also known.

God has known such people all the time. Nothing is added to God's knowledge as a result of any event or action. *"God is well aware of what you do."* (Verse 16) He, however, holds people to account only for what appears of their reality through their own actions. It is His method to test people so that their true feelings and what they harbour in their innermost hearts are made to appear. The best way to do this is to test them with hardship.

Who may tend God's houses

> *It is not for the idolaters to visit or tend God's houses of worship; for they are self-confessed unbelievers. Vain shall be their actions and they shall abide in the fire. God's houses of worship may be tended only by those who believe in God and the Last Day, are constant in prayers, pay* zakat *(i.e. the obligatory charity) and fear none other than God. It is those who are likely to be rightly guided. Do you, perchance, consider that the provision of drinking water to pilgrims and tending the Sacred Mosque are equal to believing in God and the Last Day and striving for God's cause? These are not equal in God's sight. God does not provide guidance for people who are wrongdoers. Those who believe, and leave their homes and strive hard for God's cause with their property and their lives stand higher in rank with God. It is they who shall triumph. Their Lord gives them the happy news of bestowing on them His grace, and acceptance, and of the gardens of eternal bliss where they shall reside for ever. God's reward is great indeed.* (Verses 17–22)

With the declaration and disavowal made at the beginning of the *surah* concerning the termination of the treaties with the unbelievers, there can be no excuse for anyone who refuses to fight the idolaters. Moreover, there might have been some hesitation to forbid them entry to the Sacred Mosque in Mecca, which they used to enjoy in pre-Islamic days. The *surah* questions the claims of the idolaters to visit the Sacred Mosque, for that is an exclusive right of the believers who attend to their duties of worshipping God alone. That the idolaters used to visit the Mosque and provide drinking water to the pilgrims did not alter the situation in any way. These verses address those troubled Muslims who might not as yet have fully understood this basic Islamic principle.

"It is not for the idolaters to visit or tend God's houses of worship, for they are self-confessed unbelievers." (Verse 17) It is totally wrong that this should ever happen because it is contrary to the nature of things. God's houses of worship belong to Him alone, and only His name should be glorified in them. No other name should be invoked beside His name. How could it be acceptable then that those who associate partners with Him should ever tend these houses of worship when they are self-confessed unbelievers. *"Vain shall be their actions."* (Verse 17) Whatever they do is without value, including their tending of the Ka'bah, the Inviolable House of Worship. That is because none of their actions is based on the fundamental principle of God's oneness. As a result of their open and clear rejection of the truth of faith, *"they shall abide in the fire."* (Verse 17)

Worship is simply an expression of faith. If the faith is wrongly based, then the worship offered on its basis is wrong as well. Hence any act of worship, including the visiting and tending of the houses of worship, is of little benefit unless hearts are full of faith which translates itself into action that is totally dedicated to God alone. *"God's houses of worship may be tended only by those who believe in God and the Last Day, are constant in prayers, pay* zakat *(i.e. the obligatory charity) and fear none other than God."* (Verse 18) We note that the two conditions relating to belief and action are coupled with a third stipulating that those believers who do good deeds must fear none other than God. This is not an idle condition. It is important that a believer should be totally dedicated to God alone and should rid himself of all traces of idolatry in his feelings, beliefs and behaviour. To fear anyone beside God is a subtle aspect of polytheism. Hence the *surah* warns against it specifically so that believers may make sure that their faith is pure and that their actions are intended to earn God's pleasure. When they do that they deserve to tend houses of worship and to be graced with God's guidance: *"It is those who are likely to be rightly guided."* (Verse 18) First, concepts are formulated and beliefs are held, then action is undertaken on the basis of faith. God will then reward people with His guidance and with success and prosperity.

This is a criterion which God states clearly to the believers and unbelievers alike, because it determines who may tend God's houses and provides a basis for the evaluation of actions of worship and rituals. Those who tended the Ka'bah and provided drinking water for pilgrims in pre-Islamic days when their faith was not based on submission to God alone cannot be placed in the same position as those who have accepted the divine faith and striven hard for God's cause to help make His word supreme: *"Do you, perchance, consider that the provision of drinking water to pilgrims and tending the Sacred Mosque are equal to believing in God and the Last Day and striving for God's cause? These are not equal in God's sight."* (Verse 19) It is God's scale and His measure that are the important ones. Nothing else is of any value.

"God does not provide guidance for people who are wrongdoers." (Verse 19) The wrongdoers meant here are the idolaters who reject the true faith, even though they may tend and maintain the Ka'bah, the Sacred Mosque, and provide drinking water for pilgrims. The point here is concluded with a statement which speaks of the high position of those believers who strive hard to make God's word triumph. We are also told of the eternal bliss and great reward that await them: *"Those who believe, and leave their homes and strive for God's cause with their property and their lives stand higher in rank with God. It is they who shall triumph. Their Lord gives them the happy news of bestowing on them His grace, and acceptance,*

and of the gardens of eternal bliss where they shall reside for ever. God's reward is great indeed." (Verses 20–22)

It should be pointed out here that the comparative stated in this verse, *"stand higher in rank with God,"* does not imply two positions on the same scale, or that the others have a lesser rank with God. It indicates an absolute preference. We have already been told about the others, i.e. the idolaters, and that *"vain shall be their actions and they shall abide for ever in the fire."* (Verse 17) Hence the two situations cannot be compared.

The *surah* continues to stress the need to purge feelings and relations within the Muslim community of any influence other than that of faith. It calls on the believers to give no importance to ties of kinship or to other interests. It groups together all worldly pleasures as well as family and social ties in order to weigh them against loving God and His Messenger and striving for His cause. The choice is then left to Muslims to make: *"Believers, do not take your fathers and brothers for allies if they choose unbelief in preference to faith. Those of you who take them for allies are indeed wrongdoers. Say: 'If your fathers, your sons, your brothers, your spouses, your clan, and the property you have acquired, and the business in which you fear a decline, and the dwellings in which you take pleasure, are dearer to you than God and His Messenger and the struggle in His cause, then wait until God shall make manifest His will. God does not provide guidance to the evildoers.'"* (Verses 23–24)

The Islamic faith cannot accept any partners in its followers' hearts and minds. A person can be either totally dedicated to it or can leave it altogether. There is no requirement here to cut off all ties with one's children, family, clan or neighbourhood, nor to reject wealth or different types of pleasure and enjoyment. That is not the point meant here. What is required is total dedication and wholehearted love. This means in practical terms that the faith becomes the prime mover and the paramount motivation. When this is the case, people may have their pleasures and enjoyment because they will be able to sacrifice all these whenever such sacrifice is required by their faith.

The determining factor is whether faith has the overall control over man's attitudes and actions or not. Would the final decision in any situation be based on considerations of faith or on some other interests or worldly matters? When a Muslim is certain that he has given all his heart to his faith then he may enjoy his family life and have all the happiness of having a wife and children. He may maintain and strengthen his social ties as he wishes and he may have his business and fine dwelling. He may enjoy all the pleasures of this world, without being too extravagant or adopting an arrogant attitude. Indeed to enjoy these pleasures is encouraged as a means of showing gratitude to God for His bounty.

Attitudes shaped by feelings

"Believers, do not take your fathers and brothers for allies if they choose unbelief in preference to faith." (Verse 23) All ties of blood and family relations are severed if the tie of belief does not take its place in people's hearts. Family loyalty is nullified when loyalty based on faith is non-existent. The first bond is that which exists between man and God. It is the bond which unites all humanity. When this is severed, no relationships, ties or bonds may exist. *"Those of you who take them for allies are indeed wrongdoers."* (Verse 23) The term 'wrongdoers' here means the idolaters, because to maintain ties of loyalty and alliance with family and community when they prefer unbelief to faith is a form of idolatry which believers may not entertain.

The *surah* does not merely state the principle. It goes on to list all types of ties, ambitions and pleasures, grouping them all together and putting them in the scale against faith and its requirements. Thus we have in the first group fathers, children, brothers, spouses and clan (i.e. ties of blood and family), property and business (i.e. the natural desire to have money), and comfortable houses and dwellings (i.e. the pleasures of affluence). Against all this is placed love of God and His Messenger and striving for God's cause. It is important to realize that striving here implies a great deal of hardship and sacrifice. It may mean suffering oppression, going to war and sacrificing one's life altogether. Moreover, all this striving must be purged of any desire to be known or to be publicly appreciated or recognized. Once this striving aims at such recognition, it earns no reward from God.

"Say: 'If your fathers, your sons, your brothers, your spouses, your clan, and the property you have acquired, and the business in which you fear a decline, and the dwellings in which you take pleasure, are dearer to you than God and His Messenger and the struggle in His cause, then wait until God shall make manifest His will.'" (Verse 24) What is required here is certainly hard, and it is certainly of great importance. But thus are God's requirements. Otherwise, *"wait until God shall make manifest His will."* (Verse 24) The only alternative is to have the same fate as those who perpetrate evil: *"God does not provide guidance to the evildoers."* (Verse 24) This requirement is not obligatory merely on individuals. The whole Muslim community, and indeed the Muslim state, are also required to make the same choice. There is no consideration or bond which may have priority over those of faith and the struggle for God's cause.

God does not impose this obligation on the Muslim community unless He knows that its nature can cope with it. It is indeed an aspect of God's grace that He has given human nature this strong ability to cope with great demands when motivated by dedication to a noble ideal. Indeed He has given it the ability to feel a more sublime pleasure which is far superior to all the pleasures of this world. This is the pleasure or the ecstasy of having a tie with God Himself and the hope of winning His pleasure. It is also the pleasure of rising above human weaknesses, family and social pressures while looking forward to a bright horizon. If human weakness sometimes pulls us down, the bright horizon that looms large will give us a renewed desire to break loose of all worldly pressures to give faith its due importance.

Reminder of a great event

The *surah* follows this with a quick reminder of some of the events that the first Muslim generation experienced. The Muslims are reminded of the many battles when they were weak and poorly equipped but where God granted them victory. They are also reminded of the Battle of Hunayn when they were defeated despite their numerical strength, but then God granted them His support. On that day, the army which achieved the conquest of Mecca was joined by 2,000 of its people who were pardoned by the Prophet. On that day, there was a time when, for a few seconds, the Muslims overlooked their reliance on God to admire their strength and large following. The events of that day taught the Muslims the lesson that complete dedication to God's cause and strengthening their ties with Him are the best equipment for victory. These will never fail them, while wealth, friends and even closest relatives may do so.

> *God has granted you His support on many a battlefield, and also in the Battle of Hunayn, when you took pride in your numerical strength, but it availed you nothing. For all its vastness, the earth seemed too narrow for you, and you turned back in flight. God then bestowed from on high an air of inner peace on His Messenger and on the believers, and He sent down forces whom you could not see, and punished those who disbelieved. Such is the reward for the unbelievers. God will then turn in His mercy to whom He wills, for God is Much-forgiving, Merciful.* (Verses 25–27)

The victories they achieved in many battles were still fresh in their memories, requiring only a brief reference to bring them back in all clarity. The Battle of Hunayn took place shortly after the conquest of Mecca, in the eighth year of the Islamic calendar.

When the Prophet settled matters after Mecca had fallen to him, and its people accepted Islam and were pardoned by the Prophet, he was informed that the tribe of Hawazin were mobilizing forces to fight him, under the leadership of Malik ibn ʿAwf al-Nadri. They were joined by the whole Thaqif tribe as well as the tribes of Jusham and Saʿd ibn Bakr. Also allied with them were some forces of the clans of Hilal, ʿAmr ibn ʿAmir and ʿAwf ibn ʿAmir. They marched bringing with them their women and children as well as their cattle and property to make it a battle to the bitter end.

The Prophet marched at the head of the army which conquered Mecca, estimated at the time to be around 10,000 strong, composed mostly of the *Muhajirin* and the *Ansar*. He was joined by 2,000 of the pardoned people of Mecca. The two hosts met at a valley known as Hunayn. The battle started before the break of day, as the Muslim army was going down into the valley. The Hawazin forces had been lying in ambush. They took the Muslims by surprise and showered them with arrows and put up a determined fight. In no time, the Muslim soldiers were on the retreat, as God says here.

The Prophet remained steadfast, mounting his she-camel, with his uncle, al-ʿAbbas, holding its rein on the right and his cousin, Abu Sufyan ibn al-Harith holding it on the left, trying to slow her. He was calling out to his followers to come back to him, mentioning his name and saying: "You, God's servants, rally to me, for I am God's Messenger." He also said out loud: "I am the Prophet, no doubt. I am the son of ʿAbd al-Muttalib." A number of his Companions who might have been no more than 80 or 100, according to various reports, stood firm by him. Among these were Abu Bakr, ʿUmar, al-ʿAbbas and his son, al-Fadl, ʿAli, Abu Sufyan ibn al-Harith, Ayman and Usamah ibn Zayd. The Prophet then asked his uncle, al-ʿAbbas, who had a loud voice, to shout to the Muslims reminding them of the pledge they had given under the tree, which was a pledge to fight with him until death, and for which they earned God's pleasure. He did so, adding some variations to remind the Muslims of their position. As they heard him, they would respond verbally and rally to the Prophet in his position. If any of them found his camel unwilling to turn round in the confusion, he would take his armament and dismount to join the Prophet.

When a core group of them had rallied, the Prophet told them to fight with total dedication. Soon the idolaters were in flight, arid the Muslims were chasing them, killing some of them and taking others prisoner. By the time the rest of the Muslim army had regrouped and rallied, the prisoners were in chains in front of God's Messanger.[14]

Large forces avail nothing

Such was the battle in which the Muslims had for the first time an army which was 12,000 strong. They felt confident when they looked at their numbers. They overlooked the most essential cause of victory. So God allowed defeat to befall them at first so that they might remember. He then granted them victory at the hands of the small group which remained steadfast with the Prophet and defended him with all the bravery they could muster. The *surah* portrays some scenes of the battle in order to recall the feelings experienced by those who were on the battlefield: "*When you took pride in your numerical strength, but it availed you nothing. For all its vastness, the earth seemed too narrow for you, and you turned back in flight.*" (Verse 25)

This describes how the excessive confidence felt by a large force led to spiritual defeat causing the Muslims to feel such a heavy burden that made the vast earth seem too narrow. This then led to a physical defeat and those large forces were on the retreat. But what happened next?

"*God then bestowed from on high an air of inner peace on His Messenger and on the believers.*" (Verse 26) This 'inner peace' seems as if it were a garment which people wore to pacify their feelings and give them tranquillity. "*And He sent down forces whom you could not see.*" (Verse 26) We do not know the nature of these forces and whom they really were. No one other than God Himself knows what forces He may bring in. "*And He punished those who disbelieved. Such is the reward for the unbelievers.*" (Verse 26) The killing of some of their soldiers and taking others captive, and the defeat that befell them all were part of the punishment they received in this life, which is only a fitting reward for their denial of God and rejection of the faith. However, the door to repentance is always open to receive those who wish to mend their ways. "*God will then turn in His mercy to whom He wills, for God is Much-forgiving, Merciful.*" (Verse 27)

The *surah* refers to the Battle of Hunayn in order to portray the consequences of turning away from God and relying on any power other than His. The events of the battle, however, highlight the real forces on which every faith should rely. Numerical strength is of little importance. Power lies with the hard core who are totally dedicated to their faith and cannot be shaken. Sometimes the multitude may cause defeat, because some people may join in without really knowing the truth of the faith they profess. At times of hardship, courage deserts them and this may lead to confusion within the ranks of believers. Besides, large numbers may lead to a feeling of complacency which causes people to overlook the need to strengthen their ties with their Lord. The triumph of faith has always come about through the efforts of the hard core of firm believers who are ready to sacrifice all for their faith.

At this point the *surah* concludes its statement on the unbelievers who associate partners with God and gives its final verdict concerning them. This verdict remains valid for the rest of time: "*Believers, know that the idolaters are certainly impure. So, let them not come near to the Sacred Mosque after this year is ended. If you fear poverty, then in time God will enrich you with His own bounty, if He so wills. Truly, God is All-knowing, Wise.*" (Verse 28)

The *surah* emphasizes the abstract impurity of the idolaters to make it their essential quality. This shows them to be totally and completely impure. This statement gives the feeling that we should seek to purify ourselves when we have anything to do with them, although their impurity is abstract. Their bodies are not really impure. In its unique style, the Qur'an often resorts to magnification, giving abstract matters a physical shape and entity. "*The idolaters are certainly impure. So, let them not come near to the Sacred Mosque after this year is ended.*" (Verse 28) Here we have the strictest injunction prohibiting their presence in the Haram area. The order implies that they must not even come near it, because they are impure while the Haram is a source of purity.

The whole commercial season which the people of Mecca await every year, and their business which provides livelihood for most people and the two business trips in summer and winter which are so essential for the continued prosperity of the people of Mecca will all be jeopardized as a result of banning the idolaters from pilgrimage and declaring *jihad* against them all. This may be true, but when it comes to faith, God wants people's hearts to be totally dedicated to their faith. When they do this, they will not worry about their livelihood, because God ensures that everyone gets his or her share in the normal way and through recognized means: "*If you fear poverty, then in time God will enrich you with His own bounty, if He so wills*." (Verse 28) When God wills, He may replace certain causes with others, and He may close certain doors in order to open others. "*Truly, God is All-knowing, Wise*." (Verse 28) He manages all matters and conducts all affairs in accordance with His knowledge and wisdom.

In this *surah* the Qur'an is addressing the Muslim community as it was composed immediately after the conquest of Mecca, when standards of faith were not at the same level. We can see from reading the *surah* carefully that there were gaps in that community, and we can also see how the Qur'an has set about filling these gaps and the great effort made to educate the Muslim community.

The method of the Qur'an was to guide the footsteps of the Muslim community to bring it up to the high summit of total dedication to God and to the divine faith. Faith becomes the standard by which any relationship or source of pleasure in life is accepted or rejected. All this was accomplished through educating people in the real difference between God's method which makes all people serve God alone and the methods of *jahiliyyah* which enable some people to enslave others. The two are essentially different and they cannot be reconciled.

Without this proper understanding of the nature of this religion and its method, and also the nature of *jahiliyyah*, or the state of ignorance that Islam always comes up against, we cannot recognize the true value of Islamic rules and regulations that govern dealings and transactions between the Muslim community and other communities.

6 The earth's suffocating expanse

Overview

This final passage of the *surah* outlines a number of final rulings that govern the Muslim community's relations with other groups and communities. It starts with defining the relationship between a Muslim and his Lord, the nature of Islam and an outline of Islamic duties and methods of action.

- Embracing Islam is described as a deal in which the buyer is God while the believer is the seller. Since it is a sale to God, believers have no say over anything in their lives. Neither their property nor their person can be withheld from serving God's cause. The final product is that God's word should be supreme, and all submission is made to God alone. The price a believer receives in this deal is admittance into heaven, which is far superior in value to the commodity he offers. Therefore, he receives it as a favour from God: "*God has bought of the believers their lives and their property, promising them heaven in return: they fight for the cause of God, kill and be killed. This is a true promise which He has made binding on Himself in the Torah, the Gospel and the Qur'an. Who is more true to his promise than God? Rejoice, then, in the bargain you have made with Him. That is the supreme triumph.*" (Verse 111)

- The people who enter into this deal are a select few with distinctive qualities, some of which apply to them in their direct relationship with God, their feelings and the worship they offer. Their other qualities are concerned with the duties under this deal, which requires them to work for the establishment of the divine faith on earth, enjoin what is right and forbid what is wrong, and to see to it that God's bounds are respected: "*{It is a triumph for} those who turn to God in repentance, who worship and praise Him, who contemplate {God and His creation}, who bow down and prostrate themselves, who enjoin the doing of what is right and forbid the doing of what is wrong, and keep within the limits set out by God. Give you {Prophet} glad tidings to the believers.*" (Verse 112)

- The verses that follow in this passage show that relations between the believers who make this deal and all others, including their close relatives, are severed. The two groups move in opposite directions, towards opposite ends. Those who are party to this deal go to heaven, while the others go to hell. The two meet neither in this world nor in the next. Hence, blood relationships cannot establish a bond between the two: "*It is not for the Prophet and the believers to pray for the forgiveness of those who associate partners with God, even though they may be their close relatives, after it has become clear that they are destined for the blazing fire. Abraham prayed for the forgiveness of his father only because of a promise he had made to him. But when it became clear to him that he was God's enemy, he disowned him; Abraham was most tender-hearted, most clement.*" (Verses 113–114)

- A believer's loyalty must be purely to God. It is on the basis of this unified loyalty that all ties and bonds are established. Here we have a clear statement by God clarifying all issues and leaving no room for error. It is more than enough for the believers that they have God's protection and support. With these promised by the One who is the master of the universe, they need nothing from anyone else: "*Never will God let people go astray after He has given them guidance until He has made plain to them all that they should avoid. God has perfect knowledge of all things. To God belongs the kingdom of the heavens and the earth; He alone gives life and causes death. Besides God, you have none to protect or support you.*" (Verses 115–116)

- With the nature of the deal being such, reluctance to join an expedition serving God's cause is a very serious matter. However, God has pardoned those whom He knew to have good intentions and a firm resolve to do their duty after having once failed. Thus, He turned to them in mercy: "*God has assuredly turned in His mercy to the Prophet, the* Muhajirin *and the* Ansar, *who followed him in the hour of hardship, when the hearts of a group of them had almost faltered. Then again He turned to them in mercy; for He is compassionate towards them, merciful. And {so too} to the three who were left behind: when the earth, vast as it is, seemed to close in upon them, and their own souls had become too constricted, they realized that there was no refuge from God except by returning to Him. He then turned to them in mercy, so that they might repent. God is indeed the One who accepts repentance, the Merciful.*" (Verses 117–118)

- This is followed by a clear definition of the duties of the people of Medina and the Bedouins that live nearby on account of their pledges given to the Prophet. It should be remembered that those formed the solid base of the Muslim community that was the standard-bearer of Islam. Strong objections are raised to staying behind, coupled with a clear statement of the terms of the deal and the actions to be taken in fulfilment of those pledges: "*It does not behove the people of Medina and the bedouins who live around them to hold back from following God's Messenger, or to care for themselves more than for him; for, whenever they endure thirst, stress, or hunger for the sake of God, or take any step which would irritate the unbelievers, or inflict any loss on the enemy, a good deed is recorded in their favour. God does not suffer the reward of those who do good to be lost. And whenever they spend anything for the sake of God, be it little or much, or traverse a valley {in support of God's cause}, it is recorded for them, so that God will give them the best reward for what they do.*" (Verses 120–121)

- This encouragement to go forth on *jihad* for God's cause is coupled with a clarification that shows the limits of general mobilization, particularly after the land area of the Muslim state had become much bigger and the number of Muslims, increased manifold. It is now feasible that only some of them should go to fight the enemy and acquire a more profound knowledge of the faith. The rest should stay behind to look after the needs of the community, provide logistic support and discharge other duties. All these efforts converge at the end: "*It is not desirable that all the believers should go out to fight. From every section of them some should go forth, so that they may acquire a deeper knowledge of the faith and warn their people when they return to them, so that they may take heed.*" (Verse 122)

- The next verse defines the line the *jihad* movement should follow after the entire Arabian Peninsula has become the base of Islam. *Now jihad* should mean fighting the unbelievers all together, so that all oppression is ended and people submit only to God. The same applies to *jihad* against the people of earlier revelations until they pay the submission tax: "*Believers, fight those of the unbelievers who are near you, and let them find you tough; and know that God is with those who are God-fearing.*" (Verse 123)

- Now that a full clarification of the pledge and the responsibilities it lays down, and the line the Muslim community should follow is given, the *surah* provides two contrasting pictures showing the opposite attitudes of the believers and unbelievers towards the Qur'an as it is being revealed. Needless to say, the Qur'an opens up positive responses to faith within people's hearts, outlines practical duties, and censures the hypocrites for their paying no heed to reminders and tests: "*Whenever a surah is revealed, some of them say: 'Which of you has this strengthened in faith?' It certainly strengthens the believers in their faith, and so they rejoice. But as for those whose hearts are diseased, it only adds wickedness to their wickedness, and so they die unbelievers. Do they not see that they are tested once or twice every year? Yet they do not repent, and they do not take warning.*" (Verses 124–126)

- The final two verses of the *surah* describe the Prophet's concern and compassion for the believers. The Prophet himself is directed to place his trust totally in God and to pay little heed to those who reject God's guidance: "*Indeed there has come to you a Messenger from among yourselves: one who grieves much that you should suffer {in the life to come}; one who is full of concern for you; and who is tender and full of compassion towards the believers. Should they turn away, then say to them: 'God is enough for me! There is no deity other than Him. In Him have I placed my trust. He is the Lord of the Mighty Throne.'*" (Verses 128–129)

This brief outline of this final passage reflects the strong emphasis placed on *jihad*, the alignment of loyalties on the basis of faith, the advocacy of the Islamic faith throughout the world, in line with the terms of the pledge of loyalty required of believers. This pledge is shown here as a deal by which believers sell their lives and property in return for heaven. This means fighting to establish the divine order, with the emphasis on God's sovereignty over people and land. No acknowledgement of sovereignty to anyone else can be condoned.

Perhaps this quick outline of the passage shows the extent of defeatism that overwhelms people who try hard to explain the Qur'an in such a way that limits *jihad* to the narrow sense of defending the 'land of Islam'. Yet the verses here declare very clearly the need to fight unbelievers who live next to this land of Islam, without reference to any aggression they might have perpetrated. Indeed their basic aggression is the one they perpetrate against God as they submit themselves and other people to deities other than Him. It is this type of aggression that must be fought through *jihad* by all Muslims.

A very special contract

God has bought of the believers their lives and their property, promising them heaven in return: they fight for the cause of God, kill and be killed. This is a true promise which He has made binding on Himself in the Torah, the Gospel and the Qur'an. Who is more true to his promise than God? Rejoice, then, in the bargain you have made with Him. That is the supreme triumph. (Verse 111)

I have heard this verse recited and have read it myself countless times over a long period starting from when I first memorized the Qur'an and later when I used to recite and study it over a period of more than a quarter of a century. But when I began to reflect on it in order to write about it in this commentary, I began to understand it in a way that did not occur to me previously.

It is an inspiring verse, revealing the nature of the relationship between the believers and God, and the nature of the deal they make with God when they adopt Islam and which remains in force throughout their lives. Whoever makes this deal and remains true to it is the one who may truly be described as a believer reflecting the nature of faith. Otherwise his claim to be a believer remains short of proof.

The nature of this deal, or this contract of sale, as God graciously describes it, is that He has taken for Himself the souls and property of the believers, leaving them nothing of all that. They do not retain any part of that which they would feel too dear to sacrifice for His cause. They no longer have any choice whether to spend it in furthering His cause or not. It is indeed a deal that has been concluded and sealed. The buyer may do what He likes, as He pleases, with what He has bought. The seller has no option other than to fulfil the terms of the deal. He cannot argue or make any choices. He can only do what the deal specifies. The price given for this purchase is paradise, and the way to be followed by the sellers is that of *jihad*, fighting and sacrificing their lives, and the end result is either victory or martyrdom.

"*God has bought of the believers their lives and their property, promising them heaven in return: they fight for the cause of God, kill and be killed.*" (Verse 111) Whoever is party to this deal, signing the contract, paying the price agreed is a true believer. It is with the believers that God has made this deal of purchase. He has bestowed His grace on them by specifying a price. He is, after all, the One who gives life and property to all His creation, and He has also given human beings the ability to make a choice. He then bestowed further grace on human beings by making them able to make contracts, even with God Himself, and holding them to their contracts. He makes the honouring of their contract an evidence of their humanity, while going back on it is evidence of sinking back to the level of animals, and the worst of animals: "*Indeed, the worst of all creatures in God's sight are the ones who have denied the truth, and therefore will not believe; those with whom you have concluded a treaty, and then they break their treaty at every occasion, entertaining no sense of fearing God.*" (8: 55–56) He has also made the honouring or violation of such deals the criterion of reckoning and reward.

It is indeed an awesome deal, but it remains binding on every believer who is able to honour its terms. He is not to be exempt from it unless he goes back on his faith. Hence the sense of dread that I feel now as I am writing these words. "*God has bought of the believers their lives and their property, promising them heaven in return: they fight for the cause of God, kill and be killed.*" (Verse 111) My Lord, we certainly need Your help. The deal fills us with awe. Yet those who are claiming to be Muslims everywhere, from the far east to the far west are sitting idle, unwilling to strive hard in order to establish the fundamental truth of God's Lordship on earth, or to remove the tyranny which usurps the qualities of Lordship over human life on earth. They are unwilling to fight, kill and be killed for God's cause, and unwilling to undertake a struggle that does not involve fighting and sacrificing one's life.

These words touched the hearts of the early Muslims at the time of the Prophet and were transformed into a reality that they would experience in life. They were not mere words carrying certain abstract meanings for contemplation and reflection. They were meant for immediate implementation. This is how ʿAbdullah ibn Rawahah felt at the time of the second pledge given by the *Ansar* to the Prophet at ʿAqabah as reported by Muhammad ibn Kaʿb al-Qurazi and others: "ʿAbdullah ibn Rawahah asked God's Messenger to specify God's conditions and his own conditions. The Prophet said: 'As for God, the condition is that you worship Him alone, associating no partners with Him. And as for myself, the condition is that you protect me like you protect yourselves and your property.' He said: 'What do we get in return if we fulfil these terms?' The Prophet said: 'Paradise.' They all said: 'This is a profitable deal. We accept no going back and we will not go back on it ourselves.' "

That is how they felt about the whole contract: it was a profitable deal that allows no going back by either party. They treated it as a final deal concluded and sealed, with no opting out clause. The price, which is paradise, is paid, not deferred. Is it not a promise made by God Himself? Is He not the purchaser? Is He not the One who has made an old promise specifying the price in all His revelations: *"This is a true promise which He has made binding on Himself in the Torah, the Gospel and the Qur'an."* (Verse 111)

"Who is more true to his promise than God?" (Verse 111) Indeed a promise by God is certain to be honoured. No one fulfils his promises like He does.

Jihad, or striving for God's cause, is a deal made by every believer, ever since the first Messenger was sent to mankind with a religion setting out the principles of faith. It is a course of action that is necessary to put life on a proper footing. Without it human life will not follow its right course. It is as God says in the Qur'an: *"Had it not been for the fact that God repels one group of people by another, the earth would have been utterly corrupted."* (2: 251) And He also says: *"Had it not been for the fact that God repels one group of people by another, monasteries, temples, houses of worship and mosques, wherein God's name is often praised, would have been pulled down."* (22: 40)

A true promise and a profitable deal

The truth must certainly move along its well-known way, and it is inevitable that falsehood should try to obstruct its march. The true faith revealed by God must set forth to liberate all mankind from submission to other creatures and to return them to serve and submit to God alone. Tyranny is certain to try to stop it and foil its efforts. The aim of the faith is to reach all corners of the world and liberate all mankind. The truth must set out along its way, without hesitation in order to prevent falsehood from gaining access to it. As long as unbelief and falsehood continue to exist anywhere in the world, and as long as people continue to submit to beings other than God, thus causing man to be humiliated, then striving for God's cause must continue. The deal made by every believer must be fulfilled, or else he is not a believer. The Prophet is quoted as saying: "Whoever dies without having joined a campaign of *jihad*, or at least considered joining it, betrays an aspect of hypocrisy." [Related by Ahmad, Muslim, Abu Dawud and al-Nasa'i.]

"Rejoice, then, in the bargain you have made with Him. That is the supreme triumph." (Verse 111) Yes, people should rejoice at having dedicated their souls and their property for God's cause in return for admittance into heaven, as God Himself has promised. What does a believer miss out on when he honours his part of the deal? He certainly does not miss out on anything. He is certain to die anyway, and his wealth is certain to go, whether he spends it to serve God's cause or in any other way. Being in paradise is a great gain which a believer actually gets for nothing, since the price he offers would be gone anyway, whichever course of action he follows.

We need not mention the position of honour man attains when he conducts his life in line with what God requires of him. If he attains victory, then it is a victory achieved to make God's word supreme, to establish the faith God has revealed and to liberate God's servants from subjugation by human beings. If he attains martyrdom, then he is a martyr sacrificing his life for God's cause, making a testimony that he values his faith as more precious than his life. At every moment and at every step he feels himself to be stronger than the shackles and bonds of life, and that the burdens of this earthly life cannot stop his march. His faith triumphs over pain, and over life itself.

On its own this is a great victory, because it represents the fulfilment of man's humanity through his release from the burdens of his needs. When admittance to heaven is added as a reward, then the sale he has made calls for him to rejoice as it represents a great triumph indeed: *"Rejoice then in the bargain you have made with Him. That is the supreme triumph."* (Verse 111)

We need to pause here a little to reflect on God's statement which says: *"This is a true promise which He has made binding on Himself in the Torah, the Gospel and the Qur'an."* (Verse 111) The promise God has made in the Qur'an to those who strive for His cause is well known and is repeated several times. It leaves no room for any doubt about the fact that striving for God's cause is an essential part of the Islamic way of life as revealed by God Himself. Such striving is indeed the means to counter any human situation, at any place or time. It is to be remembered that the state of ignorance, or *jahiliyyah*, is found in a human grouping or community that resorts to physical force to protect itself. It is not a theoretical concept standing in opposition to another. It takes practical steps to resist the divine faith and to overcome any Islamic grouping that upholds it. It prevents people from listening to the general declaration Islam makes which emphasizes that God is the only Lord to whom all human beings should submit; the declaration that ensures the liberation of all mankind throughout the world from submission to creatures of any sort. It actually stops people from joining the liberated Islamic community. Hence Islam has no choice but to confront the physical power that protects *jahiliyyah* groupings, which, in turn, try their utmost to crush the Muslim revivalist groups and suppress their declaration announcing the liberation of mankind.

God's promise in the Torah and the Gospel to those who strive for His cause needs clarification. The Torah and the Gospel that are today in circulation cannot be described as the ones which God—limitless is He in His glory—revealed to His Messengers, Moses and Jesus (peace be upon them both). Even the Jews and the Christians do not claim that. They agree that the original versions of these Scriptures are not in existence. What they have today was written long after the revelation of these books, when all that was left was the little committed to memory after more than one generation. Much was added to that small memorized portion.

Nevertheless there remain in the Old Testament clear references to *jihad* and much encouragement to the Jews to fight their pagan enemies in order to ensure the triumph of their faith. Having said that, we should remember that distortion has crept into their concept of God and what striving for His cause means.

On the other hand, the Gospels that circulate among Christians today do not include any reference to *jihad*. We must, however, revise the concepts people have of the nature of Christianity, because these are taken from those Gospels which are not authentic, a fact conceded by Christian scholars. Besides, their lack of authenticity has been stated by God Himself in His last book, the Qur'an, which admits no falsehood whatsoever. And in the Qur'an God says clearly that His promise to grant heaven to those who strive for His cause, kill and be killed, was spelled out in the Torah, the Gospel and the Qur'an. This is, then, the true fact which no counter argument can disprove.

What this statement means is that *jihad*, or striving for God's cause, is a deal binding on everyone who believes in God, ever since God sent messengers to mankind to preach His faith. But striving for God's cause does not mean rushing to fight the enemy. It is the practical translation of a principle of faith which influences the feelings, attitudes, behaviour and worship of the believers. Those with whom God has made this deal reflect their faith by their true characteristics outlined in the next verse.

The characteristics of true believers

Those who turn to God in repentance, who worship and praise Him, who contemplate {God and His creation}, who bow down and prostrate themselves, who enjoin the doing of what is right and forbid the doing of what is wrong, and keep within the limits set out by God. Give you {Prophet} glad tidings to the believers. (Verse 112)

The first of these qualities is that they "turn to God in repentance." They appeal to Him for forgiveness, regretting any slip they may make and resolving to turn to Him and follow His guidance in their future days. They will not revert to sin. They will endeavour to do only good actions in order to make their repentance a reality. It is then a means of purging themselves of the effects of temptation and of mending their ways so that they can earn God's acceptance.

"Who worship and praise Him." (Verse 112) They submit and dedicate their worship to Him alone, acknowledging that He is God, the only Lord. This is a basic quality of theirs which is manifested by their worship, and also by their dedicating all their actions and statements to the pursuit of God's pleasure. Their worship, then, is meant as a practical confirmation of their belief in God's oneness. They praise God acknowledging His grace which He bestows on them. They praise Him continuously, in times of happiness and in times of adversity. When they are happy they praise God for His blessings, and when they go through difficult times they praise Him because they know that the difficulty is a test which they need to pass. They realize that God will show them His mercy when they prove their metal by going through the test with their faith unshaken. True praise is not that expressed only in times of ease and happiness. It is the praise genuinely expressed in times of adversity, recognizing that God, the Just and Merciful, would not put a believer through a trial unless it is eventually for his own good. A believer may not know that at the time, but God certainly knows it.

"Who contemplate {God and His creation.}" (Verse 112) The meaning of the Arabic term which is translated here in this fashion is not readily apparent. There are several interpretations of what it means. Some people suggest that it refers to those who leave their homes to support God's cause, while others suggest that it refers to those who strive hard for its triumph. Other scholars suggest that it refers to those who travel in pursuit of knowledge, and still others say that it refers to people who fast. We feel that the interpretation we have chosen is closer to its meaning. It is in reference to such a quality that God says elsewhere in the Qur'an: *"In the creation of the heavens and the earth, and in the succession of night and day, there are indeed signs for men endowed with insight, who remember God when they stand, sit and lie down, and reflect on the creation of the heavens and the earth: 'Our Lord, You have not created all this in vain. Limitless are You in Your glory. Guard us, then, against the torment of the fire.' "* (3: 190–191) The quality of contemplation and reflection is better suited to the context here. With repentance, worship and praising of God comes the quality of reflecting on God and His dominion which will inevitably lead to turning to Him, acknowledging His wisdom manifested in all His creation. The contemplation and reflection are not meant for their own sake or for gaining more knowledge of the world around us, but they should be made the basis on which human society is built.

"Who bow down and prostrate themselves." (Verse 112) They attend to their prayers which becomes an essential part of their life. Praying is thus made one of their distinctive characteristics.

"Who enjoin the doing of what is right and forbid the doing of what is wrong." (Verse 112) When a Muslim community that conducts its life in accordance with God's law is established, making clear that it submits to God and no one else, then the quality of enjoining the doing of what is right and forbidding what is wrong is seen to be fully operative within this community. It addresses any errors of implementation of, or deviation from, the code of living God has revealed. But when there is no Islamic community which gives supremacy to the implementation of God's law, then this quality of

enjoining what is right should be addressed totally to the most important thing, which is acceptance of God's oneness, submission to His authority and the establishment of a truly Islamic community.

Similarly, the forbidding of what is wrong should also address the greatest wrong, namely, submission to authorities other than God's through enforcing laws that are at variance with His law. Those who responded to the Prophet Muhammad (peace be upon him) and believed in his message, migrated, and strove to establish the Muslim state that implements God's law and a Muslim community that is governed on its basis. When this was achieved, they continued to enjoin what is right and forbid what is wrong, addressing matters that related to the details of worship or violation of the Islamic code of living. They never spent any time addressing these details before the establishment of the Islamic state and its Muslim community, because these details only arose as a later and practical development. The concept of doing what is right and forbidding what is wrong must be understood in the light of reality. No matter of detail, whether right or wrong, need be addressed before the basic and essential one is completed, as happened when the first Islamic community came into being.

"And keep within the limits set out by God." (Verse 112) That is to say, they make sure of the implementation of God's law in their own life and in the life of the community, and they resist anyone who tries to forestall it. Like the previous one, this quality can only work in a Muslim community governed by God's law in all its affairs. By definition, such a community acknowledges God's sovereignty as the only God, Lord and Legislator, and rejects any authority which seeks to implement laws that are not revealed by God. Efforts must concentrate first of all on the establishment of such a community, Only when it comes into being, will those who *"keep within the limits set out by God"* have their rightful place in it, as happened in the first Islamic community.

Such is the Islamic community with whom God has made this deal, and such are its distinctive qualities: repentance brings a human being back to God's way, stops him from committing sin and motivates him to do what is right; worship maintains a close relationship with God and sets the winning of His pleasure as people's aim; praising God in times of happiness and in adversity is a manifestation of total submission to Him alone and complete trust in His justice and wisdom; reflecting on God's attributes and the signs that indicate His wisdom and perfection of creation; enjoining what is right and forbidding what is wrong to expand people's role so as to ensure that the whole community is set on the right course; and keeping within the limits set out by God to ensure their implementation and to prevent any violation.

Such is the believing community which is bound by a deal with God which guarantees heaven in return for their lives and property which they sell to God. It thus implements a rule that has been in force since the start of the divine faith, and the revelation of God's first message to mankind. The deal means fighting for God's cause with the aim of making His word supreme, killing those who stand in opposition to God's message or falling as martyrs in the continuing battle between the truth and falsehood, Islam and *jahiliyyah*, God's law and tyranny, divine guidance and error.

Life is not all play, or all enjoyment and eating as animals eat. Nor is it cheap, humble safety and comfort. True living means doing what is necessary in support of the truth, striving for the cause of goodness, the achievement of victory for God's cause or sacrificing one's life for that, and then earning God's pleasure and admittance into heaven. This is the true life which the believers are called upon to seek: *"Believers, respond to the call of God and the Messenger when he calls you to that which will give you life."* (8: 24)

An example to follow

The believers whose lives and property God has bought in return for His promise to admit them to paradise are a unique community, because faith is their only bond which unites them and makes of them a well-knit community. This *surah* which outlines the relationship between the Muslim community and others who do not belong to it also makes a final judgement in respect of relationships not based on this bond, particularly after the rapid expansion of the Muslim community following the conquest of Mecca, when large numbers of people embraced Islam without being fundamentally affected by its way of life. They continued to attach great importance to blood relations. The verses that follow sever the ties that existed in the past between the believers who have made this deal and those who have not taken part in it, even though they may be related to them by blood. This is because they have two different courses to follow and two widely different ends in the hereafter.

> *It is not for the Prophet and the believers to pray for the forgiveness of those who associate partners with God, even though they may be their close relatives, after it has become clear that they are destined for the blazing fire. Abraham prayed for the forgiveness of his father only because of a promise he had made to him. But when it became clear to him that he was God's enemy, he disowned him; Abraham was most tender-hearted, most clement. Never will God let people go astray after He has given them guidance until He has made plain to them all that they should avoid. God has perfect knowledge of all things. To God belongs the kingdom of the heavens and the earth; He alone gives life and causes death. Besides God, you have none to protect or support you.* (Verses 113–116)

It appears that some Muslims used to pray to God to forgive their parents who were unbelievers, and to request the Prophet to pray for their forgiveness. These verses were then revealed to state that such prayer was evidence of their continued attachment to blood relations which was unacceptable from true believers. It was not right or up to them to do so. But the question arises here: how can the believers be certain that those relatives were destined for hell-fire? Most probably that ensues once those relatives die without having accepted the divine faith, when they can no longer believe.

Faith is the great bond that regulates all human bonds and relationships. If it is severed then all other bonds are uprooted. There can be no more value for bonds of blood or marriage relationships, or bonds of race and nationality. It is either that faith unites people and maintains their bonds, or there are no relationships when faith does not exist: "*Abraham prayed for the forgiveness of his father only because of a promise he had made to him. But when it became clear to him that he was God's enemy, he disowned him; Abraham was most tender-hearted, most clement.*" (Verse 114)

Abraham's example in this regard should not be followed, because he was only fulfilling a promise which he made to his father to pray for his forgiveness in the hope that he would follow God's guidance. At the time Abraham said to his father: "*Peace be on you. I shall pray to my Lord to forgive you; for He has always been very kind to me. But I shall withdraw from you all and from whatever you invoke instead of God, and I shall pray to my Lord alone. Perhaps, by my prayer to my Lord I shall not be unblest.*" (19: 47–48) When his father died an unbeliever and Abraham realized that he was an enemy of God, he disowned him and severed all relations with him.

"*Abraham was most tender-hearted, most clement.*" (Verse 114) He used to pray to God very often and with great sincerity. He was also clement and he would forgive those who treated him badly. His father ill-treated him but he was forbearing. Yet only when he realized that there was no hope that he would ever believe in God, did he give up on him.

It has been reported that when these verses were revealed those believers who were in the habit of praying for the forgiveness of their relatives feared that they might have gone far astray because their action was against God's law. The following verse was then revealed to reassure them that no punishment could be incurred prior to a clear definition of error: *"Never will God let people go astray after He has given them guidance until He has made plain to them all that they should avoid. God has perfect knowledge of all things."* (Verse 115)

God does not hold against people anything He has not made clear that they should avoid. He does not let them go astray because of certain actions unless these are of a type which He has clearly forbidden them in advance. Human knowledge is limited and it is God alone who has perfect knowledge of all things. God has made this religion easy to follow, explaining what should be done and what should be avoided with all clarity. He has left certain things without giving a clear verdict on them. This is done on purpose to make things easier for people. He has made it clear that we need not ask about those matters where a clear verdict has not been given, lest such questioning should lead to more restrictions. Hence no one may forbid what God has not clearly forbidden.

At the end of this passage, in an atmosphere which calls for abandoning blood ties and being ready to sacrifice one's life and property, the *surah* makes a clear statement that it is God alone who protects and supports the believers. He is the One who has sovereignty over the heavens and the earth and it is He who controls life and death: *"To God belongs the kingdom of the heavens and the earth; He alone gives life and causes death. Besides God, you have none to protect or support you."* (Verse 116) All property, all human beings and all creation, the heavens and the earth, life and death, support and protection are all in God's hands. To maintain a strong tie with Him is sufficient for anyone.

These categorical statements concerning blood relations indicate the hesitation that some people might have shown and their leaning at one time to such ties and at another to their bond of faith. It is fitting that this final definition is made in this *surah* which outlines the final shape of the relationship between the Muslim community and other communities. It was not permissible to pray to God to forgive those who died unbelievers. This is meant to purge the hearts of believers from any lingering bonds. The only tie to unite the advocates of Islam is that of faith. It is an aspect of their conceptual beliefs and also of their method of action. This is made abundantly clear in this *surah*.

Acceptance of repentance

With the nature of the deal between God and the believers being such, to refrain from joining a *jihad* campaign by people who are able to do so is a very serious matter indeed. Hence it was necessary to examine why some people were reluctant to join such an expedition. The passage we are looking at explains how much grace God bestows on the believers, overlooking their hesitation and their slips, serious as these may be. It also speaks of the three people whose cases were deferred for judgement.

> *God has assuredly turned in His mercy to the Prophet, the* Muhajirin *and the* Ansar, *who followed him in the hour of hardship, when the hearts of a group of them had almost faltered. Then again He turned to them in mercy; for He is compassionate towards them, merciful. And {so too} to the three who were left behind: when the earth, vast as it is, seemed to close in upon them, and their own souls had become too constricted, they realized that there was no refuge from*

God except by returning to Him. He then turned to them in mercy, so that they might repent. God is indeed the One who accepts repentance, the merciful. (Verses 117–118)

That God turned in His mercy to the Prophet should be understood with reference to the events of this expedition as a whole. It seems to be in line with what God said earlier to the Prophet: "*May God forgive you {Prophet}! Why did you grant them permission {to stay behind} before you had come to know who were speaking the truth and who were the liars?*" (Verse 43) That was when some of them who were really able to join the expedition came to him with fabricated excuses and he allowed them to stay behind. God pardoned him for his attitude which was based on his own discretion. He is told that it would have been better to wait until he had learnt who really had valid reasons for staying behind.

As for turning in mercy to the *Muhajirin* and the *Ansar*, the verse outlines its causes. They are the ones "*who followed him in the hour of hardship, when the hearts of a group of them had almost faltered.*" (Verse 117) Some of them were slow to join the Muslim army, but they joined as it marched, as will be given in detail. These were among the most sincere of believers. Others listened to the hypocrites as they tried to dissuade the believers from going out to confront the Byzantines whom they described as fearsome fighters. Those, however, joined the army after their initial reluctance.

We will review briefly some of the events of this expedition in order to capture a sense of the prevailing atmosphere which God describes as 'the hour of hardship.' This may give us an insight into the feelings and actions that shaped the different attitudes.[1]

An earlier verse in the *surah* gives the following instructions: "*Fight against those who – despite having been given Scriptures – do not truly believe in God and the Last Day, and do not treat as forbidden that which God and His Messenger have forbidden, and do not follow the religion of truth, till they {agree to} pay the submission tax with a willing hand, after they have been humbled.*" (Verse 29) Upon receiving this revelation the Prophet instructed his Companions to get ready to fight the Byzantines. [It should be noted here that the first engagement against the Byzantines was at the Battle of Mu'tah which preceded the revelation of these verses. Hence, these orders simply outline a permanent course of action which the Muslim community should always follow.]

This call to arms occurred at the height of the summer, when resources were scarce, the weather was extremely hot, and when fruits had ripened. At such a time people would prefer to stay at home and do very little work; travelling in the desert was almost unbearable. It was the Prophet's habit, whenever he intended to attack any people that he would not specify the particular place he was going to, or the particular people he wanted to attack, hoping to take his enemies by surprise. This time, the difficulties presented by the journey made him inform the Muslims exactly where they were going, so that they could prepare themselves as best as they could for the difficult task ahead.

Some hypocrites went to the Prophet seeking leave to stay behind, giving the absurd excuse that they might be infatuated with Byzantine girls when they saw them, and he let them stay. It is in connection with this that God remonstrated with the Prophet, but this remonstration opens with the statement that God has pardoned the Prophet and turned to him in mercy: "*May God forgive you {Prophet}! Why did you grant them permission {to stay behind} before you had come to know who were speaking the truth and who were the liars?*" (Verse 43) In their reluctance to join the campaign *of jihad*, and the doubts they raised about the truth of the Islamic message and their hostility to the Prophet, the hypocrites advised one another not to join the army because the hot summer was not a suitable time for war. Commenting on this, the following verse was revealed: "*They said {to one another}: 'Do not go to war in this heat.' Say: 'The fire of hell is far hotter.' Would that they understood. They shall laugh but a little, and they will weep much, in return for what they have earned."* (Verses 81–82)

The Prophet was informed that a group of hypocrites were meeting in the house of a Jew called Suwaylim to discourage people and dissuade them from joining the expedition. He sent Talhah ibn 'Ubaydullah with a group of his Companions giving them instructions to burn the house down. Talhah carried out the Prophet's instructions. One of the people inside called al-Da111hak tried to run away from the back of the house and he fell and broke his leg, but later repented. The others also jumped to safety.

The Prophet then gave orders to his Companions to speed up their preparations and urged those with money and property to spend generously, and to provide camels and horses for those who had none. Many of those who were rich came forward with generous donations. The one who gave the greatest donation was 'Uthman ibn 'Affan. One report suggests that 'Uthman's donation was 1,000 dinars (which was the gold currency). The Prophet said: "My Lord, be pleased with 'Uthman, for I am pleased with him."

Another report transmitted by Ahmad ibn Hanbal says: "When the Prophet made his speech encouraging his Companions to donate generously, 'Uthman said: 'My commitment is to provide 100 camels with all their equipment.' As the Prophet descended one step from the pulpit, 'Uthman made a further equal commitment. The Prophet came one step further down and 'Uthman increased his commitment to 300 camels, fully equipped. The Prophet was so deeply touched by the donation made by 'Uthman that he waved with his hand to express his admiration. He also said: ''Uthman will not suffer in consequence of anything he does in future.'

Other reports mention the donations given by various people, each according to his means. 'Abd al-Rahman ibn 'Awf brought a donation of 4,000 dirhams (the silver currency at the time). He said to the Prophet: "All I own is 8,000 dirhams. I brought one half and kept the other half." The Prophet said to him: "May God bless you for what you have kept and what you have donated." Abu 'Aqil brought a quantity of dates and said: "Messenger of God, I have only some dates and I brought half of what I have, retaining the other for my family." The hypocrites spoke ill of him, saying he only did this to remind the Prophet of his poverty. They further asked: would God and His Messenger be in need of this amount of dates?

A turn of mercy

Some Muslims were so poor that they could not find transport for themselves to join the army. There were seven people, mostly from the *Ansar*, who could obtain neither a camel nor a horse. They, therefore, went to the Prophet to explain their situation and requested him to provide them with some transport. The Prophet explained that he had nothing available. All the horses and camels were allotted to other people and he had none left. The seven men went back to their homes with tears in their eyes. They were made entirely helpless by their poverty.

Two of the seven men, 'Abd al-Rahman ibn Ka'b and 'Abdullah ibn Mughaffil, were still in tears when they met a man called Yamin ibn 'Umayr. He asked them why they were crying and they told him that they were prevented from joining the army by their poverty and the fact that the Prophet did not have any spare camels to give them. He offered them a camel of his own to share between them and also gave them some dates to eat on their journey. Thus they were able to join.

Another report speaks of another man among the seven, 'Ilbah ibn Zayd. That night, knowing he could not join the army, he prayed for a long while. He reflected on the situation and tears sprang to his eyes. Then he addressed God with this emotional prayer: "My Lord, You have commanded us to go on *jihad* and You have encouraged us not to abandon this duty. Yet You have not given me what I need in order to be able to go on this campaign. Your Messenger cannot give me any means of transport. I, therefore, give in charity to every Muslim any right which I hold against him for a wrong he has done to me, whether in matters of money or self or honour."

The following morning, the man joined the dawn prayers as he always did. The Prophet asked, "Where is the man who was charitable last night?" Nobody replied. The Prophet repeated the question and said, "Let this man stand up." ʿIlbah stood up and explained to the Prophet what he had done. The Prophet said, "By Him Who holds my soul in His hand, this has been credited to you as *zakat* accepted by God."

The Prophet then ordered the Muslims who joined him to march. There were about 30,000 in the army, made up of the people of Medina and the bedouin tribes in the surrounding area. A few individuals among the Muslims did not join the army, although they did not entertain any doubt about the truth of Islam, or their duty to be in the army. Among these were Kaʿb ibn Malik, Murarah ibn al-Rabiʿ and Hilal ibn Umayyah, [these were the three whose cases will be discussed in detail shortly] and also Abu Khaythamah and ʿUmayr ibn Wahb al-Jumahi. The Prophet ordered his forces to encamp at a place called Thaniyat al-Wadaʿ, just outside Medina, while ʿAbdullah ibn Ubayy, known as the chief of the hypocrites, encamped with his followers separately a short distance apart. One report by Ibn Ishaq suggests that his group was claimed to be of similar strength, but this was highly unlikely. Other reports confirm that those who actually stayed behind were less than one hundred. When the Prophet moved on, ʿAbdullah ibn Ubayy stayed behind along with other hypocrites.

The Prophet and his army then started their march. The going was very tough indeed. It was only natural that among the 30,000 who were in the army, there would be some who might not be able to keep pace with the rest. Every time a man fell behind, his case was reported to the Prophet. Every time the Prophet gave the same answer: "Leave him alone. If he is good, God will see to it that he will catch up with you. If he is otherwise, good riddance."

At one stage of the journey, a man of no lesser standing in the Muslim community than Abu Dharr, one of the *Muhajirin* and also among the earliest of them to accept Islam, was falling behind. His camel was no longer able to keep pace with the army. Some people went to the Prophet to report the fact, but he gave them the same answer: "Leave him alone. If he is good, God will see to it that he will catch up with you. If he is otherwise, good riddance."

Abu Dharr gave his camel every chance to pick up strength. He then realized that it was useless: the camel was absolutely exhausted. Feeling that there was no alternative, Abu Dharr dismounted, took his belongings off his camel and walked at a fast pace, hoping to catch up with the Prophet.

Soon, the Prophet stopped for a short while to allow the army a little rest. This stop gave Abu Dharr the chance to catch up. Someone standing near the Prophet pointed to the direction from which Abu Dharr was coming and said, "Messenger of God, there is a man walking alone in our trail." The Prophet said, "Let it be Abu Dharr." When the man drew nearer, they said: "Messenger of God, it is indeed Abu Dharr." The Prophet said, "May God have mercy on Abu Dharr: he walks alone, dies alone and will be resurrected alone."

One of the few believers who stayed behind in Medina was Abu Khaythamah. A few days after the army had moved out, he went back home to rest on a day when it was extremely hot. He had two wives. At home, there were all the comforts one needed on such a hot day. Each of his two wives had prepared her sitting place in a well-shaded area of the yard. Each had prepared food and cold water for her husband. When he came in, he looked at his two wives and what they had prepared for him. He reflected a little, then he said to his wives: "God's Messenger (peace be upon him) is suffering the burning sun and the stormy wind, while I, Abu Khaythamah, enjoy the cool shade and delicious food in the company of two pretty women in my own home? This is unfair. By God, I will not enter either of your two places until I have caught up with God's Messenger. Prepare some food for me to keep me going on my journey." When the food was prepared, he mounted his camel and went as fast as he could. He did not manage to catch up with the army until it arrived at Tabuk.

On his way, Abu Khaythamah met ʿUmayr ibn Wahb al-Jumahi, who was also travelling fast to catch up with the army. Apparently, ʿUmayr had some good reason for his delay. The two travelled together until they were close to Tabuk. Abu Khaythamah then said to ʿUmayr: "I have perpetrated something bad. It may be advisable for you to slow down a little until I catch up with the Prophet (peace be upon him)."

ʿUmayr slowed down and Abu Khaythamah continued to travel at speed. When his figure was visible to the army encamping at Tabuk, some of the Prophet's Companions drew his attention to the person travelling alone. The Prophet said: "Let it be Abu Khaythamah." When the man drew nearer, they said: "Messenger of God, it is indeed Abu Khaythamah."

When he reached the place where the Prophet was, he dismounted and greeted the Prophet. The Prophet spoke to him a phrase which implied warning. Interpreters suggest that it meant that he, Abu Khaythamah, had brought himself very close to destruction. Abu Khaythamah related his story, and the Prophet prayed to God to forgive him.

The hour of difficulty

One factor that contributed to the difficulty facing the Muslims was the attitude of the hypocrites who not only tried to seek excuses for themselves to stay behind, but also tried to show the decision to fight the Byzantines as lacking careful planning and consideration.

A report mentions that a group of hypocrites, including Wadiʿah ibn Thabit, as well as a man called Makhshi ibn Himyar, an ally of the tribe of Salamah, were with the Muslim army when the Prophet headed for Tabuk. Some of them tried to frighten the believers and spread doubt in their ranks. They said: "Do you think fighting the Byzantines the same as internal warfare between Arabian tribes? We can even now see how you will all be taken captive tomorrow and will be put in chains." Makhshi said: "I wish we could escape with only 100 lashes each, without having verses of the Qurʾan revealed to expose us as a result of what you have said."

The Prophet was informed of this and he said to ʿAmmar ibn Yasir: "Rush to those people for they are burnt. Ask them about what they have said and if they deny it, tell them that they have said these very words." ʿAmmar went to them and told them exactly what the Prophet said. They came to the Prophet to apologize. Wadiʿah ibn Thabit said to the Prophet as he mounted his camel, and Wadiʿah holding its reins: "Messenger of God, we were only talking idly and jesting." Makhshi said: "Messenger of God, my name and my father's name prevented me from leaving these people." (This is a reference to the fact that he was only an ally occupying a weak position.) He was the one among those to whom this verse refers who was pardoned. He changed his name to ʿAbd al-Rahman and appealed to God to grant him martyrdom where his body would not be found. He was killed when he was fighting with the Muslim army at Yamamah against the apostates. His body was lost without trace.

Another report suggests that when the Prophet and the Muslim army were on the way back from Tabuk, a group of hypocrites tried to assassinate him by throwing him from the top of a high peak along the road. He was informed of their design. He ordered the bulk of the army to travel through the valley, while he went up the mountain trail, instructing two of his trusted Companions, ʿAmmar ibn Yasir and Hudhayfah ibn al-Yaman, to go with him. ʿAmmar held the rein of his she-camel while Hudhayfah drove it. They were followed by that group of hypocrites trying to catch up with them, having drawn their headcovers over their faces to hide their identities. When the Prophet heard the sound of their camels travelling close behind, he was angry. Hudhayfah recognized how angry he was, and he went back towards them. He held out his shield to stop their camels. When they saw him, they thought that their scheming was discovered. So they made haste to join the bulk of the army and mix among them. Hudhayfah went back to the Prophet who instructed him and ʿAmmar to make haste until they passed the peak of the trail, and rejoined the road. They stopped for the army to catch up with them.

The Prophet asked Hudhayfah whether he recognized those people? He said: "I could only see their camels as it was dark when I met them." The Prophet asked both his Companions: "Do you know what those people were after?" When they answered in the negative, he told them of their conspiracy, and named them asking his two Companions to keep that information to themselves. They wondered: "Messenger of God, should you not order their execution?" He said: "I hate that people should say that Muhammad is killing his Companions." Another report suggests that the Prophet told only Hudhayfah of their names.

As for the hardship encountered by the Muslims in this expedition, a number of reports give us a clear picture of it. Some of these emphasize that the expedition took place at a time of scarcity, in the height of a very hot summer, when provisions and water were in extremely short supply. Qatadah, an early scholar, says: "They set out to Tabuk when it was burning hot, and they encountered great difficulty. It is reported that two men would share a single date. Indeed a few men would all share one date, with one of them sucking it a little and drinking some water, then he would give it to another to do the same, and so on. God then turned to them in mercy and brought them back safely."

Al-Tabari, a leading historian and scholar, mentions a report that ʿUmar was asked about the difficulty. He answered: "We marched with the Prophet to Tabuk. We encamped at a place where we were so thirsty that we felt our throats were cracking with thirst. Any one of us might go out looking for water, and by the time he came back he would have felt his throat cut. Any of us might slaughter his camel and take out its inside, extracting all the fluid to drink. He would place the rest over his belly."

In his commentary on the Qurʾan, al-Tabari mentions the following comments on this verse: "*God has assuredly turned in His mercy to the Prophet, the* Muhajirin *and the* AnSar, *who followed him in the hour of hardship.*" (Verse 117) This refers to the scarcity of funds, transport, equipment, provisions and water. "*When the hearts of a group of them had almost faltered.*" (Verse 117) They almost deviated from the truth. With all the difficulties they encountered, doubts might have crept in about the Prophet's message. "*Then again He turned to them in mercy.*" (Verse 117) He guided them to revert to the truth and to show real steadfastness. "*He is compassionate towards them, Merciful.*" (Verse 117)

These reports depict for us a picture of the reality of the Muslim community at the time. We see a whole spectrum of different standards of faith. We see those who had unshakeable faith, and those who were seriously shaken as a result of the hardship, as well as those who stayed behind, although they had no doubt about the truth of Islam or their duty to join the expedition. We also see a whole range of hypocrisy, with some hypocrites adopting a soft attitude and others speaking out bluntly, and still others conspiring to kill the Prophet. This gives us an impression of the overall structure of society at the time. It also shows us how hard this expedition was, not only in respect of a fearsome enemy but also in terms of the hardship faced by the Muslim community. It was a test to the core so that people could prove their metal. Perhaps it was intended by God to serve as such.

The case of one honest man

Such was the hardship which some people tried to evade. The majority of these were hypocrites, and their case has already been discussed. Some, however, were believers who entertained no doubt about Islam or the Prophet's message. They were simply people who preferred the comforts of home when the going got tough. These include two groups, one of whom received their judgement earlier. They had added some bad deeds to their good ones and acknowledged their mistake. The case of the second group was deferred for judgement: "*God would either punish them or turn to them in His mercy.*" (Verse 106) This group included three people whose case now comes in for detailed treatment.

Before we say anything about the statement describing their case, and before we speak about the artistically miraculous picture the *surah* paints in describing it, let us look at the account given by one of them, Ka'b ibn Malik:

I have never stayed behind when the Prophet went on any expedition, except that of Badr. Neither God nor the Prophet blamed anyone for staying behind at the time of Badr, because the Prophet set out from Medina to intercept a trade caravan which belonged to the Quraysh. The battle took place without any preparation or prior planning. On the other hand, I had attended the pledge of the *Ansar* to the Prophet at 'Aqabah when we made our commitment to Islam absolutely clear. I would not exchange my attendance there with taking part in the Battle of Badr, although Badr is the more famous occasion.

Nevertheless, I failed to join the army of the expedition of Tabuk. I was never in better circumstances or more physically able than I was then. At no time did I have two means of transport except on that occasion. It was the habit of the Prophet to keep his destination secret. This time, however, setting his destination so far away, and moving in an exceptionally hot climate, he made it clear to the people that he intended to attack the Byzantines. Those who joined the Prophet were in such large numbers that no register of them could have been kept.

In the circumstances, anyone who wished to stay behind might have thought that he would not be noticed, unless God chose to inform the Prophet about him by revelation. The Prophet decided to launch that attack at a time when fruits were abundant and people preferred to stay in the shade. The Prophet and the Muslims, however, were busy getting ready for their impending task. I went out day after day to the marketplace in order to get my equipment, but I always came back having done nothing. I always thought that I was able to get whatever I needed in no time. Nevertheless, I continued in that condition until it was time to move. The Prophet and the army with him started their march and I had not got my preparations under way. I thought to myself: 'I can still get myself ready in a day or two and should be able to catch up with them.' When they had covered quite a distance, I went out to the market and came back having done nothing. This continued day after day. By this time, the army must have covered quite a long distance. I thought I must make a move now and catch up with them. I wish I had done that, but I did not. Every time I went out after the Prophet and the army had left, I was troubled by the fact that I saw only people who were known to be hypocrites or people who were physically unable to join the army. My place was not with either group. I was told that the Prophet did not mention me until he had arrived at Tabuk. He remarked once to those who were present at Tabuk: 'What has happened to Ka'b ibn Malik?' A man from the tribe of Salamah said to him: 'Messenger of God, his wealth and arrogance made him stay behind.' Mu'adh ibn Jabal said to him: 'What a foul remark! Messenger of God, we have known nothing bad of the man.' The Prophet made no comment.

I soon heard that the Prophet and his Companions had started on their journey back from Tabuk. I felt very sad. To tell a lie was paramount in my mind. I started thinking about what to say to the Prophet tomorrow, after his arrival, in order to spare myself his anger. I sought the help of everyone in my household. When it was mentioned that the Prophet was soon to arrive, all thoughts of seeking a false excuse disappeared from my mind. I realized that the only way to spare myself the Prophet's anger was to tell the truth. I was determined, therefore, to say exactly what happened.

The Prophet then arrived in Medina. It was his habit when he came back from travelling to go first to the mosque and pray two *rak'ahs* before sitting to meet the people. When he did that, those who had stayed behind went to him and stated their excuses, swearing to their truth. They were over 80 people. The Prophet accepted their statements and oaths and prayed to God to forgive them, leaving it to God to judge them by His knowledge. I then followed and greeted the Prophet. He met my greeting with an angry smile. He then told me to come forward. I went to him and sat down facing him. He said, 'What caused you to stay behind? Have you not bought your transport?'

I said to him, 'Messenger of God, had I been speaking to anyone on the face of the earth other than you, I would have been able to avoid his anger by giving some sort of an excuse. I can make a case for myself. But I know for certain that if I were to tell you lies in order to win your pleasure, God would soon make the truth known to you and I would incur your displeasure. If, on the other hand, I tell you the truth and you are not happy with me because of it, I would hope for a better result from God. By God, I have no excuse whatsoever. I have never been more physically able or in better circumstances than I was when I stayed behind.' The Prophet said to me: 'You have certainly said the truth. You await God's judgement.'

After I left, some men from the clan of Salamah followed me and said: 'We have never known you to commit a sin before this. You could certainly have given the Prophet an excuse like all those who stayed behind. You would have been spared this trouble had the Prophet prayed to God to forgive you, as he would surely have done.' They continued pressing me on this to the extent that I wished to go back to the Prophet and tell him that I was lying. Before I did that, however, I asked whether anyone else said the same thing as I did. They replied that two more people said the same and were given the same answer. When I asked their names, they mentioned Murarah ibn al-Rabi' and Hilal ibn Umayyah. I knew these two to be men of faith and sincere devotion. I realized that the proper attitude for me was to be in their company. I therefore made no further move.

The Prophet ordered all his Companions not to speak to us three. He made no similar instruction concerning anybody else of those who stayed behind. All people were now evading us. Their attitude was changed. It was very hard for me that I did not even know myself or the place I was in. This was no longer the town I lived in. My world had changed. We continued in this condition for 50 days.

My two Companions, Murarah ibn al-Rabi' and Hilal ibn Umayyah, stayed at home. I was the youngest of the three. I continued to go out and attend the congregational prayers with other Muslims. I frequented all the markets, but nobody would speak to me. I would also go to the Prophet and greet him as he sat down after prayers. I would always think to myself: 'Have I detected any movement on his lips suggesting that he has answered my greeting?' I would pray close to him and look at him stealthily. When I was preoccupied with my prayers, he would look at me, but when I looked towards him, he would turn his face the other way.

When this boycott by all the Muslim community seemed to have lasted too long, I climbed the wall of an orchard which belonged to a cousin of mine named Abu Qatadah, who was very close to me. I greeted him, but he did not answer. I said to him: 'Abu Qatadah, I beseech you by God to answer me: do you know that I love God and His Messenger?' He did not answer. I repeated my question three times, but he still did not answer.

I then beseeched him once again, and his answer came: 'God and His Messenger know better.' Tears sprang to my eyes and I came down. I went to the market and as I was walking I saw a man, apparently a stranger from Syria, enquiring about me. People pointed me out to him. He came to me and handed me a letter from the King of Ghassan, the Arab tribe in Syria. The letter was written on a piece of silk and read: 'We have learnt that your friend has imposed a boycott on you. God has not placed you in a position of humiliation. If you join us, we will endeavour to alleviate all your troubles.' When I read it, I thought it to be yet another test of my sincerity. I have reached so low that an unbeliever hopes that I would willingly join him. I put the letter in an oven and burnt it.

When we had spent 40 nights in that situation, a messenger from the Prophet came to me and said: 'God's Messenger (peace be upon him) commands you to stay away from your wife.' I asked whether that meant that I should divorce her and he answered in the negative. He told me only to stay away from her. My two Companions also received the same instruction. I told my wife to go to her people's home and stay there until God had given His judgement in this matter.

Hilal ibn Umayyah was an old man. His wife went to the Prophet and said, 'Messenger of God, Hilal ibn Umayyah is very old and has no servant. Do you mind if I continue to look after him?' He said, 'That is all right, but do not let him come near you.' She said, 'By God, these things are far from his mind. He has not stopped crying ever since this has happened to him. I indeed fear for his eyesight.' Some people in my family suggested that I should seek the Prophet's permission to let my wife look after me. I said, 'I am not going to ask him that. I do not know what his answer would be, considering that I am a young man.'

Another ten nights passed, to complete 50 nights since the Prophet instructed the Muslims not to talk to us. At dawn after the 50th night I prayed at the top of one of our houses. I was still in that condition which I have described: the world seemed to me suffocatingly small and I did not recognize myself any more. As I sat down after the dawn prayers, however, I heard a voice from the direction of Mount Sal' saying: 'Ka'b ibn Malik! Rejoice!' I realized that my hardship was over, and I prostrated myself in gratitude to God.

What happened was that the Prophet informed the congregation after finishing the dawn prayer that God has pardoned us. People moved fast to give us that happy news. A man came at speed on horseback to bring me the news, while another from the tribe of Aslam went on top of the mountain to shout it to me. His voice was quicker than the horse. When I heard that man's voice giving me the happiest piece of news I ever received, I gave him my two garments as a gesture of gratitude. By

God, they were the only clothes I had at the time. I borrowed two garments and went quickly to the Prophet. People were meeting me in groups, saying, 'Congratulations on being forgiven by God.' I entered the mosque and saw the Prophet sitting with a group of people around him. Talhah ibn 'Ubaydullah came quickly towards me, shook my hand and congratulated me. He was the only one from the *Muhajirin* to do that. I will never forget Talhah's kindness.

When I greeted the Prophet, he said to me, with his face beaming with pleasure, 'Rejoice, for this is your happiest day since you were born!' I asked him: 'Is my pardon from you, Messenger of God, or is it from God?' He said, 'It is from God.' When the Prophet was pleased at something, his face would light up and look like the moon. We always recognized that."

When I sat down facing him, I said to him, 'Messenger of God, I will make my repentance complete by giving away all my property in charity.' The Prophet said, 'Keep some of your property, for that is better for you.' I answered that I would keep my share in Khaybar. I then added that I was forgiven only because I told the truth, and I would make my repentance complete by never telling a lie at any time in my life.

I feel that the greatest grace God has bestowed on me ever since He guided me to accept Islam is my telling the truth to the Prophet on that day. Had I invented some false excuse, I would have perished like all those who told him lies. God has described those people in the worst description ever. He says in the Qur'an: '*When you return to them they will swear to you by God so that you may let them be. Let them be, then: they are unclean. Hell shall be their abode in recompense for what they used to do. They swear to you trying to make you pleased with them. Should you be pleased with them, God shall never be pleased with such transgressing folk.*' (Verses 95–96) I have never knowingly or deliberately told a lie ever since I said that to the Prophet. I pray to God to help me keep my word for the rest of my life.[2]

Vacillating between extremes

This is then the story of the three people whose cases were deferred, as related by one of them, Ka'b ibn Malik. There is a lesson in it at every juncture. It gives us a very distinct picture of the solid base of the Muslim community, how closely knit it is, the purity of its people, the clarity of their vision with respect to their community and their duties towards their faith, the importance of the commands issued to them and their need to obey these commands.

Those three people stayed behind at a time of hardship. Human weakness got the better of them when they preferred the shade and comfort of their own homes. That seemed much more preferable than enduring the summer heat and a long traverse. Yet when the Prophet and his Companions had left Medina, Ka'b felt that he was committing a terrible error. Everything around him pointed to it: "Every time I went out after the Prophet and the army had left, I was troubled by the fact that I saw only people who were known to be hypocrites or people who were physically unable to join the army." Those in the latter group were people who were either sick or weakened by old age, or those who could not find any means of transport. This means that the hardship did not cause the Muslims to give a cold shoulder to the Prophet's command to get ready for a very tough expedition. The only ones who stayed behind were those suspected of hypocrisy, or those who had genuine excuses. The solid base of the Muslim community was strong enough to overcome the hardship and to give the right response.

The second point is that of fearing God. When a sinner is truly God-fearing, he will certainly acknowledge his error, and leave judgement in his case to God. In his account Ka'b states why he did not try to give the Prophet a false excuse: "Had I been speaking to anyone on the face of the earth other than you, I would have been able to avoid his anger by giving some sort of an excuse. I can make a case for myself. But I know for certain that if I were to tell you lies in order to win your pleasure, God would soon make the truth known to you and I would incur your displeasure. If, on the other hand, I tell you the truth and you are not happy with me because of it, I would hope for a better result from God. By God, I have no excuse whatsoever. I have never been more physically able or in better circumstance than I was when I stayed behind."

This shows how an errant believer was keen to watch God and seek not to incur His anger. He was certainly keen to win the Prophet's pleasure, which in those days could lift a person to the highest standard or allow him to fall into an abyss, and make a Muslim enjoy high esteem or leave him in total oblivion. Nevertheless, fearing God was a stronger motivation, and the hope to win His forgiveness was more deeply entertained.

Let us look at another aspect of the story: "The Prophet ordered all his Companions not to speak to us three. He made no similar instruction concerning anybody else of those who stayed behind. All people were now evading us. Their attitude was changed. It was very hard for me that I did not even know myself or the place I was in. This was no longer the town I lived in. My world had changed. We continued in this condition for 50 days.

"My two Companions, Murarah ibn al-Rabi' and Hilal ibn Umayyah, stayed at home. I was the youngest of the three. I continued to go out and attend the congregational prayers with other Muslims. I frequented all the markets, but nobody would speak to me. I would also go to the Prophet and greet him as he sat down after prayers. I would always think to myself: 'Have I detected any movement on his lips suggesting that he has answered my greeting?' I would pray close to him and look at him stealthily. When I was preoccupied with my prayers he would look at me, but when I looked towards him he would turn his face away.

"When this boycott by all the Muslim community seemed to have lasted too long, I climbed the wall of an orchard which belonged to a cousin of mine named Abu Qatadah, who was very close to me. I greeted him, but he did not answer. I said to him: 'Abu Qatadah, I beseech you by God to answer me: do you know that I love God and His Messenger?' He did not answer. I repeated my question three times, but he still did not answer. I then beseeched him once again, and his answer came: 'God and His Messenger know better.' Tears sprang to my eyes and I came down."

These details give us a clear impression of the level of discipline and obedience in the Muslim community, despite all the looseness that crept in after the fall of Mecca to the Muslims, and the confusion that accompanied the preparations for the expedition to Tabuk. The Prophet gave his instructions that nobody should speak to those three, and hence no one uttered a word to them. None would even meet Ka'b with a smiling face, and none would give or take anything from him. Even his closest cousin and friend would not return his greeting or answer his question, after Ka'b had climbed the fence to enter his garden. When he answered after much beseeching, his answer was far from reassuring. He only said: "God and His Messenger know better."

In his eagerness to know his position, after his whole world had changed, Ka'b would try to detect a faint movement on the lips of the Prophet to know whether he had answered his greetings. He would look sideways to find out whether the Prophet had looked at him in a way which would renew his hopes, and tell him that his situation was not totally desperate.

Left all alone, with no one saying a word to him even as a gesture of charity, he receives a letter from the King of Ghassan offering him a position of honour and influence. He turns his back on all this in a single movement. His only reaction is to throw the letter into the fire, considering this tempting offer as part of his trial.

Yet the boycott is extended and he is ordered not to go near to his wife, so that he is totally alone, isolated, hanging in the air. He feels too shy to request the Prophet to let his wife look after him, because he was unsure what the answer would be like.

The whole world seems too narrow

This should be contrasted with the piece of really happy news subsequently given to the three offenders. It is the news of rehabilitation, acceptance of the three men's repentance and their return to the fold and to life. Let us remind ourselves of Ka'b's own account of that happy moment:

> I was still in that condition which I have described: the world seemed to me suffocatingly small and I did not recognize myself any more. As I sat down after the dawn prayers, however, I heard a voice from the direction of Mount Sal' saying: 'Ka'b ibn Malik! Rejoice!' I realized that my hardship was over, and I prostrated myself in gratitude to God.
>
> What happened was that the Prophet informed the congregation after finishing the dawn prayer that God had pardoned us. People moved fast to give us that happy news. A man came at speed on horseback to bring me the news, while another from the tribe of Aslam went on top of the mountain to shout it to me. His voice was quicker than the horse. When I heard that man's voice giving me the happiest piece of news I ever received, I gave him my two garments as a gesture of gratitude. By God, they were the only clothes I had at the time. I borrowed two garments and went quickly to the Prophet. People were meeting me in groups, saying, 'Congratulations on being forgiven by God.' I entered the mosque and saw the Prophet sitting with a group of people around him. Talhah ibn 'Ubaydullah came quickly towards me, shook my hand and congratulated me. He was the only one from the *Muhajirin* to do that. I will never forget Talhah's kindness.

Such was the true value of events in that community. An accepted repentance was given such importance that a man would ride on horseback to deliver the news to its recipient, and another would go to the top of a mountain to shout it over so that he could be faster than the herald on horse. Joy felt by a brother and genuine congratulations are felt as a kindness that will never be forgotten by yesterday's outcast who has just been rehabilitated. His is a day that is fittingly described by the Prophet: "Rejoice, for this is your happiest day since you were born!" As Ka'b says, the Prophet's face was shining with delight. How kind and compassionate the Prophet was that his face beamed with pleasure because three of his Companions had been returned to the fold.

This, then, was the story of the three people who were left behind until God accepted their repentance. We have highlighted some of the impressions it gives us of the life of the early Muslim community and its values. As related by one of the three people who went through its experience, the story brings clear before our minds the meaning of the verse which states: *"when the earth, vast as it is, seemed to close in upon them, and their own souls had become too constricted, they realized that there was no refuge from God except by returning to Him."* (Verse 118)

"When the earth, vast as it is, seemed to close in upon them." (Verse 118) What is the earth? Its world is that of its inhabitants and the values that are upheld by them. Its expanse is

as vast as the relationships between its people make it to be. Hence the description here is very truthful in its practical significance, as much as it is truthful in its artistic beauty. It shows the whole expanse of the earth becoming too narrow for those three. Its outer limits are brought too near to make it extremely tight, closing in on them. *"And their own souls had become too constricted."* (Verse 118) It is as if their souls are a sort of a container that has become too small and tight. They can hardly breathe as it tightens over them. What happened then was that *"they realized that there was no refuge from God except by returning to Him."* (Verse 118) That applies to all creation. None can have any refuge from God except in Him, because He has power over the whole universe. Yet stating this fact at this point, in an atmosphere of sadness imparts an air of stress and despair that can only be cleared by God Himself.

Then hope is restored and release is granted: *"He then turned to them in mercy, so that they might repent. God is indeed the One who accepts repentance, the Merciful."* (Verse 118) He has turned to them in mercy with regard to this particular error, so that they might make a general repentance which covers all their past sins. This means that they would watch God eagerly to guard against any future error. This is explained by Ka'b:

> When I sat down facing him, I said to him, 'Messenger of God, I will make my repentance complete by giving away all my property in charity.' The Prophet said, 'Keep some of your property, for that is better for you.' I answered that I would keep my share in Khaybar. I then added that I was forgiven only because I told the truth, and I would make my repentance complete by never telling a lie at any time in my life. I feel that the greatest grace God has bestowed on me ever since He guided me to accept Islam is my telling the truth to the Prophet on that day . . . I have never knowingly or deliberately told a lie ever since I said that to the Prophet. I pray to God to help me keep my word for the rest of my life.

That is all that we can say in comment on this highly inspiring story and the unique style in which it is reported in the Qur'an. We praise God for what He has guided us to write about it here, and we hope to make a longer discussion of it in future.[3]

A reward for every little thing

The element of truth is highly significant in the story of those three Companions of the Prophet. To give this element its due importance, all believers are advised to fear God and to align themselves with those truthful people of the early believers. On the other hand those people in Medina and the surrounding desert who stayed behind are strongly criticized. This is followed by a promise of generous reward to those who strive for God's cause: *"Believers, have fear of God and be among those who are truthful. It does not behove the people of Medina and the bedouins who live around them to hold back from following God's Messenger, or to care for themselves more than for him; for, whenever they endure thirst, stress, or hunger for the sake of God, or take any step which would irritate the unbelievers, or inflict any loss on the enemy, a good deed is recorded in their favour. God does not suffer the reward of those who do good to be lost. And whenever they spend anything for the sake of God, be it little or much, or traverse a valley {in support of God's cause}, it is recorded for them, so that God will give them the best reward for what they do."* (Verses 119–121)

The people of Medina were the ones who rushed to support the Islamic message, which meant that they were truly its basic core of supporters. They had given shelter to God's Messenger, pledged their total loyalty to him and constituted the hard nucleus of the Islamic faith in the Arabian Peninsula. The bedouin Arabs in the surrounding area, having also adopted Islam as a faith and a way of life, formed the outer belt of defence. Hence those two groups could not refrain from joining the Prophet or spare themselves from any risk to which they might be exposed. When God's Messenger set out to attend to a certain task that served Islamic interests, then the people of Medina, the vanguard of the Islamic message, and those of the surrounding area could not but join him. Whether this happened to be in the burning summer heat or the extreme winter cold, in times of strict hardship or easy affluence, it does not behove them, being so close to the Prophet, to try to spare themselves a difficulty that God's Messenger is undertaking. They could not excuse themselves by protesting ignorance or lack of awareness of the real task in hand.

The *surah* appeals to them to fear God and to join the truthful believers who have never entertained any thoughts of staying behind and who have maintained their strong commitment to their faith at times of hardship. Those were the cream among the early believers and those who followed in their footsteps: "*Believers, have fear of God and be among those who are truthful.*" (Verse 119)

The *surah* follows this appeal by a strong censure of the very thought of staying behind when God's Messenger is setting out: "*It does not behove the people of Medina and the bedouins who live around them to hold back from following God's Messenger, or to care for themselves more than for him.*" (Verse 120) The statement implies a strong reproach. No Companion of God's Messenger can be reproached in a stronger way than by saying that he puts his own safety ahead of the Prophet's. How could he when he is the Prophet's Companion and follower? The same applies to the advocates of Islam in all generations and periods. It does not behove a believer to try to spare himself a risk that the Prophet himself was willing to undertake for the cause of Islam. How could he when he claims that he is an advocate of the cause of Islam, and a follower of the Prophet Muhammad (peace be upon him)?

Taking up such a responsibility is a duty imposed by God's order and emphasized by our love of the Prophet that makes any believer too ashamed to put himself ahead of him. At the same time it earns a very generous reward indeed: "*Whenever they endure thirst, stress, or hunger for the sake of God, or take any step which would irritate the unbelievers, or inflict any loss on the enemy, a good deed is recorded in their favour. God does not suffer the reward of those who do good to be lost. And whenever they spend anything for the sake of God, be it little or much, or traverse a valley {in support of God's cause}, it is recorded for them, so that God will give them the best reward for what they do.*" (Verses 120–121)

Every feeling is rewarded, be it thirst, hunger or mere stress and tiredness. Taking up a position which irritates the unbelievers and inflicting any loss or damage on them is credited as a good deed. When a believer goes out on a *jihad* campaign, he is included among those who do good. God will not suffer the reward of such servants of His to be lost. Furthermore, any financial contribution, be it little or much, and the mere walking across a valley are also rewarded as God rewards the best of His servants. By God, this is a rich reward indeed. It is a reward by God whose generosity is beyond any limit. How embarrassing to us all that such a great reward is given for something that is much less than the hardship suffered by the Prophet himself for the cause of Islam. It is the advocacy of this cause that we should now assume. Most certainly, we must be true to our trust.

A task akin to fighting

As we have seen in this *surah*, the Qur'an repeatedly denounces, in very clear terms, those who stay behind at the time when a *jihad* campaign is announced, particularly those from Medina and the bedouins in the surrounding area. This denunciation made people come to Medina in large numbers, particularly from the tribes living nearby, so that they would be ready to join the Prophet at any moment. Hence it was necessary to spell out the limits of all-out mobilization at the appropriate time.

The Muslim area had expanded. With the whole of Arabia practically adopting Islam, large numbers were ready to fight. At Tabuk, there were about 30,000 of them, which was a much larger number than at any earlier battle the Muslims had fought. It was time that different people should attend to different tasks, so that no area, such as agriculture or trade or social concerns, was neglected. All these are necessary for an emerging nation, whose needs are far more sophisticated than those of a tribal community. Hence the present verse was revealed to set out certain limits: "*It is not desirable that all the believers should go out to fight. From every section of them some should go forth, so that they may acquire a deeper knowledge of the faith and warn their people when they return to them, so that they may take heed.*" (Verse 122)

Several reports have been mentioned in explaining the meaning of this verse, giving different views on which group is to acquire deeper knowledge in faith so as to warn their people when they return. The view which we find to be soundest suggests that a section from each group in the Muslim community should go out to fight, with a system that allows alternation between the fighters and those who stay behind to attend to other tasks. The group of fighters acquires a more profound understanding of this faith as they take practical action seeking to consolidate its base. Hence these fighters are the ones who, on their return, warn their people against any complacency in attending to their duties.

This interpretation is based on views expressed by such leading commentators as Ibn ʿAbbas, al-Hasan al-Basri and Ibn Kathir. It is also the view of Ibn Jarir al-Tabari. Its central point is that this faith has its own method of action, and it cannot be properly understood except by those who actively implement it. Hence those who go out to fight for its cause are the ones most likely to understand it best. Its underlying meanings, its implications, its practical implementation and its main features unfold to them as they move under its banner. Those who stay behind are the ones who need to be informed by those who take practical action, because the latter are the ones who witness and learn all these aspects. They are the ones who probe its secrets. This is particularly so, if the campaign they join is one led by the Prophet himself. However, every *jihad* campaign is a means to acquire a better understanding of this faith.

This is perhaps the reverse of what may appear at first sight, with those who are not on a *jihad* campaign being the ones who devote time to studying and understanding this faith. But this is a delusion that does not fit with the nature of this faith, which makes action one of its basic requirements. Hence it is understood more profoundly by those who take action and strive to establish it as a code of living in spite of the opposition they encounter from the forces of *jahiliyyah*. Experience confirms that those who are not involved in the method of action to serve this faith do not understand it properly, no matter how much time they spend in studying it from books. That is a cold study, while real insight is acquired only by those who join the efforts aiming to establish it as a practical code of living. It is never acquired by those who only look at books and papers.

Proper understanding of this faith does not evolve except where action is taken to serve its cause. It cannot be taken from a scholar who stays idle when action is needed. Those who occupy their time with studying books to deduce rulings and 'renew' or 'develop' Islamic law, as the Orientalists say, do not really understand the nature of this faith. They take no part in the movement which aims to liberate humanity from different tyrannical authorities, and from submission to others, so that they may submit to

God alone. With such lack of action, they cannot put its laws and concepts into, their proper form.

Islamic law came about after Islamic action had moved ahead. First, submission to God was properly established when a community had determined to submit itself to God alone and to abandon the laws, customs and traditions of *jahiliyyah*. That community also decided that no aspect of its life could be governed by human law. The community then started to shape its life on the basis of the main Islamic laws, without neglecting the details outlined in the sources of this law. As the community continued to do so, new issues came up in its practical life that needed to be sorted out on the basis of Islamic law. At this point new rulings were deduced and *Fiqh*, or the formal study of Islamic law, started to develop. It is then the action itself which allowed *Fiqh* to develop and flourish. It did not develop as a cold academic study that had no bearing on active and practical life. Thus scholars were able to develop a profound insight into this faith based on interaction with a real community shaping its life on the basis of this religion and striving to make its cause triumphant.

What do we find today in place of that? No one can claim that a proper Islamic community, determined to submit to God alone and to live by His law, rejecting any laws and regulations that are not based on His guidance exists anywhere. Hence no true Muslim, who has an insight into this religion of Islam, its method of action and its history would try to 'develop' or 'renew' Islamic law in communities that are unwilling to declare that they recognize no other law. Serious Islamic action should start by making submission to God alone the first step, followed by acknowledging that sovereignty belongs only to Him. Hence no legislation is acceptable unless it is based on His law. To do otherwise is no more than a silly joke. Moreover, to imagine that one can have a proper understanding of this faith looking only at books and papers, without being involved in real action to serve the Islamic cause betrays deep ignorance of this religion.

Submission to God alone gives rise to an Islamic community, which in turn helps Islamic scholarship to flourish. This is the proper order. There can be no situation where specially tailored Islamic laws are prepared in advance for an Islamic community that is expected to be established. The fact is that every ruling seeks to implement the Islamic law, and its basic principles, in a practical case that has its own clear shape, dimensions and circumstances. Such cases arise from practical life within the Islamic community which gives it its particular shape, dimensions and circumstances. Hence a ruling that addresses each particular case is deduced. The rulings that we find today in books of *Fiqh* addressed similar practical cases in the past, when Islamic law was implemented by an Islamic community. They were not ready made in advance. Today we need to have similar rulings that address our own issues, provided that the community decides first of all to submit to God alone and to accept no ruling unless based on God's law.

When this happens, then our efforts will yield proper fruits. Striving for God's cause, or *jihad*, will open people's eyes and give them real knowledge and understanding of the faith. Unless we do this, then we are evading our real duty of *jihad*, seeking flimsy excuses of 'developing' or 'renewing' the study of Islamic *Fiqh*. It is far better to acknowledge our weakness and lack of effort, seeking God's forgiveness, than to resort to such evasiveness.

Uncompromising fight

We then have a verse outlining the plan and extent of *jihad*, which was implemented by the Prophet Muhammad (peace be upon him) and his successors generally. The only exceptions were limited cases dictated by special circumstances: "*Believers, fight those of the unbelievers who are near you, and let them find you tough; and know that God is with those who are God-fearing.*" (Verse 123)

The *jihad* movement marched on, confronting those who were near to the land of Islam, one stage after another. When practically the whole of Arabia had adopted Islam, after Mecca itself fell to Islam, leaving only scattered individuals and groups who did not form any threat to the land of Islam, the Tabuk Expedition took place, threatening the outer areas of the Byzantine Empire which were closest to the Muslim state. This was followed by open warfare, with the Muslim armies moving far into the lands of both the Byzantine and Persian Empires, leaving no pockets behind them. The areas that were now under Islam were united, having continuous borders. It was a vast land area with solid loyalty to one authority.

Weakness only crept in after its division into different units, with artificial borders to allow the governments of certain ruling families or certain races and nationalities. This was the outcome of plans that the enemies of Islam tried hard to bring to fruition, as they still do today. The different ethnic communities which Islam united in a single nation or community in the land of Islam, superseding the divisions of race, language and colour, will continue to suffer from inherent weaknesses until they return to their faith. Only when they once again follow the guidance of God's Messenger, the Prophet Muhammad (peace be upon him), and allow only a single banner to unite them shall they recognize the implications of divine leadership which will once again bring them power and victory. When that happens, it will ensure that they are held in awe by other nations and powers.

Let us now reflect on this verse: "*Believers, fight those of the unbelievers who are near you, and let them find you tough; and know that God is with those who are God-fearing.*" (Verse 123) What we find here is an order to fight those unbelievers who are near to the Muslim state, without specifying whether these have launched any aggression on the Muslims or their land. We understand that this is the final situation which makes the need to carry Islam forward the basis of the principle of *jihad*. This will ensure that Islam is available to mankind. It does not have a defensive outlook, as was the case with the provisional orders in the early days after the establishment of the Muslim state in Medina.

Some of those who speak about the Islamic view of international relations or about the rulings that govern *jihad*, as well as those who write essays interpreting the Qur'anic verses speaking about *jihad*, try to show this verse, which is the final one, limited by the earlier provisional rules. Hence they impose on it a restriction, limiting its application to cases of aggression being launched or expected against the Muslim community. But this statement is general and has no restriction attached to it. Besides, it is the final one. What we have learnt is that when the Qur'an lays down legal provisions, it states them in a clear and precise way, without referring one situation to another. It resorts to precise expression, adding at the same point any exceptions, limitations or restrictions it wants the Muslim community to observe.

We have already commented in detail, in the Prologue and Chapters 1 and 2, on the meanings of the verses and the final rulings they provide, shedding light on the nature of the Islamic method of action.

However, those speakers and writers find it incomprehensible that Islam lays down such an order commanding the believers to fight those unbelievers who are near to them, and to continue to do so as long as there remain unbelievers in their vicinity. Hence they try to find limits restricting this general statement, but they can only find these in the earlier statements which were, by nature, provisional.

We understand why they find it so incomprehensible. They simply forget that *jihad* is meant to serve God's cause. It aims to establish God's authority and to remove tyranny. It liberates mankind from submission to any authority other than that of God. *"Fight them until there is no more oppression, and all submission is made to God alone."* (8:39) *Jihad* does not aim to achieve the hegemony of one philosophy or system or nation over another. It wants the system laid down by God to replace the systems established by His creatures. It does not wish to establish a kingdom for any one of God's servants, but to establish God's own kingdom. Hence it has to move forward throughout the earth in order to liberate the whole of mankind, without discrimination between those who are within the land of Islam and those who are outside it. The whole earth is populated by human beings who are being subjected to different types of tyrannical authority wielded by fellow human beings.

When they lose sight of this fact they find it odd that one system and one nation should move forward to remove all systems and dominate all communities. If things were such, that would be odd indeed. But the systems that exist today are all man-made. None of them has any right to say that it alone should dominate the others. The same does not apply to the divine system which sets out to overthrow all man-made systems in order to liberate all mankind from the humiliation of submission to other human beings, so that they can submit to God alone and worship Him only without any partners. Moreover, they find it odd because they face a concentrated and wicked crusade which tells them that the Islamic faith managed to spread only because it used the sword. *Jihad*, it claims, wanted to force other people to accept Islam, depriving them of the freedom of belief.

Had things been so, they would have been odd indeed. But the truth is totally different. Islam lays down a rule stating that *"There shall be no compulsion in religion. The right way is henceforth distinct from error."* (2:256) Why does Islam, then, move forward to fight, and why has God bought the believers' souls and property, so that *"they fight for the cause of God, kill and be killed"*? (Verse 111) The answer is that *jihad* has a reason which is totally different from compelling other people to accept Islam. Indeed *jihad* seeks to guarantee the freedom of belief.

As we have stated on several occasions, Islam is a declaration which liberates mankind throughout the earth from submission to human beings. As such, Islam always faces tyrannical forces and systems which seek to subjugate people and dominate their lives. These systems are backed by regimes and powers of different sorts, which deprive people of the chance to listen to the Islamic message and to adopt it if they are convinced of its truth. Or they may force people, in one way or another, to turn away from the Islamic message. That is an ugly violation of the freedom of belief. For these reasons, Islam moves forward, equipped with suitable power, to overthrow these systems and destroy their forces.

What happens then? It leaves people entirely free to adopt the faith they like. If they wish to be Muslims, they will have all the rights and duties that apply to all Muslims. They will have a bond of real brotherhood with those who have been Muslims long before them. On the other hand, if they wish to maintain their religions, they may do so. They only have to pay a tribute, i.e. *jizyah*, which has a clear purpose: to acknowledge the freedom of movement for Islam among them, to contribute to the treasury of the Muslim state which is required to protect them against any outside aggression, and to look after those of them who are ill, disabled and elderly in the same way as Muslims are looked after.

Never in its history did Islam compel a single human being to change his faith. That is alien to Islamic beliefs and practice. On the other hand, crusades were launched to kill, slaughter and eliminate entire communities, such as the people of Andalusia in the past and the people of Zanzibar in recent history, in order to compel them to convert to

Christianity. Sometimes, even conversion was not accepted. They were killed only because they were Muslims, or because they followed a brand of Christianity which was different from that of the dominating Church. For example, 12,000 Egyptian Christians were burnt alive only because they differed with the Byzantine Church over matters of detail, such as whether the soul originated with the Father alone, or with the Father and the Son together, or whether Jesus had a single divine nature or a united one in which both the divine and the human combine. These are basically the causes which make some writers about Islam find the general statement in this verse rather odd, and they try to explain it away by limiting the *jihad* movement to a defensive strategy only.

Moreover, the thought of moving forward to confront the unbelievers who are near to the Muslim state sounds too awesome to those defeatists who look at the world around them today and find this requirement totally impractical. Are those who have Muslim names in communities that are weak, or subject to foreign domination, to move forth in the land, challenging all nations in open warfare, until there is no more oppression and all submission is declared to God alone? That is totally unrealistic. It cannot be imagined that God would give such an order.

All such people forget the timing and the circumstances leading to this order. It was given after Islam had established its state, and the whole of Arabia adopted the Islamic faith and started to organize its life on its basis. Prior to that a community was established which dedicated itself totally to its cause, with everyone in that community ready to sacrifice his life and property in order for Islam to triumph. This community was given victory in one battle after another, stage after stage. Today we are in a situation which is highly similar to that which prevailed at the time when Prophet Muhammad was sent to call on mankind to believe in God's oneness and to declare that *"There is no deity other than God, and Muhammad is His Messenger."* Together with the small band who believed in him, the Prophet strove hard until he managed to establish the first Muslim state in Medina. The orders to fight the unbelievers were modified stage after stage, facing the prevailing situation at each stage, until it reached its final version.

The gulf that separates people today from that final version is wide indeed. Hence, they have to start again at the beginning, with the declaration that *"There is no deity other than God, and Muhammad is His Messenger."* They will have to move forward on the basis of this declaration until they reach, in their own good time and with God's help, the final stage. At that time they will not be the sort of powerless multitude divided by a variety of creeds and desires, and declaring their affiliation to different races and nationalities, as they are today. They will be a united Muslim community that accepts no banner, or man-made creed or system. They will only move with God's blessings to serve His cause.

Encumbered with their pathetic weakness, people will not understand the rules of this religion. It is only those who strive in a movement dedicated to the establishment of God's sovereignty on earth, and the removal of false deities, that fully understand its rules. Understanding this religion in its true nature cannot be taken from those who deal only with books and papers. Academic study is insufficient on its own to formulate any real understanding of Islam, unless it is coupled with striving in a movement.

Finally, this verse, giving such a clear order, was revealed in circumstances that suggest that the first to be meant by it were the Byzantines, who belonged to an earlier religion, or, to use the Islamic term, People of the Book. The *surah*, however, has already made it clear that they had distorted their faith and obeyed man-made laws and systems, so they were truly unbelievers. We should reflect here on the line of action Islam takes towards communities of the People of the Book who have turned away from their faith and adopted man-made laws. This line of action applies to all such communities everywhere. God has commanded the believers to fight those unbelievers who are near to them, and to be tough on them, but then concluded the verse making this order by saying: *"Know that God is with those who are God-fearing."* (Verse 123) This is a significant comment on the order preceding it. The type of fearing God that He appreciates and gives His support to those who have it is the same that emboldens believers to show toughness in fighting the unbelievers. This means that there is no compromise *"until there is no more oppression and all submission is made to God alone."* (8:39)

Nevertheless, everyone should know that this toughness is directed against only those who fight, and it remains controlled by Islamic ethics. Before Muslims fight, they give a warning and offer the other party a choice between three alternatives: to adopt Islam, or to pay the tribute, i.e. *jizyah*, or to fight. If there is a treaty between the Muslim state and another community and the Muslim state fears that there may be treachery on the latter's part, then a notice terminating the treaty should be served on them. It is useful to mention here that treaties may be given only to communities that are ready to be bound by a peace agreement and to pay the *jizyah*. The only other situation where a treaty may be signed is that when the Muslim community is lacking in power. In this situation, some provisional rules are applicable to it.

The Prophet himself set out the ethics of war which must be observed by the Muslim community in any battle it may fight.

Islamic war ethics

Buraydah, a Companion of the Prophet, reports:

> When the Prophet appointed someone to command an army or an expedition, he would recommend him to be God-fearing in his public and private affairs, and to take good care of those who were under his command. Then he would tell them: 'March by God's name and to serve His cause. Fight those who deny God. March on; but do not be unfair, and do not commit any treachery. Do not disfigure the bodies of any enemy soldiers killed in battle. Never kill any children. When you meet your enemies, call upon them to choose one of three alternatives. If they choose one of them, accept it from them and do not fight them. Call on them first to accept Islam. If they agree, accept their pledges and do not fight them. Then ask them to move over to the land of the *Muhajirin*, and tell them that they would then have the same duties and privileges of the *Muhajirin*. If they do not wish to move from their quarters, tell them that they would then be in the same position as the bedouin Muslims. They will be subject to God's orders that are applicable to all believers, but they will have no share of any booty that is gained through war or peaceful campaigns, unless they fight with the Muslims. If they refuse to accept Islam, then offer them the alternative of paying *jizyah* [or tribute]. If they agree, accept it from them and do not fight them. If they refuse, then seek God's help and fight them.

'Abdullah ibn 'Umar, a Companion of the Prophet reports: "A woman was found killed in one of the Prophet's expeditions. He immediately issued an order that no women or children may be killed." [Related by al-Bukhari and Muslim.]

The Prophet sent his Companion Mu'adh ibn Jabal to the Yemen to teach the people there. As he departed the Prophet said to him: "You will be among people who follow earlier revelations. Call on them to believe that there is no deity other than God and that I am God's Messenger. Should they accept that from you, then tell them that God has commanded them to pray five times every day. If they accept that from you, then tell them that God has imposed on them the payment of *zakat*, i.e. a charity which is to be levied from the rich and given to the poor among them. If they accept that, then do not touch their good earnings. Guard against an appeal to God by a person who suffers injustice, for such an appeal goes straight to God, without any hindrances."

Abu Dawud relates that the Prophet said: "You may fight some people and overcome them. They may then try to protect themselves and their children from you by their money, and they may make an agreement with you. Do not take anything from them over that, for it is not lawful to you."

Al-Irbad ibn Sariyah reports: "We arrived at Khaybar Castle with the Prophet when he had a large number of Muslims with him. The chief of Khaybar, an arrogant gigantic man, came to the Prophet and said, 'Muhammad! Do you permit yourselves to slaughter our cattle, devour our produce, and force our women?' The Prophet was very angry. He said, 'Ibn ʿAwf! Mount your horse and announce: Only believers are admitted into heaven. Then, gather around for prayers.' They were all gathered and the Prophet led the prayers. When he finished, he stood up and said, 'Does any of you think as he reclines over his couch that God has not forbidden anything other than what is stated in the Qurʾan? I have certainly admonished you, given certain orders and forbidden certain things. These are as much prohibited as those in the Qurʾan or even more so. God has not permitted you to go into the homes of the people of the earlier revelations without first having permission, nor has He allowed you to force their women or devour their produce when they have paid what is due from them."

After a certain battle, it was reported to the Prophet that a few boys were killed during the fighting. He was very sad. Some of his Companions said, "Why are you so sad when they are only the sons of unbelievers?" The Prophet was angry and said words to this effect: "These were better than you, because they still had uncorrupted natures. Are you not the children of unbelievers. Never kill boys. Never kill boys."

These instructions by the Prophet were strictly followed by his successors. Abu Bakr is reported to have said: "You will find people who claim that they have dedicated themselves to God. Leave them to their dedication. Never kill a woman, a child or an elderly man." Zayd ibn Wahb reports that the army he had joined received written instructions from the Caliph, ʿUmar, in which he said: "Do not be unjust; or commit treachery; or kill a young person. Fear God in your treatment of peasants." His instructions to his commanders always included the following: "Do not kill an elderly person, a woman or a child. Guard against accidentally killing them when you engage your enemy in battle and when you launch any attack."

Reports are numerous which make clear the general method Islam adopts in fighting its enemies, as well as its commitment to a high standard of ethics in war, giving high respect to human dignity. Fighting is targeted only against real forces which prevent people's liberation from subjugation by other creatures, so that they submit to God alone. Kind treatment is extended even to enemies. As for toughness, this applies only to fighting when Muslims are expected to fight hard. It has nothing of the barbarism against children, women and elderly people who do not fight in the first place, or the disfigurement of dead bodies. These practices are often committed by the barbaric armies of countries which these days claim to be highly civilized. Islam has given more than adequate orders to ensure the safety of those who do not fight, and to respect the humanity of the fighters. The toughness required is that sort of attitude which ensures that the confrontation does not fizzle away. As Muslims have been ordered time and again to show mercy and kindness, an exception needs to be made in the state of war, in as much as that state requires, without allowing any extreme practices of torture or disfigurement of bodies.

Hypocritical attitudes

Since the *surah* has spoken extensively about the hypocrites, we have here some verses showing how those hypocrites used to receive any new revelation outlining certain duties imposed by the faith they falsely claimed to accept. This is contrasted with the way believers used to receive the revelation of new verses of the Qur'an: "*Whenever a surah is revealed, some of them say: 'Which of you has this strengthened in faith?' It certainly strengthens the believers in their faith, and so they rejoice. But as for those whose hearts are diseased, it only adds wickedness to their wickedness, and so they die unbelievers. Do they not see that they are tested once or twice every year? Yet they do not repent, and they do not take warning. Whenever a surah is revealed, they look at one another {as if to say}: 'Is anyone watching?' Then they turn away. God has turned their hearts away, for they are people devoid of understanding.*" (Verses 124–127)

It is a strange and suspicious question the first verse quotes: '*Which of you has this strengthened in faith?*' It is asked only by one who has not felt the impact of the new *surah* as it is revealed. Otherwise he would have spoken about its effect on him instead of wondering how it has affected other people. At the same time, it betrays a sense of belittling the importance of the new revelation and its effect on people's hearts and minds. Hence a decisive reply is given by the One who has the ultimate knowledge: "*It certainly strengthens the believers in their faith, and so they rejoice. But as for those whose hearts are diseased, it only adds wickedness to their wickedness, and so they die unbelievers.*" (Verses 124–125)

The believers receive with every new *surah* and new revelation a new pointer to the truth of the faith. They also remember their Lord when they listen to His revelations, and they appreciate the care He takes of them by sending down these revelations. All this adds to the strength of their faith. On the other hand, those who have sickness in their hearts, the hypocrites, will have their wickedness increased. They will die unbelievers. This is a true piece of information given by God who knows everything.

Before the *surah* portrays the opposite picture, it wonders at those hypocrites who never take an admonition, and never reflect on an event to gather the lesson that may be learnt from it: "*Do they not see that they are tested once or twice every year? Yet they do not repent, and they do not take warning.*" (Verse 126) The test may have taken the form of exposing their reality, or that the believers achieve victory without those hypocrites taking any part. There could be many other forms of test, which were all too frequent at the time of the Prophet. Still hypocrites today are tested and they pay no heed.

The next verse portrays a vivid scene, full of details, showing their behaviour: "*Whenever a surah is revealed, they look at one another {as if to say}: 'Is anyone watching?' Then they turn away. God has turned their hearts away, for they are people devoid of understanding.*" (Verse 127)

When we read this verse, the scene of these hypocrites is large in front of us. We see them at the moment when a new *surah* is revealed, with some of them looking at each other winking and wondering: "*Is anyone watching?*" (Verse 127) Then they feel that the believers are preoccupied with their own business, so they go out stealthily, hoping not to be noticed: "*Then they turn away.*" (Verse 127) But the eye which never loses sight of anything follows them with a curse that suits their suspicious deed: "*God has turned their hearts away.*" (Verse 127) Their hearts are turned away from the right guidance. They deserve to remain deep in error, "*for they are people devoid of understanding.*" (Verse 127) This is because they have kept their hearts and minds idle, unable to function properly. All of this scene is portrayed so skilfully and vividly using only a few words.

The Prophet's relationship with the believers

The *surah* concludes with two verses which different reports suggest were revealed in Mecca or Medina. We are inclined to support the latter view, as these verses fit with various aspects of the last passage in the *surah* and with its general message. The first of these two verses explains the bond between God's Messenger and his people, and how compassionate and full of concern he was for them. This is perfectly fitting with the tasks assigned to the Muslim community who are required to support the Messenger, convey his message, fight his enemies and endure whatever trouble or hardship they may face in doing so. The final verse directs the Messenger to rely only on his Lord when people turn away from him. It is sufficient for him to have God's help and support.

"Indeed there has come to you a Messenger from among yourselves: one who grieves much that you should suffer; one who is full of concern for you; and who is tender and full of compassion towards the believers. Should they turn away, then say to them: "God is enough for me! There is no deity other than Him. In Him have I placed my trust. He is the Lord of the Mighty Throne.'" (Verses 128–129) The statement here does not say 'a Messenger from among you' has come to you. Instead it describes the Messenger as being one 'from among yourselves' to add connotations of closer contact and firmer ties. It shows the type of bond that exists between them and their Messenger. He is one of them, with very close contact between them, and he feels for them.

Another characteristic of this Messenger is that he is *"one who grieves much that you should suffer."* (Verse 128) He is keen that you should come to no hardship. He is also *"full of concern for you . . . tender and full of compassion towards the believers."* (Verse 128) He would never lead you to ruin. If he calls on you to strive for God's cause, and to endure any difficulty in doing so, then you should know that he does not take this lightly, and that there is no cruelty in his heart. His call is a manifestation of compassion. He simply does not like to see you humiliated. He is too concerned that you should not suffer the ignominy of sin. He is keen that you should have the honour of conveying this message, earn God's pleasure and admittance into heaven.

The *surah* then addresses the Prophet, showing him what attitude to take when people turn away from him and his message. It points to the source of power which gives him all the protection he needs: *"Should they turn away, then say to them: 'God is enough for me! There is no deity other than Him. In Him have I placed my trust. He is the Lord of the Mighty Throne.'"* (Verse 129) To Him belong all power, dominion, greatness and honour. His support is sufficient for everyone who seeks His patronage.

The *surah* which concentrates mainly on fighting and striving for God's cause is thus concluded with the directive to rely on God alone, trust Him and seek His powerful support. After all *"He is the Lord of the Mighty Throne."* (Verse 129)

Conclusion

This *surah* outlines the final rulings on the permanent relations between the Muslim community and the outside world, as explained in our commentary on its various passages. Hence we have to refer to its latest statements since these represent the final say on these relations. These statements must not be restricted or narrowed down in their applicability on the basis of earlier statements and rulings, which we described as provisional. In doing so, we have relied on the chronological order of the revelation of these verses and statements, and on the progress of the Islamic movement at the time of the Prophet, as well as the events marking that progress.

We have also been guided by our understanding of the nature of the Islamic message and its method of action which we have explained in our presentation of the *surah* and our commentary on its verses. This method of action is only understood by those who deal with this faith of Islam as a movement striving to establish itself in human life. As we have explained, the goal of that striving is to liberate mankind from submission to others so that they submit to God alone.

There is a wide gap between an understanding based on active striving and one based on academic study which is bound to ignore action. The first type of understanding looks at Islam as it conducts its direct confrontation with the system of *jahiliyyah*, taking one step after another and moving from one stage to the next. It also looks at it as it proclaims its legislation to deal with the changing situation in its confrontation.

Moreover, these final laws and verdicts outlined in this last *surah* were actually revealed when the general situation of the Muslim community and the world around it required such legislation. Prior to that, when the situation required different rulings, these were given in earlier *surahs* to serve as provisional rulings.

When a new Muslim community emerges again and starts to strive for the establishment of this faith in human life, it may be appropriate for this community to apply the provisional rulings, provided that it remains well aware that these are only provisional. It should also be aware that it must strive to reach the stage when only the final rulings govern its relations with the world around it. God will certainly help that community and guide it on its way.

7 Religion and society in Christianity and in Islam

In the world of economics an individual who has private means does not resort to borrowing before he has examined his means to see what resources he has there; nor does a government resort to importing until it has scrutinized its native resources and examined its raw materials and their potential. And so in the case of spiritual resources, intellectual capabilities, and moral and ethical traditions—are not these things on the same level as goods or money in human life? Apparently not; for here in Egypt and in the Muslim world as a whole, we pay little heed to our native spiritual resources and our own intellectual heritage; instead, we think first of importing foreign principles and methods, or borrowing customs and laws from across the deserts and from beyond the seas.

We have only to look in order to see that our social situation is as bad as it can be; it is apparent that our social conditions have no possible relation to justice; and so we turn our eyes to Europe, America, or Russia, and we expect to import from there solutions to our problems, just as from them we import goods for our industrial livelihood. With this difference—that in industrial importing we first examine the goods which are already on our markets, and we estimate our own ability to produce them. But when it is a matter of importing principles and customs and laws, we do no such thing; we continually cast aside all our own spiritual heritage, all our intellectual endowment, and all the solutions which might well be revealed by a glance at these things; we cast aside our own fundamental principles and doctrines, and we bring in those of democracy, or socialism, or communism. It is to these that we look for a solution of our social problems, although our circumstances, our history, and the very bases of our life-material, intellectual, and spiritual alike-are quite out of keeping with the circumstances of people across the deserts and beyond the seas.

At the same time we profess Islam as a state religion, we claim in all sincerity to be true Muslims—if indeed we do not claim to be the guardians and propagators of Islam. Yet we have divorced our faith from our practical life, condemning it to remain in ideal isolation, with no jurisdiction over life, no connection with its affairs, and no remedy for its problems. For, as the popular saying goes, "Religion concerns only a man and his God." But as for ordinary relationships, the bonds of society and the problems of life, and political or economic theory—religion has nothing to do with these things, nor they with it; such is the view of those who are not actively hostile to religion. As for the others, their reaction is: Make no mention of religion here; it is nothing but an opiate employed by plutocrats and despots to drug the working classes and to paralyze the unfortunate masses.

How have we arrived at this strange view of the nature and the history of Islam? We have imported it, as we import everything, from across the deserts and beyond the seas. For certainly the fable of a divorce between faith and life did not grow up in the Muslim East, nor does Islam know of it; and the myth that religion is but a drug to the senses was not born of this faith at any time, nor does the nature of the faith even sanction it. We merely repeat these things like parrots, and accept them second hand like monkeys; we never think of looking for their origin and their sources, nor of learning their beginning or their results. Let us see first, then, whence and how these strange opinions came about.

*   *   *   *   *   *   *

Christianity grew up in the shadow of the Roman Empire, in a period when Judaism was suffering an eclipse, when it had become a system of rigid and lifeless ritual, an empty and unspiritual sham. The Roman Empire had its famous laws, which still live as the origin of modern European legislation; the Roman public had its own customs and social institutions. Christianity had no need then—nor, indeed, had it the power—to put before a powerful Roman government and a united Roman public laws and rules and regulations for government or for society. Rather, its need was to devote its power to moral and spiritual purification; and its concern was to correct the stereotyped ritual and the empty sham of ceremonial Judaism, and to restore spirit and life to the Israelite conscience.

Christ (upon whom be peace) came only to preach spiritual purity, mercy, kindness, tolerance, chastity, and abstinence, and to moderate certain restrictions that had been imposed on the Children of Israel or that they themselves had invented. He showed by his behavior and by his opinions that he attached no importance to the narrow traditions of the priests and the scribes; they were concerned only with external acts, while his concern was with the moral and the spiritual realms. Thus he made the Jewish sabbath lawful to his disciples; and thus he allowed them to eat anything which entered the mouth, because it was not that which defiled, but rather that which came forth in the way of "deceit, falsehood, and adultery." Thus, while he made it lawful for his disciples to break the fast on the Jewish fast-days, yet he would not stone the adulterous woman who was brought to him for questioning; for of those who should have been responsible for her stoning, according to the Mosaic Law, not one was free from guilt. He once said, "You have heard that it has been said 'An eye for an eye and a tooth for a tooth'; but I say to you 'Resist not evil; but whoever strikes you on the right cheek, turn the other to him also. And whoever wishes to quarrel with you and to take your undergarment, give him your overgarment also; and whoever forces you to go one mile, go with him two."

The same spirit is apparent also in the words, "You have heard that it was said to those of old, 'Do not kill; for whoever kills is liable to judgment.' But I say to you, Indeed, everyone who is angry with his brother without cause is liable to judgment; whoever says to his brother "Fool" is liable to the Council; and whoever says "Imbecile" is liable to the fire of Gehenna. So if you bring your offering to the altar, and if you remember there that your brother has some cause of complaint against you, then leave your offering there in front of the altar, go first and settle your quarrel with your brother and. then come and present your offering. Be reconciled with your opponent quickly while you are in the way."

Or again: "You have heard that it was said to those of old, 'Do not commit adultery'. But I say to you that whoever looks at a woman with desire has already committed adultery with her in his heart; if your right eye causes you to stumble, pluck it out and cast it from you, for it is better for you that one of your members should perish than that your whole body should be thrown into hell-fire; or if your right hand causes you to stumble, cut it off and cast it from you, for it is better for you that one of your members should perish than that your whole body should be thrown into hell-fire."

Or: "Again ye have heard that it hath been said by them of old, 'Thou shalt not forswear thyself, but shalt perform unto the Lord thine oaths.' But I say unto you, Swear not at all. Not by Heaven, for it is God's throne; nor by the earth, for it is His footstool; nor by Jerusalem, for it is the city of the Great King. Nor shalt thou swear by thy head, for thou cannot make one hair white or black. But let your speech be, Yea; nay, nay. Whatsoever is more than that cometh of evil."

Accordingly, Christianity forgot about "Render unto Caesar the things that are Caesar's, and unto God the things that are God's," and it turned its full strength towards spiritual purity and pious discipline. It took its stand upon the ground that "Religion concerns only a man and his God," while the temporal law is concerned with the relationship between the individual and the state. And this was the more natural since Christianity grew up in the embrace of the Roman Empire, and since it was a reaction against Judaism.

Accordingly, the Christian faith pushed to the uttermost limit its teachings of spiritual purity, material asceticism, and unworldly forebearance. It fulfilled its task in this spiritual sphere of human life, because it is the function of a religion to elevate man by spiritual means so far as it can, to proclaim piety, to cleanse the heart and the conscience, to humble man's nature, and to make him ignore worldly needs and strive only for holy objectives in a world of shades and vanities. But it left society to the State, to be governed by its earthly laws, since to it society was connected with the outer and temporal world, whereas the faith had its realm in the soul and the conscience. In this, Christianity was logical on three counts; first, because it grew up in a strictly limited area; second, because of the particular needs of the Jewish people to whom Jesus was sent in that they formed only a tiny fragment of the totality of the great Roman Empire; and thirdly, because of the limited time allotted to Christianity before the appearance of the new world religion—the faith of Islam.

Then God so willed it that Christianity should cross the seas to Europe, taking with it all its sublimity and purity and denial of the material world. There it met the Romans, inheritors of the pagan and material culture of Greece, and there it met also the peoples of the remoter parts of Europe, its first contact with the barbarian world. They were peoples of immense numbers, fighting bitterly over their narrow territories, ruthless and merciless in nature, mean and selfish in outlook. Among them none could taste the savor of ease for a moment, nor could put away his weapons for a minute, nor could find time in the struggle of life for the speculations of Christianity, this unselfish, excessively self-denying faith. "Whoever smite thee on the right cheek, turn to him the other also; and whoever wisheth to sue thee and take away thy undergarment, give him your overgarment also." Such peoples early saw that religion was of no profit to life, and they concluded that "Religion concerns only a man and his God." Accordingly, they found it natural to seek the refuge of religion while they were in the church and to breathe its air in the sanctuary, and after to return to the battle of life with all their barbarian customs; so they settled their quarrels by the judgment of the sword, or on occasion by that of the local law. And religion was left in pious isolation, to deal only with heart and conscience in the holy sanctuary and in the confessional.

Hence arose that division between religion and the world in the life of Europe; for the actual truth inherent in the nature of things is this, that Europe was never truly Christian. Hence religion there has remained in isolation from the business and the customs of life from the day of its entry to the present day.

But the churchmen, the priests, the cardinals, and the popes were unable thus to guarantee their own prosperity or to preserve their influence so long as the Church remained isolated from the economic, social, and administrative life. So it became inevitable that the Church should become a power comparable to the power of kings and rulers—with an inevitable weakening of its spiritual authority in the sphere of everyday life. Then came the age when the Church had princes with armies and authority not less than the most powerful of kings with their troops and their sovereignty. Thus inevitably there arose the dispute between the Church and temporal power, between the popes and the emperors, with the common people largely on the side of the Church. But to this—again inevitably—there succeeded the alliance between these two powers, for each had a common interest in keeping the masses in subjection and in the exploitation of the common people. This alliance lasted as long as prosperity remained essentially economic and material, and as long as the dispute was basically concerned with temporal power. It was under these circumstances, and because of despots and religious tyrants, that the saying arose that: "Religion is the opiate of the masses." For it was thus that it happened in Europe.

So the Church remained the supreme spiritual power, with full authority over men, in this world and the next. It continued to sell its "plenary indulgences," and to preach its "eternal damnation"; it continued to hold sway over men's bodies and minds alike; further, it even had the power of inquisition to kill or burn anyone who raised his head in revolt, or who even inclined to doubt or heresy. Then came the age of the Renaissance, and the Church was quick to perceive the threat to its power which must result from the enfranchisement of mind and sense after the Dark Ages; there was no slight danger that it would be deprived of its power by the pride of the thought and knowledge now coming into being. So the Church set itself in opposition, striving to muzzle liberty of thought and freedom of speech which contradicted its ancient and threadbare doctrines. And so from that time there has been bitter hostility between the Church and free thought. For the Church was unwilling to limit itself to spiritual affairs, which are the true sphere of Christianity; nor was it content to hold sway merely over the world to come, as is the claim of the Papacy. Therefore, its doctrines have come into conflict with those of science on such matters as the world, the universe, and the nature of existence. But the teachings of science are based on study and trial and experiment, and they are corroborated by experience and by proof, so that the discoveries of science leave no room for doubt concerning the strength of this new weapon; and so there have grown up generations of scientists and thinkers who dislike and even despise the Church, and who have in their hearts only hostility and loathing for Church and churchmen. Hence has arisen the bitterness between religion and science, between the Church and the intellectual world in the life of Europe.

With the advance of time the new science bore its fruits, and there grew from it in the sphere of technology what is known as mass production. Capital increased and in the arena of industry there appeared two sharply divided camps, that of capital and that of labor. The cleavage between the interests of these two soon became apparent, and the real authority passed from the hands of the state to those of the capitalists; and since the Church had no chance of sharing that authority, it joined itself to the capitalist camp.

I should not care to denigrate the whole body of European churchmen. There are some self-seekers who want only power and who devote themselves to its acquisition. To this end they draw from their religion an opiate for the masses of the workers, in order to restrain them from revolution in search of their rights; or they wean them from the pursuit of justice in this world by the promise of compensation in the next. But the majority must be sincere, by reason of their faith in the tenets of Christianity which is essentially acetic. By its nature a denial of worldly life, it is a summons to avoid materialism, to despise the world, and to seek rather the Lord's kingdom in the Heavenly world.

But be that as it may, the laboring classes who contemplate a class struggle have concluded that religion will not serve their cause in that struggle. They affirm that the Church uses religion only as an opiate for the working classes, and they have turned completely against religion, saying of it that, "It is the opiate of the millions." Hence there has arisen the manifest Communist hostility to religion.

* * * * * * *

On the other hand, what of ourselves; what has all this to do with us? The conditions of our history and the nature and circumstances of Islam have nothing in common with any of these things. Islam grew up in an independent country owing allegiance to no empire and to no king, in a form of society never again achieved. It had to embody this society in itself, had to order, encourage, and promote it. It had to order and regulate this society, adopting from the beginning its principles and its spirit along with its methods of life and work. It had to join together the world and the faith by its exhortations and laws. So Islam chose to unite earth and heaven in a single system, present both in the heart of the individual and the actuality of society, recognizing no separation of practical exertion from religious impulse. Essentially Islam never infringes that unity even when its outward forms and customs change.

Such was the birth of Islam and such its task; so it was not liable to be isolated in human idealism far removed from practical worldly life; nor was it compelled to narrow the circle of its action out of fear of an empire or a monarch. For the center of its being and the field of its action is human life in its entirety, spiritual and material, religious and worldly. Such a religion cannot continue to exist in isolation from society, nor can its adherents be true Muslims unless they practice their faith in their social, legal, and economic relationships. And a society cannot be Islamic if it expels the civil and religious laws of Islam from its codes and customs, so that nothing of Islam is left except rites and ceremonials.

"No, by thy Lord, they do not believe until they make thee judge in their disputes, and do not afterwards find difficulty in thy decisions, but submit to them fully." (4:68) "What the Apostle gives you, receive it; and what he forbids you, refrain from it." (59:7) "And whoever does not judge by what Allah has sent down—is an unbeliever." (5:48)

One of the characteristic marks of this faith is the fact that it is essentially a unity. It is at once worship and work, religious law and exhortation. Its theological beliefs are not divorced in nature or in objective from secular life and customs. Thus its prayers, which are the highest expression of the theological side of religion, express the turning of the individual and of the congregation towards one single, mighty, and powerful God, and they entail submission to none save to Him. So, too, the direction of prayer is uniform, nor can any deviate from it. Similarly, Muslim prayers infer a kind of equality, since they express one faith to which all are obedient, and in view of which all are equal. Nay, more: "The credo is that there is no god save Allah," which is the most distinctive tenet of the faith, implying as it does for the worshippers a freedom of religion from any kind of servitude. Such a freedom is the fundamental basis of a righteous and dignified community, in which all men are equals.

However we approach the question, there can be no shadow of doubt that the theory of society is obviously reflected in the beliefs and the customs of this religion, and that these latter represent the basic, powerful, and universal theory of all social life. So, if in any age we find a desire to overemphasize the pietistic aspect of this faith and to divorce it from the social aspect, or to divorce the social aspect from it, it will be the fault of that age rather than of Islam.

Now, these statements on Islam are not a new theory which is being propounded, nor is a reinterpretation of the faith here being made; this is Islam as it has manifested itself in history and as it was understood by its first exponent, Muhammad (upon whom be the blessings and the peace of Allah), as well as by his sincere Companions and all those close to its original source. There is a passage in the glorious Qur'an: "O ye who believe, when proclamation is made for prayer on the day of assembly, strive towards remembrance of Allah and leave off business. That is better for you if you are wise. But when the prayer is finished, scatter abroad in the land and seek the bounty of Allah." (62:9–10) Now all of us know how much time in the day is taken up by the statutory prayers and how much remains for business and trade. The time given to prayer is but a small proportion of man's life, while for the needs of society and life there remains the whole length of day and night. So it is said in another place: "We have appointed the night for a cover, and We have appointed the day for a livelihood." (78:10–11) For the major activity during the day is the making of a living, rather than any prescribed acts of worship.

So Islam does not prescribe worship as the only basis of its beliefs, but rather it reckons all the activities of life as comprehending worship in themselves—so long as they are within the bounds of conscience, goodness, and honesty. A man once passed by the Prophet, and the Companions of Muhammad noticed in him an eager intentness on his business which set them talking about him; they said, "O Messenger of Allah, would that this man had been in the path of Allah. Then said Muhammad, "If he has come to work for his young children, then he is in the path of Allah; or if he has come to work for his aged and infirm parents, then he is in the path of Allah; or if he has come to work for himself in all moderation, then he is in the path of Allah. But if he has come to work only for luxury or for self-glory, then he is in the path of Satan." Similarly the two following stories are authoritative indications of the spirit of Islam as understood by its founder, the Messenger of Allah. It is related on the authority of Anas that he said: We were on a journey with the Prophet, some of us having fasted and some having eaten. We alighted somewhere in a day of scorching heat, and he who had a garment gave us its shade, but many of us had to shade ourselves from the sun with our hands. So those who had fasted lay helpless, but those who had eaten arose and went from door to door till they got water for the party. Then said the Messenger, "Those who did not fast have this day carried off the full reward." And again, a certain man, noted for his piety, was mentioned to the Prophet, who said, "Who lives with him? His brother." Then said he, "His brother is then more pious than he."

Now all this does not mean that Muhammad, who surely knew his own religion better than any other, scorned the whole matter of fasting and prayer; it means rather that the essential spirit of this religion is found in this—that practical work is religious work, for religion is inextricably bound up with life and can never exist in the isolation of idealism in some world of the conscience alone. This is what 'Umar ibn al-Khattab had in mind when, seeing a man making a parade of asceticism and enfeeblement, he struck him with his whip, crying, "Do not kill our religion to our face, may Allah destroy you." Or on another occasion, when a certain man was giving evidence before him, 'Umar said to him, "Bring hither some one who knows you." So the man brought another who praised him highly. Then said 'Umar to the second man, "Are you this man's nearest neighbor, to know his comings and goings?" "No." "Have you, then, been his companion on a journey, whereon he gave evidence of nobility of character?" "No." "Have you perhaps had dealings with him in money matters, wherein he showed himself a man of self-control? "No." "Then I suspect that you have only seen him in the mosque, murmuring the Qur'an, and now and then lowering and raising his head in prayer." "That is so." Then said 'Umar, "Away. You do not really know him." And turning to the man himself, "Go, and bring hither someone who really knows you."

In such stories 'Umar is at one with his Prophet, Muhammad. And such give a reliable indication of the nature of this faith, its opinion of worship and of asceticism, of faith which is hidden in the heart and of work which is apparent to the sight. "In the midst of what Allah hath given you seek the future world, but forget not your portion in this world." (28:77)

And, "Work for this world as if you were going to live forever, but work for the future world as if you were going to die tomorrow." "Whoever among you sees a stranger, let him make provision for him." "And were it not that Allah sets some men against others, the cloisters had been destroyed, and the churches and the synagogues and mosques in which the name of Allah is often repeated." (22:41) "And fight in the 'way of Allah against those who fight against you, but do not provoke hostility; verily Allah loveth not those that provoke hostility." (2:186) "Piety lies not in turning your faces to East or West; but piety is this, that a man believe in Allah and the Day of Judgment, in the Angels, and the Book and the Prophets; that he give generously and for love alone to kindred and to orphans, to the poor and the wayfarer, to beggars and to those under oppression; that he be constant in prayer and that he give alms; that such men stand to their word when they pledge their word, and that they have fortitude in poverty, in distress, and in time of evil." (2:172)

Such is the position of Islam in regard to works and faith; and hence it is clear that there can be no separation between the faith and the world, or between theology and social practice, as was the case in early Christianity.

Furthermore, in Islam there is no priesthood, and no intermediary between the creature and the Creator; but every Muslim from the ends of the earth or in the paths of the sea has the ability of himself to approach his Lord without priest or minister. Nor again can the Muslim administrator derive his authority from any papacy, or from Heaven; but he derives it solely from the Muslim community. Similarly, he derives his principles of administration from the religious law, which is universal in its understanding and application and before which all men come everywhere as equals. So, the man of religion has no right to oppress Muslims; nor has the administrator any power other than that of implementing the law, which derives its authority from the faith. As for the world to come, all men are making their way to Allah, "and all of them will come before Him singly on the Day of Judgment." (19:95) Hence, too, there can be no quarrel between men of religion and the state concerning the control of the faithful or of their possessions. They cannot contend for economic or spiritual profits, for Islam has no knowledge of one spiritual power and another temporal power. So there is no possibility of disagreement here, as was the case with the emperors and the popes.

Islam is not hostile to learning, nor in opposition to the learned; on the contrary, it accepts learning as a divine and sacred possession which forms a part of religious duty. "The seeking of knowledge is a duty for every Muslim." "Seek learning even if it be found as far as China." "He who treads the path of the search for learning, Allah will facilitate his path to Paradise." So Islamic history has never known those evil, organized persecutions of thinking men or learned men, such as were known in the lands of the Inquisition; the short, scattered periods in which men have been victimized for their theories may be accounted as anomalous in Muslim history. In general, such occurrences were the outcome of political conditions, the result of concealed party differences, and on the whole were not a normal feature of Islamic life. Also, they arose among peoples who neither knew nor comprehended Islam fully.

Such a tolerance was no more than natural in a religion, which did not depend for its proof on wonders and miracles, which did not rely on strange events for the very heart of its message, but which relied rather on the examination and scrutiny of the evidence of life itself and its facts. "Surely in the creation of heaven and earth, in the division of night and day, in the ship which runs on the sea, carrying what is of profit to men, in the water which Allah has sent down from heaven to revive the earth after its death, spreading abroad in it every kind of cattle, in the changing of the winds and the clouds made to do service between heaven and earth—in all these are signs for a people who have intelligence." (2:159) "He bringeth forth the living from the dead, and He bringeth forth the dead from the living; as He quickeneth the earth after it is dead, so will you be brought forth. Among His signs is that He hath created you from dust, and lo, you are human beings, spreading abroad. And among His signs is that He hath created for you wives of your own kind that you may dwell with them, and hath set love and mercy between you; surely in that there are signs for a thoughtful people. Again, among His signs is the creation of the heavens and the earth, and the divergence of your tongues and complexions. Surely in that there are signs for those who know. Among His signs is your sleeping by night and by day, and your seeking a share of His bounty; surely in that there are signs for a people who hearken. Among His signs is that He makes you to see the lightning in fear and desire, and that He sends down water from heaven, and thereby quickens the earth after it has been dead; surely in that there are signs for a people who understand." (30:18–23)

And again, this tolerance is but natural in a religion which associates piety with learning, making the latter the pathway to a knowledge and a reverence of Allah. "Only the learned among His servants truly fear Allah" (35:25); and so He exalts the station of the learned above that of the unlearned. "Say: Are they who have knowledge equal with them who have none?" (39:12) "Surely the learned man surpasses the merely pious man in excellence, as the moon on the night of its fullness surpasses the remainder of the stars." So there is no gulf yawning between religion and learning, either in the nature or in the history of Islam, comparable to that which existed between the Christian Church and the liberal scholars during the Renaissance.

As for men of religion associating themselves with the power of the state or with the power of wealth and thus keeping the workers and the deprived drugged by means of religion, there is no denying that this did happen in some periods of Islamic history. But the true spirit of the faith disavows such persons; the faith indeed threatens them with dire punishments for having exchanged the signs of Allah for a trifling price. And furthermore, history has preserved beside the memory of such men examples of another type of religious scholar, men who without fearing the reproach of anyone confronted rulers and the rich to assert the claims of the poor and the rights of Allah. They encouraged the underprivileged to demand the rights that they expounded to them, and as a result were themselves exposed to the oppression of the rulers as well as occasional banishment and persecution.

*   *   *   *   *   *   *

We have, then, not a single reason to make any separation between Islam and society, either from the point of view of the essential nature of Islam or from that of its historical course; such reasons as there are attach only to European Christianity. And yet the world has grown away from religion; to it the world has left only the education of the conscience and the purification of the soul, while to the temporal and secular laws has been committed the ordering of society and the organizing of human life.

Similarly we have no good grounds for any hostility between Islam and the struggle for social justice, such as the hostility which persists between Christianity and Communism. For Islam prescribes the basic principles of social justice and establishes the claim of the poor to the wealth of the rich; it lays down a just principle for power and for money and therefore has no need to drug the minds of men and summon them to neglect their earthly rights in favor of their expectations in heaven. On the contrary, it warns those who abdicate their natural rights that they will be severely punished in the next world, and it calls them "self-oppressors." "Surely the angels said to those who died when they were oppressing themselves, 'In what circumstances were you?' They answered, 'We were poor in the earth.' The angels said, 'Was not Allah's earth wide enough for you to migrate?' The abode of such is Hell—an evil place to go." (4:99) Thus Islam urges men to fight for their rights: "And he who is killed while attempting to remedy injustice, the same is a martyr. "So, while Europe is compelled to put religion apart from the common life, we are not compelled to tread the same path; and while Communism is compelled to oppose religion in order to safeguard the rights of the workers, we have no need of any such hostility to religion.

But can we be certain that this social order, which was established by Islam in one specific period of history, will continue to have the potential for growth and renewal? Can we be sure that it is suitable for application to other periods of history whose circumstances differ to a greater or lesser degree from those which obtained in the age which gave birth to Islam?

This is a fundamental question. It is not possible to give an exhaustive answer to it here, as it will be answered in detail in what is to follow; first we must examine this social order itself, define its sources and roots, and scrutinize its applications in everyday life. Suffice it here—for we are still in the stage of general discussion—to say that Islam (which is the product of the Creator of the universe, the One who established its norms) has already experienced such an historical process, and the social, economic, and intellectual developments connected with it. This process Islam has traversed by laying down the general, universal rules and principles, and leaving their application in detail to be determined by the processes of time and by the emergence of individual problems. But Islam itself does not deal with the incidental related issues of the principle, except insofar as such are expressions of an unchanging principle whose impact is felt universally. This is the limit of the authority which can be claimed by any religion, in order that it may guarantee its flexibility and ensure the possibility of its own growth and expansion over a period of time.

For this reason the jurists of Islam devoted themselves with a strong and praiseworthy effort to the science of application of the principle, to analogy, and to deduction; most of their work is, in our opinion, in agreement with the spirit of Islam. But in the case of a small proportion, a certain looseness appeared in some of their works, resulting in a greater or lesser divergence from the spirit of Islam. Still, in the majority of cases, it may safely be said that the principles of the faith have kept pace with the needs of the time. To this period of production of jurisprudence there succeeded a long interval during which the growth of law came to a halt, until at the beginning of the present century, new life began to pervade the subject as the Muslim world as a whole started to awake.

The conclusion from this is that we should not put away the social aspect of our faith on the shelf; we should not go to French legislation to derive our laws or to Western or Communist ideals to derive our social order without first trying to reconnect with our Islamic legislation, which was the foundation of our first form of society. Moreover, we should not despair of the ability of the *shari'a* to govern modern society, because the organic and natural growth of any system within a given environment makes it at the very least more fitted for that environment than a system alien to it or imposed upon it. However, there is a wide ignorance of the nature of our faith as well as the nature of societies and the laws governing life; there is a psychological and intellectual laziness that is opposed to a return to our former resources; there is a ridiculous servility to the European fashion of divorcing religion from life—a separation necessitated by the nature of their religion, but not by the nature of Islam. For, with them there still exists that gulf between religion on the one hand and learning and the State on the other, the product of historical reasons which have no parallel in the history of Islam.

This does not mean that our summons is to an intellectual, spiritual, and social avoidance of the ways of the rest of the world; the spirit of Islam rejects such an avoidance, for Islam reckons itself to be a message for the whole world. Rather, our summons is to return, to our own stored-up resources, to become familiar with their ideas, and to test their validity and permanent worth, before we have recourse to an untimely and baseless servility which will deprive us of the historical background of our life, and through which our individuality will be lost to the point that we will become merely the hangers-on to the progress of mankind. Our religion demands that we should be ever in the forefront. "You are the best nation which has been brought forth for men; you enjoin the good, and you forbid the evil." (3:10)

It may well become apparent to us if we look back on our heritage that we have something to give to this unhappy, perplexed, and weary world, something which it has lost in the present material and unspiritual frame of mind that led to two world wars within a quarter of a century; something which the world is continually trampling under foot in its progress towards a third war, which all the present portents indicate will end in complete ruin.

Such is our position on this question. But, we must not proceed to speak of the value of Islam for modern society until first we have examined the nature of its relation to life and to all human problems; and particularly in the field of social justice, which is the main theme of this book.

8   Sorrows of the countryside

The child's small heart knew the bitterness of sorrow too soon. It was that day when he returned from school and entered the house as usual and there was his mother lamenting, grieving audibly, repeating in a soft voice one of those many poetic phrases that are used when lamenting, and tears were flowing copiously from her eyes. She tried to fight them back when she saw him, but could not. He was no more than ten years old and this was the first time he had seen her crying. He had seen her dejected before, but as soon as he would ask her, "What is wrong, mother?" she would put on a smile and answer, while clasping him to her breast, "Nothing! Nothing! Just a bit tired."

But this time she was crying openly. The tears cascaded from her eyes, and now she was not putting on a smile or hiding her pain. Here he was, standing perplexed a few steps away from her, as if he sensed something evil and so did not utter a word but stood silently before her. She noticed him there staring at her and tried to fight back her flowing tears but could not. Then she pulled herself together and called him to her, and he threw himself into her lap and buried his face in her breast. The blackness of her grief had communicated itself to his small heart, and here he was crying without knowing the cause of his crying or of hers.

At this point the mother's heart was aroused, as was her anxiety for her only son. At that time he was still her only son, having a sister who was three years older and another three years younger. She had not yet been granted his younger brother or his two younger sisters, as a result of which their family's continued existence would be assured. Now she was caressing him and hugging him to her with tenderness while he was lost in his tears. When she asked him to calm down, he asked her not to cry again. She said if he could calm his fears perhaps she could calm hers.

"I will not cry, my son, as long as you live. The *baraka* is in you. And, I swear by your lives"—she meant him and his two sisters—"you children and your father are sufficient for me."

The boy became quiet. He looked at his mother's face and saw that her tears had dried and that she was really active and cheerful. Her cheerfulness infected him and gave him the courage to ask her, "What is wrong, mother?"

She looked him in the eyes. It seemed as if she felt that her child had become a man and that the time had come to acquaint him with some of her worries, so she said to him:

"If I speak to you, sir, do you promise me that you will be a man?"

This word "man" jolted him, for he wanted very much to grow up quickly, and he said:

"Most certainly."

She said, "Today your father sold a piece of land."

Up to that time he had not really known the meaning of this. He had been sent to school when young and had been immersed in school life. He had not concerned himself with the conditions of agriculture or the *fellahin* as had others of his age in the village, who would have understood the meaning of that sentence if it had been uttered to one of them.

As he seemed somewhat puzzled about the meaning of this information and its connection with his mother's crying, she added:

"This means that our land is decreasing and, in fact, has decreased a number of times before by such sales, for your father sells a portion of our soil from one year to another, and if things continue this way the day will come when we will have no land, no fields, and no house, no animals, and nothing of all that you see now."

Now he had understood—or sensed—the magnitude of the catastrophe that threatened him, threatened him personally. Would he lose this "field" where he used to go on Fridays to run and jump merrily and play with the people who worked there and with those who took care of their animals? Their animals! Would he lose these animals? And especially, would he lose the cow that he cherished, which they kept even while they changed the other animals, because she had the special quality of providing milk and cream in abundance? More important than that was the firm friendship that bound him to her as it also did his sisters and his mother. She had been there almost the whole time he and his sisters were growing up and had become a "personality" dear to him and to all in the house.

And the house . . . would he lose this house? At this point he felt for it affection such as he had never felt before. Their spacious, beautiful house. And the well that belonged to it, that well from which their animals and all the animals of the street drank. He took pride in this well because it was on their property and was needed by the people. These people complimented them when they brought their animals to its trough and flattered him in particular when he looked them and their animals over. He felt greatly elated that their house had this great and unique distinction, namely, that their cows and their other animals did not have to leave their property to drink as other people's animals did.

Then the "oven porch," that room specifically set aside for the second floor oven, to be distinguished from the oven on the first floor—and this was another special advantage, because other people had only one oven due to the limited space in their houses. Their house, however, which they were threatened with losing, had two ovens, one used in the winter for warmth, located on the first floor, and the other used only for bread in the summer. The latter was in a room whose ceiling had an opening to let the smoke out and whose wall was partly cut away for the same purpose. This allowed him and his older sister to jump off and back onto the wall where it was cut away while their younger sister tried but could not. So they would tease her a bit while she cried and then they would take hold of her together and pass her up and down between them.

Then there was the *makhash*, a very long, unroofed space along the side of the house where they stored the straw and the stalks of dry maize and the cotton stalks, so as to avoid the danger of fire that resulted from using the roof for storage as was the custom in the village. Their property was large enough to give their house this other special advantage, this *makhash* in which the piled straw brought one closer to the first floor roof terrace. This enabled him and his older sister easily to jump from the roof of the first floor onto the straw without danger and then race each other back up the ladder to the roof to jump again. Then there was the private alley in front of the house, which was his playground where he and his young playmates would play ball and the various simple village games.

Dozens of these beloved images passed through his mind in a fleeting instant. He wished he could put his hands around each one of these images and hold onto it for fear that it would slip away. Were they really in danger of losing all of this? He did not believe anything that had been said, and he turned toward his mother as if angry and said: "But why is my father selling this land?"

She said: "Because he owes money to people and has to repay it."

But that answer was not adequate, for why did he owe people money? How could that be when the boy always saw plenty of money in his father's long white purse, with which he bought everything?

Perhaps she realized at that moment that she had made a mistake and told the small child these things too soon, so she tried to end the discussion and distract him from it, but he insisted on knowing. So she gave him a full explanation, which allowed him to understand that his father spent more each year than he took in and had to make up the difference by selling some of the land. Now he understood the whole situation and sensed the true nature of the danger, but it was more than his small mind could do to imagine the final outcome of things, so he said: "No, mother. We will not sell our house and our field, or these animals of ours. And we will not sell our old cow!" His mother seemed to relax and take hope in these simple words of her child. She said: "May God listen to you, my son."

Then she clasped him to her, then pushed him away a bit and looked into his eyes. Concentrating in the tone of her voice all the warmth of her faith, she said: "Listen, sir, you must get back what your father has lost!"

Although the warmth of her conviction penetrated to his heart, standing there in her presence he still could not understand how he could undertake such a marvelous task, and he looked at her seeking an explanation!

She said: "When you get older you will go to Cairo and stay with your uncle and you will get an education there and become an *effendi* and receive a salary. Then you will remember that our lands in the village were sold because your father spent too much and you will be careful with your money. Likewise, you will not waste it like your older brother but will spend only what is necessary. Then you will have lots of money in your pocket and you will buy back these lands that we have lost."

And while she was going on and on about her sweet dreams, which she expected her small child to fulfill, his imagination was dwelling on the trip to Cairo and on the *effendi* that he would be, and he did not pay attention to the rest of what she said.

He snapped back to attention, however, and was dumbfounded as she continued: "You must not be a spendthrift like your uncles, for they are like your father in their spending, perhaps even worse. Let me tell you that they sold their vast lands and all their many houses except for one small one."

Now he paid attention because he was already aware of these painful facts. He had not witnessed the beginning of the tragedy, but he was well aware of it as he went about the village and heard it from the mouths of the women and some of the men, just as he heard his mother recount it bitterly again and again. His grandfather on his mother's side had been very wealthy, but as soon as his four uncles grew up, two of them going to the Azhar and two of them remaining as farmers, they all became extremely extravagant. As soon as his grandfather died they squandered the wealth left and right until it was all gone. It turned out that the best-off of them was this uncle who worked as a teacher and a journalist in Cairo. With him lived the boy's grandmother, whom he loved almost to the point of worship and whom he saw on rare occasions. When his mother depicted the fate that awaited his father's house if things continued as they were going, he could see the yawning abyss. Thus the first seed of real responsibility was sown in his soul. He knew now why his mother was pushing his education so fast and why she had been so eager for him to go to the primary school rather than the *kuttab*. He had to repair the building before it collapsed.

Many women in the village bore the same worries and fears that his mother did, but did not have the hope she had in her young children, because they did not have a brother in Cairo. Cairo, in the minds of the villagers, was always associated with great happiness and a radical change of condition. That was because for many middle-class families in the village wealth was limited, because it was divided up by inheritance generation after generation, and by the third or fourth generation had almost dwindled away, unless there was an unexpected change of fortune. A good family could find itself in financial straits, and sometimes miserable poverty, while dwellings once inhabited and full of life could become melancholy ruins. The memory of these things would persist in the soul of each individual and particularly among the women, and so grief would dominate the house and gloom close it off, unless a new hope dawned.

The sorrows of the countryside are long and drawn out because time there moves with slow and plodding steps. Death, which assails one member of the family after another, always casts a thick black shadow, perching on every breast and appearing in every gesture. The country people hold onto their sorrows for a long time, finding in them nourishment for their souls, which are overshadowed by miseries on all sides: There are the bitter miseries of poverty following wealth, the painful miseries of poverty inherited from previous generations, and the miseries of death and its ceremonies. The death rate in the countryside is high, as is the birthrate, which compensates for it. But each death is a lasting memory in the heart of the mother or spouse or sister, which continues to exude grief whenever it is triggered by a funeral or some incident. She then takes refuge in sorrowful and melancholy lamentation.

When the men are in the fields they can forget. The bright sunlight fills their souls and brightens them, and the sprouting of the seeds in the black earth causes dim hopes to grow in their souls even though in their profound simplicity they cannot fully perceive them. But the women, who generally do not leave the houses—except for the very poor who on rare occasions go into the field in the Upper Egypt—these women have nothing to make them forget their sorrows. The houses are dark and their rooms are gloomy, especially when night falls and the houses are lit only by those dim, small kerosene lamps, which give forth their weak, pale light onto the dark walls, so that people's shadows dance upon them like specters, and a gloomy feeling of distress and sorrow settles over the house and those in it.

Then there is the dark-colored clothing. Only a bride in the early years of her marriage is allowed in this environment to adorn herself and wear beautiful clothes and to act lightheartedly. When the years pass and she gets older and reaches thirty, she must behave "modestly." If she continues with her adornment and beautiful clothes and her gaiety, tongues wag about her behavior and she becomes the object of criticism from all sides, and this at the age when her city cousin is just beginning to really enjoy life.

The economic factor enters into all of this, for it costs money to have beautiful clothes and to keep them clean all of the time, but dark clothes wear well and do not show the dirt, and so are more economical. The people, however, do not like to admit that it is economic considerations that determine their behavior, so they turn it into an ethical matter. The girl or woman who does not adorn herself and does not keep her clothes clean is the desired ethical model!

There is one month in the year when the village rejoices and forgets its sorrows, and that is the month of Ramadan. The secret of this rejoicing is, in the first place, the light—the light that shines from the many houses that are hosting parties at night, where doors are opened to visitors and the Qur'an is recited throughout the month. Then there are the lamps that hang from some of the doors to guide the many passersby who stay out late at night because they feel safe from the *'afarit*, which are fettered during the month of Ramadan in accordance with their ancient pact with the prophet Solomon.

The rejoicing is not only because of the light, however, but also because of the food. The whole town, both rich and poor, prepares for this blessed month with special and excellent food, both for *iftar* and *subur*. People cook almost every day and they eat meat and fruit in ample quantities, and there is plenty of activity in preparing for all of this. So when the village finds light and food during the month of Ramadan, it buries and forgets its sorrows and rejoices in life, free from deprivation and gloom.

This phenomenon is repeated during other festivals and special occasions, especially the *mawlid* of the Prophet, because of the abundance of the two basic ingredients of happiness. Then the unaccustomed activity dies down and the town returns to its dark gloom, to its inherited deprivation and its traditional sorrows, for it likes to dwell on these sorrows, which it calls "the burdens of fortune."

Among the "the burdens of fortune" may be listed the burden of poverty, the burden of deprivation, and the burden of the rulers' injustice. For the countryman is always oppressed by the rulers, oppressed by the taxes on his small bit of earth, oppressed by the endless demands of the *'umda* to meet the orders of the government, which include donations for charitable associations collected from the neediest people, the ones who should be receiving assistance from the charitable associations, tickets for the Red Crescent, tickets for the first aid service. Then there is the corveé labor on the dikes and in the fields of the rich to clear the caterpillars, and guard duty outside the village, and the struggle against locusts, and countless other "tasks" besides these, which make the villager feel like a beast of burden forever. Then there is the burden of unremitting toil in the soil and the fields, to supply maize for his food, if only he could do so for the whole year. Then there is the burden of tradition—especially on the woman—who is never more than a commodity in the eyes of the man. If she stays on good terms with her family and it is prosperous, then she receives some respect because there is money coming to her sometime, but if her family has been ruined—and many families have been ruined, as we have seen—then she suffers such humiliation and abuse as to turn her life into the blackest darkness.

Between that gloomy and oppressive sorrow and these "burdens of fate," the wrinkles on the face of fate opened up to show one smile. It was those children who romped and played for a large part of the year free of toil and labor until some time after their tenth year.

That was a quarter of a century ago. When the boy returned to his beloved village for a visit and inquired among other things about the romping of the children, he was told that that is all finished. That last smile on the gloomy face of fortune has gone out. It is now too hard to earn a livelihood, so the children and young boys are no longer allowed to laugh and romp and play, but are sent to work in the fields from the age of seven or eight, and their innocent gatherings and beautiful games have vanished from the village. This age has overburdened them and scourges their backs to drive them to labor from a young age. The whole "burden of fate" is on one shoulder, while on the other shoulder is the law of compulsory education, which takes the children from their work and thus takes the snacks out of their mouths while giving them neither knowledge nor food!

Notes

Preface

1 Others have also noted the significance of Qutb's writings: "Egypt's most influential writer in the radical Muslim political tradition" (Mark Juergensmeyer); "the Trotsky of the modern Islamic movement . . ." (Geneive Abdo); "Many Muslims had been profoundly influenced by the writings of Sayyid Qutb, a Muslim Brother . . ." (Karen Armstrong); "the most influential thinker of fundamentalist Islam" (Dinesh D'Sousa), "Qutb's analysis was rich, nuanced, deep, soulful, and heartfelt . . . the analysis asked some authentically perplexing questions—about . . . Western thought . . . the soullessness of modern power and technological innovation; about social injustice." (Paul Berman), and "a leading ideologue of Muslim fundamentalism" (Bernard Lewis). In particular, see Mark Juergensmeyer, *Terror in the Mind of God: The Global Rise of Religious Violence* (Berkeley: University of California Press, 2000); and Paul Berman, *Terror and Liberalism* (New York: Norton, 2003).

2 A recent study of *jihadi* websites by McCants suggests that next to the thirteenth-century work of Ibn Taymiyya, Qutb is the most quoted Islamist theorist. His ideas continue to be used to legitimate militant Islamic causes. See William McCants, *Militant Ideology Atlas: Executive Report* (West Point: Combating Terrorism Center, 2006), www.ctc.usma.edu/atlas/Atlas-ExecutiveReport.pdf; William McCants, *Militant Ideology Atlas: Research Compendium* (West Point: Combating Terrorism Center, 2006), www.ctc.usma.edu/atlas/Atlas-Research Compendium.pdf; Aboul-Enein, "Sheikh Abdel-Fatah Al-Khalidi Revitalizes Sayid Qutb" (West Point: Combating Terrorism Center, 2007), http://www.ctc.usma.edu/Khalidi-Qutb3.pdf.

3 See William E. Shepard, *Sayyid Qutb and Islamic Activism: A Translation and Critical Analysis of Social Justice in Islam* (New York: Brill, 1996); Olivier Carre, *Mysticism and Politics: A Critical Reading of Fi Zilal al-Qur'an by Sayyid Qutb (1906–1966)* (Boston: Brill, 2003).

4 Of the 1063 paragraphs in the last edition of *Social Justice in Islam* only 442 are completely without change. See Shepard, 1996: xxiii.

5 For literature on Qutb's life and ideas see, among others: Gilles Kepel, *Muslim Extremism in Egypt: The Prophet and Pharoah* (Berkeley: University of California Press, 1986); Gilles Kepel, *Jihad: The Trail of Political Islam* (Cambridge: Harvard University Press, 2002); Gilles Kepel, *Muslim Extremism in Egypt* (Berkeley: University of California Press, 2003); Gilles Kepel, *The War for Muslim Minds: Islam and the West* (Cambridge: Harvard University Press, 2004); Malise Ruthven, *Fundamentalism: The Searchs for Meaning* (Oxford: Oxford University Press, 2004); Yvonne Haddad, "The Qur'anic Justification for an Islamic Revolution: The View of Sayyid Qutb" *The Middle East Journal* 37: 14–29 (1983); Yvonne Haddad, "Sayyid Qutb: Ideologue of Islamic Revival," In *Voices of Resurgent Islam*, John Esposito, Ed. (New York: Oxford University Press, 1983); Gabriel A. Almond, R. Scott Appleby, and Emmanuel Sivan, *Strong Religion: the Rise of Fundamentalisms Around the World* (Chicago: University of Chicago Press, 2003); Mark Juergensmeyer, *Terror in the Mind of God: The Global Rise of Religious Violence* (Berkeley: University of California Press, 2000); Fuller, 2003; Noah Feldman, *After Jihad: America and the Struggle for Islamic Democracy* (New York: Farrar, Straus and Giroux, 2003); Paul Berman, *Terror and Liberalism* (New York: Norton, 2003); Roxanne L. Euben, *Enemy in the Mirror: Islamic Fundamentalism and The Limits of Modern Rationalism* (Princeton: Princeton University Press, 1999); Ahmad S. Mousalli, *Radical Islamic Fundamentalism: The Ideological and Political Discourse of Sayyid Qutb* (Beirut: American University of Beirut, 1992); I. M. Abu-Rabi, *Intellectual Origins of Islamic Resurgence in the Modern Arab World* (State University of New York Press, 1996);

William McCants, *Militant Ideology Atlas: Executive Report* (West Point: Combating Terrorism Center, 2006), www.ctc.usma.edu/atlas/Atlas-ExecutiveReport.pdf; William McCants, Militant Ideology Atlas: Research Compendium (West Point: Combating Terrorism Center, 2006), www.ctc.usma.edu/atlas/Atlas-ResearchCompendium.pdf; Aboul-Enein, "Sheikh Abdel-Fatah Al-Khalidi Revitalizes Sayid Qutb" (West Point: Combating Terrorism Center, 2007), http://www.ctc.usma.edu/Khalidi-Qutb3.pdf.

1 Sayyid Qutb in historical context

1 This brief history is a compilation of information taken from a variety of secondary sources.
2 Olivier Carre, *Mysticism and Politics: A Critical Reading of Fi Zilal al-Qur'an by Sayyid Qutb (1906–1966)* (Boston: Brill, 2003): 7
3 Carre, 2003: 6.
4 Qutb's prison experience was part of a larger canvas of violent political struggle over control of the Egyptian state. "For the period of their existence up to 1966, the Brothers count their martyrs as follows: 263 killed (including deaths in combat in Palestine and in Canal guerilla warfare); 1,450 imprisoned for life, with or without forced labor, 61,000 questioned and arrested" (Carre, 2003: 7).
5 Carre, 2003: 7.
6 Gilles Kepel, Muslim Extremism in Egypt (Berkeley: University of California Press, 2003); Carre, 2003; Ahmad S. Mousalli, *Radical Islamic Fundamentalism: The Ideological and Political Discourse of Sayyid Qutb* (Beirut: American University of Beirut, 1992); William E. Shepard, "Introduction," In *Social Justice in Islam*, Translated by William E. Shepard (Brill Academic Publishers, 1996); John Calvert and William Shepard, "Translator's Introduction." In Sayyid Qutb, *A Child from the Village*. Edited, Translated, and with an Introduction by John Calvert and William Shepard (Syracuse: Syracuse University Press, 2004): xiii–xxxii.
7 Calvert and Shepard, 2004: xx.
8 Kepel, 2003: 28.
9 Kepel, 2003: 28.
10 Moussalli, 1992: 36.
11 Shepard, 1996: lv.
12 Antonio Gramsci, *Prison Notebooks* [1929–1935]. (New York: International Publishers, 1990).
13 Sayyid Qutb, *Milestones* (Chicago: Kazi Publications, 1991) 24.
14 Sayyid Qutb, *This Religion of Islam* (Riyadh: International Islamic Publishing House, Nd.): 47, 59.
15 Marc Sageman, *Understanding Terror Networks* (Philadelphia: University of Pennsylvania Press, 2004): 14, 15.
16 Lawrence Wright, "The Man Behind Bin Laden" *The New Yorker*, September 16, 2002; Lawrence Wright, *The Looming Tower: Al-Qaeda and the Road to 9/11* (New York: Knopf, 2006); Paul Berman, *Terror and Liberalism* (New York: Norton, 2003); Gilles Kepel, *Muslim Extremism in Egypt: The Prophet and Pharoah* (Berkeley: University of California Press, 1986); Gilles Kepel, *Jihad: The Trail of Political Islam* (Cambridge: Harvard University Press, 2002); Gilles Kepel, *The War for Muslim Minds: Islam and the West* (Cambridge: Harvard Univ. Press, 2004); Aboul-Enein, "Sheikh Abdel-Fatah Al-Khalidi Revitalizes Sayid Qutb," (West Point: Combating Terrorism Center, 2007), http://www.ctc.usma.edu/Khalidi-Qutb3.pdf.
17 Emanuel Sivan, *Radical Islam: Medieval Theology and Modern Politics*. (New Haven: Yale University Press, 1985): 18.
18 Carre, 2003: 6.
19 Salim Yaqub, *Containing Arab Nationalism: The Eisehnower Doctrine and the Middle East* (Chapel Hill: University of North Carolina Press, 2004): 270.
20 Yaqub, 2004: 33.
21 Yaqub, 2004: 34.
22 Sivan, 1985: 91.
23 Michael Bonner, *Jihad in Islamic History* (Princeton: Princeton University Press, 2006); Rudolph Peters, *Jihad in Classical and Modern Islam* (Princeton: Markus Weiner, 1996).
24 These positions were also staked out by the regime in power, given the diffusely socialist and pro-Soviet stance of the Nasser government.
25 Sivan, 1985: 97.
26 Sivan, 1985: 92.
27 Quoted in Sivan, 1985: 21.

28 Although it is impossible to trace the origins of the Islamic Revival/Protestant Reformation analogy with any certainty. See Charles Kurzman and Michalle Browers, "Introduction: Comparing Reformations." In Michaelle Browers and Charles Kurzman, *An Islamic Reformation?* (Lanham, MD: Lexington Books, 2004): 2.

29 Carl L. Brown, *Religion and State: The Muslim Approach to Politics* (New York: Columbia University Press, 2000): 4.

30 Francis Robinson, "Other Worldly and This Worldly Islam and the Islamic Revival" *Journal of the Royal Asiatic Society* (Series 3, 14:1. pp. 47–58): 50.

31 Albert Hourani, *Arabic Thought in the Liberal Age, 1789–1939* (Cambridge: Cambridge University Press, 1983).

32 John L. Esposito, *Voices of Resurgent Islam* (New York: Oxford, 1983).

33 See the papers in Michaelle Browers and Charles Kurzman, *An Islamic Reformation?* (Lanham, MD: Lexington Books, 2004).

34 Ellis Goldberg, "Smashing Idols and the State: The Protestant Ethic and Egyptian Sunni Radicalism," *Comparative Studies in Society and History* 33: 3–35 (1991).

35 Max Weber, *The Protestant Ethic and the Spirit of Capitalism* [1904–1905] (Los Angeles, Roxbury, 2002).

36 Robinson, 2003: 55.

37 George Williams, *The Radical Reformation* (Philadelphia: The Westminister Press, 1962).

38 Mark Segwick, "In Search of a Counter-Reformation: Anti-Sufi Stereotypes and the Budshishiyya's Response." pp. 125–146 in Michaelle Browers Michaelle and Charles Kurzman, *An Islamic Reformation?* (Lanham, MD: Lexington Books, 2004): 126.

39 Carl W. Ernst, *Following Muhammad: Rethinking Islam in the Contemporary World* (Chapel Hill: University of North Carolina Press, 2003): 104.

40 Ernst, 2003: 207.

41 Sedgwick, 2004: 127.

42 Quoted in Kurzman and Browers, 2004: 5.

43 Robinson, 2003: 53.

44 Burke, *Al-Qaeda: The True Story of Radical Islam* (London: I. B. Tauris, 2004): 121.

45 Sedgwick, 2004: 128.

46 Quoted in Sedgwick, 2004: 128.

47 Sedgwick, 2004: 129.

48 Sedgwick, 2004: 129.

49 Brown, 2000: 32.

50 John O. Voll, "Renewal and Reform in Islamic History: *Tajdid* and *Islah*." pp. 32–47 in John L. Esposito, ed., *Voices of Resurgent Islam* (New York: Oxford, 1983): 42.

51 Brown, 2000: 33.

52 Voll, 1983: 37.

53 Fred McGraw Donner, *The Early Islamic Conquests* (Princeton: Princeton University Press, 1981): 34.

54 Donner, 1981: 35.

55 Bonner, 2006: 173.

56 Patricia Crone, *God's Rule Government and Islam. Six Centuries of Medieval Islamic Political Thought* (New York: Columbia University Press, 2004): 12.

57 Crone, 2004: 13.

58 See Joseph E. B. Lumbard (ed.), *Islam, Fundamentalism, and the Betrayal of Tradition* (World Wisdom, 2004); Bruce B. Lawrence, *Shattering the Myth: Islam Beyond Violence* (Princeton University Press, 1998); Faud S. Naeem, "A Traditional Islamic Response to the Rise of Modernism," pp.79–116 in Joseph E. B. Lumbard (ed.), *Islam Fundamentalism, and the Betrayal of Tradition* (Bloomington: World Wisdom, 2004).

59 Edward Said, *Orientalism* (New York: Random House, 1978): 3.

60 Said, 1978: 3.

61 Gayatri Chakravorty Spivak, *A Critique of Postcolonial Reason: Toward a History of the Vanishing Present* (Cambridge: Harvard University Press, 1999); Homi K. Bhabha, ed., *Nation and Narration* (London: Routledge, 1990); Ashcroft, et. al., eds., *The Post-Colonial Studies Reader* (London: Routledge, 1995); Gregory Castle, ed., *Postcolonial Discourses: An Anthology* (Oxford: Blackwell, 2001); A. L. Macfie, ed., *Orientalism: A Reader* (New York: New York University Press, 2000).

62 Lawrence, 1998: xiii, 4.

63 Lawrence, 1998: 4.
64 Said, 1978: 206.
65 Lawrence, 1998: 4.

2 Qutb's core ideas

 1 Sayyid Qutb, *The Islamic Concept and Its Characteristics* (Plainfield, IN: American Trust Publica-
    tions, 1991): 2.
 2 Qutb, 1991: 3.
 3 Qutb, 1991: 184.
 4 Qutb, 1991: 31.
 5 Qutb, 1991: 9.
 6 Qutb, 1991: 7.
 7 Qutb, 1991: 187.
 8 Qutb, 1991:188.
 9 Qutb, 1991: 9.
10 Qutb, 1991: 26.
11 Qutb, 1991: 9.
12 Qutb, 1991: 9.
13 Quoted in Russell Shorto, "The Anti-Secularist: Can Pope Benedict XVI Re-Christianize
    Europe?" The New York Times Magazine (April 8, 2007): 58.
14 Qutb, 1991: 8, 9.
15 quoted in Shorto, 2007: 42.
16 Shorto, 2007, 40, 41.
17 Qutb, 1991: 9.
18 quoted in Shorto, 2007: 58.
19 Qutb, 1991: 191.
20 Sayyid Qutb, *Milestones* [1964] (Chicago: Kazi Publication Inc.): 60.
21 Qutb, 1991: 201.
22 Qutb, nd: 60.
23 Qutb, nd: 61.
24 Qutb, 1991: 155.
25 Qutb, 1991: 155.
26 Qutb, nd: 39.
27 Qutb, 1991: 11.
28 Qutb, 1991: 155.
29 Qutb, 1991: 156, 157.
30 Qutb, 1991: 158.
31 Qutb, 1991: 159.
32 Qutb, 1991: 160.
33 Qutb, 1991: 201.
34 Qutb, 1991: 1.
35 Qutb, 1991: 2.
36 Qutb, nd: 11.
37 Qutb, 1991: 78.
38 Mark 12:17.
39 Qutb, nd: 11, 31.
40 Qutb, nd: 11.
41 Qutb, 1991: 200.
42 Qutb, 1991: 201.
43 Qutb, 1991: 198.
44 Qutb, 1991: 198.
45 Qutb, nd: 11
46 Qutb, 1991: 200.
47 Qutb, nd: 158
48 Qutb, nd: 9.
49 Qutb, nd: 18.
50 Qutb, nd: 18.
51 Qutb, nd: 20.
52 Qutb, nd: 21.

53 Qutb, nd: 21.
54 Qutb, nd: 21.
55 Qutb, nd: 24.
56 Qutb, nd: 24.
57 Qutb, nd: 25.
58 Qutb, nd: 25.
59 Qutb, nd: 25.
60 Qutb, nd: 26.
61 Qutb, nd: 26.
62 Qutb, nd: 27.
63 Qutb, nd: 30.
64 Qutb, nd: 30.
65 Qutb, nd: 31.
66 Qutb, nd: 31.
67 Qutb, nd: 46.
68 Qutb, nd: 46, 47.
69 Qutb, nd: 47.
70 Qutb, nd: 47.
71 Qutb: nd: 48.
72 Qutb, nd: 48.
73 Qutb, nd: 45.
74 Qutb, 1991, 1, 2.
75 Qutb, nd: 62.
76 Qutb, nd: 62.
77 Qutb, nd: 65.
78 Qutb, nd: 71.
79 Qutb: nd: 63.
80 Qutb, nd: 63.
81 Qutb, nd: 64
82 Qutb, nd: 63.
83 Qutb, nd: 64.
84 Qutb, nd: 64, 65.
85 Qutb, nd: 70.
86 Qutb, nd: 53.
87 Qutb, nd: 71.
88 Qutb, nd: 71.
89 Qutb, nd: 71.
90 Qutb, nd: 74, 75.
91 Qutb, nd: 76.
92 Qutb, nd: 55.
93 Qutb, 1991: 12.
94 Sayyid Qutb, *In the Shade of the Qur'an*. Vol VII, Surah 8. Translated and edited by Adil Salahi
    (Leicestershire: The Islamic Foundation, 2003): 24.
95 Qutb, 2003: 24.
96 Qutb, 2003: 22.
97 Qutb, 2003: 7:12.
98 William McCants. *Militant Ideology Atlas: Executive Report*. (West Point: Combating Terrorism
    Center, 2006), http://www.ctc.usma.edu/atlas/Atlas-ExecutiveReport.pdf; William McCants,
    Militant Ideology Atlas: Research Compendium. (West Point: Combating Terrorism Center, 2006)
    http://www.ctc.usma.edu/atlas/Atlas-ResearchCompendium.pdf.
99 Here the term *Muslims* will refer to ". . . people who follow the Qur'an and the example of
    Muhammad. This includes Sunnis (people who follow the example of the Prophet) and Shi'is
    (people who follow the example of the Prophet and his descendents through his son-in-law
    Ali), and ranges from secularists to fundamentalists. . . . *Islamists* [refer to] . . . people who
    want Islamic law to be the primary source of law and cultural identity in a state. They differ
    over the meaning of this objective and the means of achieving it. Among Sunnis (the vast
    majority of the world's Muslims), the Muslim Brotherhood is the most influential group;. . . .
    Salafis [refer to] . . . Sunni Muslims who want to establish and govern Islamic states based
    solely on the Qur'an and the example of the Prophet as understood by the first generations of
    Muslims close to Muhammad. Salafis differ over the final form of these stats and the proper

mans for achieving them. This movement is ideologically akin to the . . . Puritan movement in England and America," [and *Jihadis* refer to] . . . the holy warriors and today's most prominent terrorists, whose movement is part of the larger Salafi Movement (but note that most Salafis are not Jihadists)" (McCants, 2006a:5–6).

100 Qutb, nd: 159.
101 Qutb, nd: 159.
102 Qutb, nd: 160.
103 Qutb, nd: 160.
104 Mike Davis, "Planet of Slums." NLR. March/April, 2004: 30
105 quoted in Davis, 2004, 30, 31.
106 Davis, 2004: 30.

3 Milestones

1 *Shirk* is an Arabic word which refers to ascribing the attributes, power, or authority of God to others besides Him and/or worshipping others besides Him.

4 Prologue to Al-Anfal

1 Ibn al-Qayyim, *Z111d al-Ma*'111d*, Mu'assasat Al-Risalah, Beirut, 1994, Vol. 3, pp. 158–161.
2 Ibn al-Qayyim, Ibid, p. 161.
3 For details of this expedition with our commentary on this verse please refer to Vol.I, Chapter 13.
4 This translation of Mawdudi's quote relies on the Urdu version of his paper, which was originally a speech given in Lahore in 1939. Sayyid Qutb quoted from an Arabic translation which appears to have been expanded in some places and abridged in others. It also appears that the Arabic translation utilizes an expansive style, using many synonymous phrases and expressions. Hence, a reader who compares this text with the Arabic quote is bound to notice differences in many paragraphs. However, the ideas expressed are the same, and the lines the two versions follow are identical. – Editor's note.
5 For a full discussion of the Battle of Badr, its events and consequences, see Adil Salahi, *Muhammad: Man and Prophet*, The Islamic Foundation, Leicester, 2002, pp. 253–295. —— Editor's note.
6 Muhammad ibn Ishaq was one of the earliest biographers of the Prophet. His report of the Battle of Badr is the basis of its account in *al-Bidayah wa'l-Nihayah* by Ibn Kathir. In his book, *Imta' al-Asma'*, al-Maqrizi provides more or less the same account. Similarly, Imam Ibn al-Qayyim gives a summarized version of it in *Zad al-Ma'ad*, as does Imam 'Ali ibn Hazm in *Jawami' al-Sirah*. We have incorporated parts of all these accounts into our summary of the events of this battle.
7 Ibn al-Qayyim, Ibid, p. 188.
8 When the Prophet went to Tā'if some four years earlier to address its people with the message of Islam, they treated him very badly, and set on him their slaves and children to stone him, and his two feet bled as a result. He sought refuge in an orchard belonging to 'Utbah and Shaybah, and when they saw him, they sent 'Addas to him carrying a bunch of grapes. When 'Addas spoke to the Prophet he recognized his position and kissed his hands and feet.
9 That was the incident in which the expedition led by 'Abdullah ibn Jahsh was involved.
10 As mentioned earlier, they were only 30–40 men according to Ibn Ishāq's report.
11 Al-Maqrizi, Ahmad ibn 'Ali, *Imta' al-Asma'*, Dar al-Kutub al-'Ilmiyyah, Beirut, 1999, Vol. I, pp. 85–89.
12 Ibn Sayyid al-Nas, *'Uyun al-Athar*, Dar al-Turath, Madinah, Vol. I, p. 389.
13 Ibn Hisham, *Al-Sirah al-Nabawiyyah*, Dar al-Qalam, Beirut, Vol. II, pp. 264–270.
14 That pledge was given at the time of the second 'Aqabah commitment, which was the basis of the migration to Medina by the Prophet and his Companions.—— Editor's Note
15 This exchange is reported somewhat differently by Ibn Ishaq. According to him, al-Hubab asked the Prophet: "Are we encamping here because God has told you to do so and we are not to move forward or backward from here? Or is it your own judgement that this is the right place to gain advantage against the enemy?" The Prophet answered that it was the latter. Therefore, al-Hubab said that it was not the right place, and gave the Prophet his advice as reported in the text. – Editor's Note

16 Al-Maqrizi, Ibid, pp. 93–98.

17 Ibn Hisham, Ibid, pp. 191–195.

18 Al-Maqrizi, Ibid, p. 103.

19 ʿUmar comments as he reports on this incident that it was the first time the Prophet called him Abu Hafs, following the Arabian tradition of calling a man as the father of his child, with Abu meaning father and Hafs a short version of his daughter's name.

20 The Prophet refused ʿUmar's request, as he refused to allow any killing of people that professed to be Muslims, even though they were known to be hypocrites. Abu Hudhayfah might have said this after seeing his father, brother and uncle being killed at the start of the battle, but he was a good Companion of the Prophet. May God be pleased with him.

21 Abu al-Bakhtari was nevertheless killed in this battle, because he refused to be taken prisoner.

22 What he meant was that if he was taken prisoner, he would then buy his freedom with several camels that would produce much milk.

23 Ibn Hisham, Ibid, pp. 196–199.

24 Abu al-Hakam was Abu Jahl's name among the Quraysh, and it has the opposite meaning of the nickname given to him by the Muslims, i.e. Abu Jahl, which means 'the father of ignorance.' — Editor's note.

25 This is a reference to ʿAbdullah ibn Masʿud's background who was a small man working as a shepherd in Mecca.

26 Ibn Hisham, Ibid, pp. 201–202.

27 Ibn Hisham, Ibid, p. 202.

28 Dates were the most common food in Medina, while bread was not always available. Bread is also filling; thus someone who ate bread would not feel the pangs of hunger like someone who ate only dates. – Editor's note.

29 Ibn Hisham, Ibid, pp.204–209.

5 The basis of inter-communal relations

1 Muhammad ibn Jarir al-Tabari, *Jamiʿ al-Bayan*, Dar al-Fikr, Beirut, 1984, Vol. 10, pp. 62–63.

2 Al-Tabari, ibid., pp. 61–62.

3 It should be stated here that Shaikh Rashid Rida was a proponent of the same school of Imam Muhammad ʿAbduh, which is clearly influenced by Descartes and his philosophy, which is alien to Islam. This school places very strong emphasis on reason, allowing it great scope in matters of faith. Hence, it is important to add to rational and scientific proofs the simple, instinctive and natural evidence which appeals to the entire human make up, including mind and feeling.

4 *Surah* 8 is discussed in Volume 7. – Editor's note.

5 This is true if it means that the initial and basic standpoint is to try to spread the faith by argument and conviction. However, it goes too far if it means to argue that *jihad* is only a defensive strategy to protect the Muslims, and that peace is obligatory in any other situation as Shaikh Muhammad Rashid Rida (may God shower His mercy on him) seems to have maintained.

6 Shaikh Rida (may God bless his soul) touches here on the fundamental truth that it is impossible for the Muslims to coexist with idolaters and the people of earlier revelations on the basis of treaties, except for a certain period. Nevertheless, he is more inclined to argue that relations between the Muslim state and other camps should generally be based on peace agreements, unless the Muslims are victims of aggression in their own land. He feels that this is always possible while the lack of such peace treaties is the exception. He says that the whole question concerns the idolaters in Arabia at the time of the Prophet. While this is basically true, what applied to them applies to all idolaters everywhere.

7 Muhammad Rashid Rida, *Tafsir al-Manar*, Dar al-Maʿrifah, Beirut, Vol. 10, pp. 149–150.

8 Reference may be made to the Prologue of Vol. 7, pp. 1–64, where this is discussed at length.

9 Al-Tabari, op.cit., p. 62.

10 Al-Tabari, ibid., pp. 62–63.

11 Al-Tabari, ibid., p. 66.

12 Ibn Kathir, *al-Bidayah wal-Nihayah*, Beirut, 1996, Vol. 13, pp. 199–203.

13 This was written in 1962 or 1963. – Editor's note.

14 Ibn Kathir, *Tafsir al-Qurʾan al-ʿAzim*, Beirut, Al-Maktabah al-ʿAsriyah, 1996, Vol. 2, p. 314.

6 **The earth's suffocating expanse**

1 This account is a consolidated summary of the detailed reports of the Tabuk Expedition given in *Al-Sirah al-Nabawiyyah* by Ibn Hisham, *Imta'al-Asma'* by al-Maqrizi, as well as *Al-Bidayah wa'l-Nihayah* and *Tafsir al-Qur'an al-'Azim*, both by Ibn Kathir.

2 This account is related in detail in all early biographies of the Prophet Muhammad (peace be upon him) but we have retained its English account as given by Adil Salahi, *Muhammad: Man and Prophet*, The Islamic Foundation, Leicester, 2002, pp. 711–717. – Editor's note.

3 The author apparently intended to write a whole book discussing the events that took place at the time of the Prophet and his Companions and highlighting the lessons that could be learnt from them and how Muslims today can benefit by them in shaping their lives in accordance with Islamic guidance. He did not live to see that project implemented. – Editor's note.

Index